C000264999

FORTRESS LONDON

FORTRESS LONDON
WHY WE NEED TO SAVE THE COUNTRY FROM ITS CAPITAL
SAM BRIGHT

Harper
North

HarperNorth
Windmill Green
24 Mount Street
Manchester, M2 3NX

A division of
HarperCollins*Publishers*
1 London Bridge Street
London SE1 9GF

www.harpercollins.co.uk

HarperCollins*Publishers*
1st Floor, Watermarque Building, Ringsend Road
Dublin 4, Ireland

First published by HarperNorth in 2022

1 3 5 7 9 10 8 6 4 2

A catalogue record for this book
is available from the British Library

HB ISBN: 978-0-00-847422-5

Printed and bound in the UK using 100%
renewable electricity at CPI Group (UK) Ltd

MIX
Paper from
responsible sources
FSC™ C007454

This book is produced from independently certified FSC™ paper
to ensure responsible forest management.

For more information visit: www.harpercollins.co.uk/green

To Mum and Dad.

I will forever be standing on
the shoulders of giants.

CONTENTS

Preface

THE FORTRESS

If you stand in the foyer of King's Cross station at approximately 7:30 p.m. most evenings, you will witness a unique natural event.

When the boarding call sounds for the 7:48 p.m. train to Bradford Interchange, a flock of people move in unison to the platform, expelling a melodic Northern hum as they reach the sanctuary of the waiting train.

Yes, daily migrations of Northerners happen across London every day, but the 7:48 p.m. to Bradford Interchange is different. It surges out of the capital and does not stop until it crosses the Yorkshire border; an elongated, steel snake gliding back to its nest. Other trains on the eastern line pause in Stevenage, Peterborough and Grantham. But not the 7:48 p.m. to Bradford Interchange. This train is in such a blind hurry to deliver its cargo to Yorkshire that it ignores the rest of the country.

This creates a strange, rare atmosphere on the train – a kinship forged among people broadly from the same place, escaping an alien city. I've had a number of conversations with people on this two-hour journey, sat on the geometric grey and orange upholstery. I have made friends with people who would probably never make eye-contact with a stranger, much less strike a bond with them, in any other environment.

Often, we talk about London. We sit upright and fold our arms across our chests, like teachers reproaching an unruly student, talking in earnest clichés about how unfriendly the city is, how expensive it is and how busy it is. When we reach our respective endpoints, we hit the platform as strangers again – two people with seemingly little in common.

The 7:48 p.m. to Bradford Interchange is a rare forum for frank conversations between random people about place, region and nation; a form of social engineering or a psychological experiment. On this train, our differences seem trivial in comparison to the foreign world that we are departing.

Our towns are proud and the people are plucky. Even as our high streets degenerate and the people seem greyer and poorer than they used to be, there's a residual belief that we could still punch above our weight – as we did in the past.

London, by contrast, is the switchboard of Britain. A dizzying array of lights, noise and bodies emanate a thick perfume of money, stress and opportunity. One of the most noticeable aspects of London to an outsider is the sheer number of people. Before the Pandemic, rush hour tubes were so busy that stray body parts had to be forcibly pushed into their respective carriages, like pickles in a jar. Navigating every pavement is an Olympic slalom event, finding the pockets of air in a seemingly infinite human wall. London is a vast, sprawling metropolis, little resembling the rest of the country; a towering, bulbous ant-hill.

Our capital houses nearly 9 million people within the limits of the city and the entire metropolitan area covers 14 million. Birmingham, the second largest conurbation in the UK, has a population of just over 1 million. Bristol, the largest city in the South outside London, has a population of barely 500,000.

London is exceptional; an anomaly against any yardstick. Its economic output per head is between 30 per cent and 50

2

per cent higher than the rest of the country, depending on which criteria you use. Its education system reaches higher standards than other regions, particularly from secondary level onwards. Its house prices are nearly double the England-wide average. It is considerably more diverse than anywhere else: the non-White British population constitutes 55 per cent of the capital, compared to just 20 per cent in the second most diverse region, the West Midlands.[1] Government (Westminster), the economy (the Bank of England and the Treasury), finance (the City), the performing arts (the West End), the media and 'the professions' are all headquartered in London.

There is no denying that London deviates from the norm. The question is whether London's unique position is a good thing, for both the country and the capital. Given that you have presumably glanced at the cover of this book, there's no use in setting up an elaborate cliff-hanger. You already know my position. So, let's get to the point.

Among the most developed countries in the world, the UK is the most regionally divided – by virtue of the economic gap between London (and in some regards the broader South East) and everywhere else. London is so dominant – in terms of output, income and wealth – that Britain is now more divided than Germany, a country whose eastern bloc was under Soviet patronage until the early 1990s.

Shortly after the Second World War, geographer Jean-François Gravier wrote of his home city that Paris was suffering from 'congestive swelling'.[2] The same can be said of present-day London, which has devoured the nation's assets over the last forty years. Yet London hasn't just eaten from its own plate; Britain's bloated gut is the product of regional cannibalisation.

Traditional industries were crushed by the invisible hand of the free market during the 1980s, only 'free' in the sense that it offered no compensation for its vandalism. Industry and manufacturing were consciously and rapidly depleted, a new economy constructed in their wake. Thatcher's post-industrial settlement was fostered by the growth of professional services and deregulated high finance, based in the capital and stocked by the graduates of Britain's burgeoning academic factories. This balance of power has been under-written by disproportionate levels of government infrastructure spending in the capital – new Tube lines, rail networks and cultural institutions – on the basis that London is the engine of the British economy through which our collective prosperity is ensured.

Yet, when the finance bubble burst in 2008, the provinces were called before the jury. Stripped of their assets by Thatcher two decades earlier, former industrial areas were asked to account for their reliance on the public sector. The jurors, Prime Minister David Cameron and his chancellor George Osborne, handed down their punishment: government austerity. State services were starved of resources, punishing nurses and low-wage workers for the problems stoked in London's banks. And while the wealth of home-owners in the capital has mushroomed over the last decade – properties flogged to luxury development companies and offshore billionaires – wages have stagnated for the longest period in 200 years.[3]

Bankrupting traditional industries and concentrating national resources in London has created extreme regional imbalances that have intensified over time. As businesses and public institutions have assembled in one place, amassing vast amounts of wealth, more and more people are encouraged to join the throng. As London expands, so does its gravitational pull – reducing opportunities for work and prosperity else-where.

The end of every university year sees an exodus of students from their university towns to the capital. London is now the only viable destination for us. All of the main career paths in the post-industrial economy cascade to the metropolis. Banking, law, politics, advertising, architecture, the arts and – in my case – the media, all inhabit this one place. You can of course work in these professions outside the capital, but it's next to impossible to reach the top of your field without joining the grey hoards queuing for the next Tube.

Given the state of the London housing market, the capital therefore has a profoundly damaging effect on economic and social mobility in Britain – returning the country to a previous stage of development. In an aristocracy, status is drawn from patronage, typically provided by parents in the form of wealth or inherited titles, but also through private, elite schooling. In modern Britain, we now have an aristocracy of place, whereby success is dependent on the patronage of London. If your parents own a home in the capital, for example, you can extract London's riches without having to worry about paying for a roof over your head. London is a launch-pad for your career, and your later wealth (a healthy inheritance almost guaranteed).

Yet, if you're not part of London's asset class, your opportunities are obstructed by the mountain of cash required to enter the capital's rental market. In the year prior to the Pandemic, the median monthly rent in London was £1,425, more than double the England-wide average.[4] By 2030, the average price of a property in London is expected to exceed £1 million, benefiting the current and future inheritors of this wealth, while excluding those trapped outside the property bubble.

However, public discourse about London neglects the issues of inequality, opportunity and injustice. Instead, it focuses on the city's 'wokeness'. For those of you who are (blissfully) unaware, right-wing figures commonly accuse London of propagating a liberal, left-wing, 'woke' attitude that is cosmopolitan, multicultural and supposedly anti-patriotic. The capital voted against Brexit, by a healthy margin, and has consistently supported Labour in recent elections – facts that have been used by Conservatives who seek to divide the country into competing cultures. London is the home of the 'liberal metropolitan elite' according to the likes of Nigel Farage, who was ironically educated at one of London's poshest private schools, Dulwich College. This debate is an intellectual desert; it entirely and consciously misses the point.

Yes, London is the most diverse city in Britain – and its politics is currently orientated towards left-wing liberalism – even if the relationship between ethnic diversity and liberalism is complicated. Maria Sobolewska and Rob Ford describe in their book *Brexitland* how immigrants typically hold more socially conservative beliefs than British-born liberals, often due to their religious convictions, but tend to vote for liberal parties that defend ethnic minority groups from xenophobia.[5]

However, rather than rejecting prevailing narratives about London, the Labour Party has danced to the Right's tune. The Left has valiantly defended London as a bastion of enlightened politics, suggesting that Britain would be improved if it were more reflective of its capital. Conservatives strategically exaggerate the political and cultural differences between London – supposedly an avocado-eating Remainer paradise – and the anti-Brexit peripheries. Yet, instead of rejecting this false dichotomy, the Left has deployed its soldiers to the trenches of the Right's Culture War. The Conservatives have led Labour from its heartlands to the banks of the Thames, and the party has dutifully plunged into the electoral abyss.

In the process, the Left now occupies an ideologically ludicrous position – aggressively defending a central artery of global capitalism. London is the international capital of property speculation, financial deregulation, money laundering and inequality. In a report released by Parliament's Intelligence and Security Committee in July 2020, MPs described London as a 'laundromat', due to its popularity among Russian oligarchs seeking to clean their dirty money.[6] Yet, it is politically risky to raise these concerns; to criticise the almighty capital, even from a social justice standpoint. Critics are accused of smearing London and bolstering the rhetoric of the Conservative Party. The Left has become so tangled in its own contradictions that it now instinctively attacks those who protest regional inequality.

It is also ironic that a group of liberal-minded 'lefties' – so avidly opposed to the border walls advocated by right-wing populists – have constructed a figurative wall around London, as not merely a place but an idea that should be defended and protected.

Those who criticise London are roundly attacked by the capital's foot-soldiers, but as economist John Kenneth Galbraith wrote in 1958: 'The man who makes his entry by leaning against an infirm door gets an unjustified reputation for violence. [Yet] something is to be attributed to the poor state of the door.'[7]

These are the political circumstances in which recent elections and referendums have taken place. Vote Leave's victory and the Conservative Party's success at the 2019 general election have been attributed to a political rebellion in Labour's former industrial heartlands – a revolt against their loss of status and wealth over the last forty years, and the perceived neglect of Westminster.

This sense of injustice, rooted in certain parts of the country, did not suddenly and spontaneously detonate; Labour's support had been dwindling in these seats since 1997, while apathy has risen dramatically. The EU Referendum triggered a landmine that had been lying just beneath the surface for years, foregrounding political chameleons whose ability to exploit regional inequality far outranks their appetite and imagination to fix it.

Ever since the shock of 2016, the same journalists who failed to predict these political reverberations have been diagnosing their causes from the same Westminster hideouts. As Robert Peston writes in *WTF?*, his psycho-political analysis of what happened in 2016, 'we fucked up, didn't we, all of us who prospered in a borderless world for capital and labour? We ignored the complaints of those whose way of life was being dismantled.'[8]

Peston and others were chastened by their failure to predict Brexit, they admit. The outcome is a further lack of insight, for the writer is fearful of being wrong again. Predictable explanations are reiterated; the writer's guilt assuaged. It's assumed that Boris Johnson – the primary beneficiary of recent regional anger – is capable of fixing the inequalities created by his political and ideological predecessor, Margaret Thatcher. In all cases, London's role is marginalised.

In large part, this is the product of a media ecosystem that has been captured by London. Covering national events, the media squats in a city that bulges with the sites of political, economic and cultural importance. The decimation of advertising revenue in the industry over the last two decades has created a crisis in journalism, exacerbated among local and regional outlets that have always drawn their revenues from a limited readership, compared to national titles. Journalism is therefore one of the professions that has been swallowed by London – staffed by the city's inhabitants, stifling voices outside the metropolis.

'We all know what life is like in London, because it's on every single TV programme,' says Jess Phillips, the Labour MP for Birmingham Yardley. She recalls watching a segment on a national news programme a few years ago about the fabled Garden Bridge – the proposed £200 million floral walkway over the River Thames, keenly supported by then London Mayor Boris Johnson – causing her to launch a cushion at the TV in frustration. 'It didn't even get built!' she says. 'Seriously, we can't afford to pick up the bins where I live and you're quibbling over a bridge. Take it to your local news station – I have no interest in hearing about this in Birmingham. I have kids living in abject poverty; fuck off with your bridge on my national news.'

London is depicted as a microcosm of the nation, as journalists fill their columns with convenient stories and interviews from the capital. In reality, the opposite is true. London is an outlier – an alternate universe – and the media is stuck in its orbit. 'Journalists go out of their own door to cover stories,' says Dorothy Byrne, the former editor-at-large of Channel 4, born in Paisley, Scotland. 'So journalists will often cover the issue of commuting to work by going on the London Underground. If journalists had been forced to experience the horror of trying to travel regularly between Manchester and Leeds on a train or any road, they would soon be writing different stories.'

London is aware of its exceptionalism. It is a global city, a vast agglomeration of different nationalities and cultures. It self-identifies, whether accurately or not, as cosmopolitan and outward-looking. Using David Goodhart's definition, London is populated by proud 'citizens of anywhere'.[9] Yet, Londoners have a complex relationship with their city, and their roots. They recognise that London is unique, in a domestic context, and are keen to distance themselves from people outside the city, who they see as conservative and small-minded. And they identify primarily as Londoners, rather than as British or English. A YouGov survey in 2018 found that eight out of ten people in England identify strongly as English, falling to some 40 per cent in London,[10] while a British Future poll in 2012 reported that 90 per cent of Londoners are proud of their city.[11]

This relates to the demographic makeup of London. Some 37 per cent of Londoners were born outside the UK, and polling shows that young inhabitants of the Capital are considerably less likely to harbour patriotic instincts.[12] The average (median) age in London is 35.6, compared to 40.3 in the UK overall. Almost half of London's inner-city population is made up of those who are in their early twenties to early forties.[13]

However, a lack of contact with the rest of the country also explains London's superstitions. With many Londoners lacking a first-person understanding of places outside the capital, they have glanced at the results of recent elections and have decided – with a helping hand from the media – that peripheral Britain is bigoted and parochial. This attitude has a kernel of truth; there's no denying that the Brexit vote was motivated in part by anti-immigration sentiments. But London's sense of exceptionalism is also a product of its own parochialism. The capital is a magnet, pinning its population to the fortress. This reduces the need for Londoners to experience or learn about the rest of the country – leading to slapdash assumptions about the character of other places. Londoners see themselves as open-minded, when in fact their understanding of Britain is often limited.

Jess Phillips, for example, tells me that she is regularly mistaken for Ashton-under-Lyne MP Angela Rayner, even by journalists, such is their level of ignorance towards places outside the capital (quite apart from their misogyny). On one occasion, she recalls, on the night of the 2017 general election, Phillips was invited to appear on BBC Newsnight, under the premise that the programme was filming 'in her area' – allegedly shooting in the vicinity of her constituency. 'They sent me the details of the event and it was in Bolton,' she says. 'I don't live anywhere near Bolton!'

Even though London's values promote a rootless existence, people from the capital are largely embedded in one place. Regional identities matter to all parts of the country – triggering place-based values and political choices. Parochialism is not reserved to the areas that voted for Brexit. The late Christopher Hitchens described New York as a place of 'rooted cosmopolitanism' and this characterisation likewise applies to London. The city is not simply an empty vessel for the projection of different social and national backgrounds; it's a place that actively celebrates its diversity and believes in the righteousness of its cultural carousel. Try slagging off the capital in front of a Londoner and you will understand how passionately they feel about their birthplace and its values.

This isn't necessarily a criticism. Rather, an acknowledgement that we're all the same. Most of us have an affinity with our birthplace and where we live, even in parts of the country that claim to be vagabonds and outcasts. That's why it's important to map the contours. The UK is not a homogenous blob; understanding regional circumstances and the inequalities that exist between different places helps us to understand not just political events but also our national identity.

This task is complicated by the North–South divide, a time-honoured concept that lingers in our collective subconscious despite being almost entirely divorced from the lived reality of modern Britain. 'I get quite cross about the idea of the North–South divide,' says Labour councillor Kate Ewert, who represents Rame and St Germans in Cornwall. 'I think people in Cornwall have far more in common with people in the ex-industrial North than anyone who lives in Hampshire or Surrey or Oxford. Although we're not an organised working-class area, we do have an industrial background.'

The North–South divide also sidelines Scotland, Wales and the Midlands – reducing regional inequalities to a simplistic football match between two easily-demarcated teams. 'People in the North regard the Midlands as belonging to the South and people in the South think the Midlands belongs to the North,' says broadcaster Adrian Goldberg, born and bred in Birmingham. 'People haven't really paid attention to the Midlands, or at least that's how we feel.'

So, while there is a romantic attachment to the North–South divide, the sentimentality of the idea exceeds its substance. In reality, on pretty much every metric – productivity, education, house prices, poverty, ethnic and economic makeup – London stands alone, shadowed at a distance by the broader South East.

More recently, a distinction has been made between small towns and cities, as a way of explaining place-based inequalities in modern Britain. This theory has merit. On visiting small towns in poorer parts of the North, Midlands and the South, their common features are immediately obvious, from their pollution-stained town halls to their graffitied shop-fronts. However, London is so removed from other cities in the UK – in particular its population size and economic output – that it cannot be paired with other urban conurbations, aside from perhaps to establish broad trends in voting patterns.

Ultimately, members of all political camps have concentrated on the perceived differences in values between people in different parts of the country, while ignoring the real-life inequalities that actually matter.

According to the Resolution Foundation, the richest 1 per cent of the population holds a quarter of all household wealth.[14] This wealth has accumulated not through spectacular innovation or ingenuity, but through the inflation of assets. Between 76 per cent and 93 per cent of wealth gains since the 2008 financial crisis have been delivered through the rising value of assets such as housing. Britain's wealth is increasingly hoarded by a property-owning aristocracy whose investments have bloated while austerity has been inflicted on public-sector workers and the low-paid.

This has buttressed enduring forms of social prejudice. As George Orwell wrote in *The Lion and the Unicorn* in 1941: 'England is the most class-ridden country under the sun. It is a land of snobbery and privilege, ruled largely by the old and silly.'[15] The leadership of the country since 2010 proves the longevity of Orwell's observation.

'The only way that a Culture War can grow and fester is if people feel hard done by and start blaming others, instead of blaming those in power,' says Dawn Butler, Labour MP for Brent Central. 'If everyone felt they were being treated fairly, the Conservative Party wouldn't be able to create a Culture War and divide people for their own twisted advantage.' Ergo, the material deprivation of some people allows expedient actors to channel this public rage into the resentment of other groups based on who they are and what they seem to believe – creating the perception that Britain is divided by values, rather than social circumstances.

Ironically, these expedient actors exploit the grievances of the poor while downplaying their own privilege – failing to mention their education at expensive private schools in London and/or the South East. Yet their attitudes pervade the corridors of power, says Jess Phillips. 'The way the Midlands and the North gets talked about' in Parliament 'is commonly irritating and underwritten by basic snobbery,' she says. Ruled by a landed aristocracy, British society mirrors the nineteenth and twentieth centuries (up until the 1970s), though stripped of industrial prestige and deprived of the steep, mass inflation of living standards.

Thus, the Culture War concocted by the Conservative Party and amplified by Labour is not a fair representation of our values as a nation. While there are profound differences between political parties – greater differences than at any time in the twenty-first century – voters are more clustered than we imagine.

A vast political divide exists between Jeremy Corbyn and Nigel Farage, for example. On immigration, nationalisation, healthcare, multiculturalism, taxation, they hold radically different opinions. But this Culture War cannot be extrapolated to the rest of the country; to people who will never hold ideological passions equivalent to those of Farage or Corbyn. Most people are indifferent to politics, and, for a variety of reasons, little coverage is devoted to the ways that we agree with one another. Those who benefit from the Culture War (both politically and financially) cherry-pick examples that exaggerate supposed conflicts between different ideologies and different regions. What bleeds, leads.

For all the profound material differences between London and the rest of the country, shaping life chances from cradle to grave, there is still an enduring moral consensus between our different nations and regions. We are more economically divided, and less ideologically opposed, than we currently care to admit.

At this point, it's worth setting some ground rules. National and regional identity are volatile subjects, and we're each guided by our own experiences. I was born and brought up in Yorkshire, and this identity (plus my general affinity with the North of England) informs the way I see regional inequalities.

I have an instinctive, emotional attachment to Yorkshire that is entirely irrational yet makes perfect sense when I stand beneath the grand, ornate façade of York Minster or the barren beauty of the Dales. It's a feeling of home, of sanctuary and belonging, that is sentimental rather than scientific.

People from other parts of the country have a similar emotional attachment to their home, informed by different histories, cultures and idiosyncrasies. I've gained some appreciation of these differences during my life: I have been taught elementary Welsh by colleagues in Cardiff, lectured about Rugby League by relatives in Widnes and taken on tours of London's urban mosaic by my fellow inmates of the capital. I have also consciously supplemented this book with a number of interviews, calling on the experiences of those who know their local areas far better than I ever could.[16]

However, I will inevitably have made generalisations that more accurately describe some areas than others. I wish that I could absorb and articulate the full complexity of Britain's human geography, but such a task would probably be impossible – and would almost certainly prevent me from forming any sort of useful, overarching conclusions that may help to repair the landscape.

Also, you will notice that I have variously used 'the UK', 'Britain' and 'the country'. This book substantially refers to Britain: England, Scotland and Wales, given that Northern Ireland has a unique constitutional and historical relationship with both the Republic of Ireland and the rest of the UK. However, I will still refer to 'the UK' either when I am referencing a study that has set its parameters across the whole of the UK, or when I am discussing a particular issue that has direct, unobstructed relevance to Northern Ireland. Scotland and Wales of course also differ from England's regions by virtue of their devolved parliaments, and I hope these nuances are properly acknowledged in what follows.

Finally, although I am hacking at the roots of regional injustice in Britain, this is not an attack on the people of London. In a single night in the capital, you can tour the cuisines and cocktails of the world and mingle with scores of interesting, tolerant, progressive people – even if the city has an overabundance of ex-private school boys who now work as 'creatives' and dress like side-characters in a Wes Anderson movie.

I believe that regional inequalities are sustained by two behaviours that are prevalent in the capital: a failure to acknowledge the destructive effects of London's supremacy; and an instinctive (almost involuntary) assumption that places outside the capital are populated by xenophobes.

However, while these two attitudes have helped to preserve London's command of the country, Londoners did not make the monster. Politicians have poured jet fuel into London for the last forty years; a city that has ruled the domestic economy, and occasionally the world economy, over the course of several centuries. This has occurred at the expense of those living outside the capital, as well as the ordinary people who seek to live and work in London without selling their soul for a place to live.

Indeed, gold-plated Lamborghinis roam around the boulevards of West London, yet the city has the highest levels of poverty in Britain. Some 30 per cent of people in London live on the breadline – because the city's breadline is pegged to its outrageous property costs.[17] The capital is increasingly a playground for the rich, rather than a place where ordinary people can live. For property developers and bankers, it is a land of opportunity. For most other people, it is plagued by insecurity.

The capital is overheating; cooling its temperature can only be achieved by kindling other regions. The country – including London – needs to be saved from its capital.

1.

EDUCATION, EDUCATION, EDUCATION

Before giving an appraisal of the education system in the UK, I feel it's only fair to begin by telling you about mine.

Our class awareness is bound up in the type of education we received – perhaps more than any other developed country. Elite, fee-paying institutions have funnelled students into the upper echelons of business, law and politics for centuries – a rigged system that the Labour Party has variously attempted to knobble, with little success. Perhaps it's no wonder that schooling is so important to us, individually and collectively. It's how we have been sorted throughout history.

It's rare to find someone who isn't weighed down by their schooling – even if they have graduated from the highest stratifications of the UK's steeply contoured system. When worlds collide, particularly at university, the former inmates of fee-paying schools are met with animosity from those who were educated by the state – those who are naturally and justifiably resentful about an education system that bestows opportunities based on birthright rather than merit. The privately schooled argue, equally justifiably, that they had no choice in the matter – they were sent by their parents – and therefore the comprehensive kids must simply be jealous and boorish. A cycle of mutual resentment flows down through generations.

In order to trust the words that follow, you want to know how I was educated. I can feel your judgement piercing through these words, even as I write them. That's fine, I don't blame you. Judgement of each other's education is a knee-jerk impulse of this country as much as our road rage or our adoration of David Attenborough. There's nothing you can do to stop it.

My schooling was not particularly unique. I was educated at three state schools and a state sixth-form college. The catchment of the schools comprised a village network on the outskirts of Huddersfield in West Yorkshire. The kids I went to school with came from normal families: the majority were not well-off in relative terms, but their existence was comfortable. Their parents worked as nurses, teachers, accountants, physiotherapists and occasionally lawyers. Families owned their own cars and their own houses. The area was semi-rural, safe, and although it wasn't exactly exciting for young people – there were more bingo halls than nightclubs – none of us felt as though we were missing out on anything. We had fields big enough to host football games and nice houses to which we could retreat, with grass-stained tracksuits and sore shins, when we were inevitably drenched by rain.

The schools themselves were decent, in the truest sense of the word. By and large, the teachers did not drag down the performance of their students, but neither did they elevate them. A number of parents had attended the same school as their kids. In fact, the school lineage was so strong, and the facilities so bog-standard, that our school football team kits – i.e. the actual jerseys – had been worn by some teachers and parents when they had donned the school's colours some twenty or thirty years prior.

Indeed, an underlying assumption pervaded: that you did not need to outperform your circumstances. There were worse things in life than getting decent grades, working in a comfortable job and settling down in the area, eventually filming your kids in the nativity play you had starred in at the same school years earlier.

There were no private schools in the area; there didn't seem to be any need for them. The sports field provided our only exposure to class conflict. Our high school cricket team was particularly good, and I featured as a disciplined right-arm medium pace bowler. We progressed through to the final of the county championship at under-15 level – some achievement in a county that is both the nation's largest and its most cricket obsessed. We didn't have a cricket pitch at our school, so we agreed to play the final on enemy turf, at Scarborough College.

It was an important game and we were playing against a posh private school with a history of producing top cricketers. So, ditching the school's polo-shirt uniform, our coach instructed us to wear a white shirt and a blue tie for the occasion. The problem was, the coach did not specify which shade of blue. Players turned up with ties hastily swiped from their dad's closet, featuring every size and shade from turquoise to navy. The clown in the team, Josh, even appeared at school wearing a garish pink tie featuring a blue stripe, beaming at his ingenuity. After the two-hour drive to Scarborough, the boys rolled out of our beaten-up Volkswagen bus with shirts untucked, half having removed their ties entirely and half choosing instead to undo the noose – hanging the tie in a low listless knot, more like a mayor's medallion. The social differences between our rabble and the prim Scarborough boys with their pressed blazers and prefect robes could not have been starker. Even so, we won the game comfortably.

I left my leafy high school behind at 16, attending Greenhead College in the centre of Huddersfield. This was my equivalent of leaving for the big city, swapping my local school for a 7:30 a.m. train ride into the centre of town – embarking on a two-year academic training camp with fifteen of my friends and 2,000 kids from other schools who we didn't know.

We were lucky to attend somewhere like Greenhead. The school has consistently been rated as one of the best sixth-form colleges in the country, and in 2020 it recorded a better Oxbridge acceptance ratio than Eton, one of the world's most venerated and expensive private institutions, if one looks at the number of applications to acceptances.[1]

However, while Greenhead received the ninth most Oxbridge offers of any school in 2020, only one other Northern establishment mounted a charge into the top twenty – namely Manchester Grammar school, which costs roughly £13,000 a year to attend. Eleven of the top twenty schools are located in London, eleven are independent institutions and seventeen are based in the broader South East of England stretching from Cambridge to Brighton.

This triggers the two basic questions that frame this chapter: in what ways do regional inequalities manifest through the education system, and why has this happened?

Anecdotally, my school days provide some pointers now that I can reflect on my experiences with a reasonable level of distance and objectivity.

In year nine, every student was handed their predicted GCSE grades – a clever trick that allowed teachers to flay anyone who was straying away from their expected performance. My five or six closest friends were all justifiably predicted A* grades across the board. Perhaps partly saddled by the weight of expectation, none achieved this target, or even came close. As their relative performance gradually waned over the succeeding years, two of the most talented among the group eventually graduated college and attended a former polytechnic university, which are generally considered to be non-academic establishments.

There is of course nothing wrong with going to a polytechnic – it is not a mark of failure and it certainly does not carry the stigma that it once did. However, I've often wondered how my school friends, who were among the brightest 15-year-olds in the country, did not fulfil their academic potential. Especially when London's most expensive private schools seem to specialise in producing A* morons who end up running the country.

The principal reason, for my friends at least, was that high academic achievement was synonymous with leaving their home area. In many ways, they saw aspiration as foolhardy, given that we lived so comfortably. It's hard to argue with this case: not many areas of the country boast an abundance of natural beauty, good state schools, affordable homes and decent jobs – while maintaining a brutal Yorkshire realism that dissuades snobbery and privilege.

My friends were also correct in the sense that, if the aim were to pursue a different life – perhaps in the upper ranks of a profession or the arts – Huddersfield was never going to be the midwife of these dreams. Whereas Huddersfield and its mills once fuelled the economic engine of the country during the Industrial Revolution, we knew that London was the only game in town for those who wanted to stand at the vanguard of the information age.

For people in small Northern towns like mine, this detachment from the all-powerful capital city incubates a collective ignorance towards the treasures that it holds. People don't aspire towards it – whatever *it* may be – because they simply don't know it exists. The names of corporate institutions, other than those on the high street, were alien to me until I ventured to university. And even then, in my first year, fellow students talked about their father's promotion at KPMG as though I was supposed to know that it's an international accountancy firm and not some sort of Class A drug.

Similar observations are made, although not so crass, by the 2018 Children's Commissioner report on the prospects of children growing up in the North. 'Overwhelmingly, the young people we spoke to were planning to go into a career of someone known to them personally,' it notes. 'This meant the aspirations of the young people we spoke to were reflective of the local labour market – and its limitations. Very few professional or office-based occupations were mentioned in any of our sessions.'[2]

Of course, the second-generation immigrant son or daughter of a cleaner in Tower Hamlets will also feel estranged from the glistening glass façades of Canary Wharf. But it's difficult to be ignorant about the economic opportunities provided by the UK's financial sector when you live within spitting distance of the HSBC Tower, or apathy towards art or politics after your school trip to the Tate Modern or the Houses of Parliament. London is a melting pot, as we're often told, and that bestows advantages on everyone growing up in the city – even if the benefits amassed by the rich far outweigh those of the poor.

There has been a stark reversal of regional fortunes in the British education system over recent decades. In the early 2000s, London had the worst performing schools in the country – inner London being the only area in which less than 40 per cent of children achieved five or more good GCSEs.[3] There was a fear that London's poorest boroughs were experiencing a brain drain, as more affluent families repatriated to the suburbs or packed their kids on trains out of the city centre.

By 2013, however, the three London regions (inner, outer and everywhere else) had cartwheeled into the three top positions in England, comfortably exceeding 60 per cent of students achieving five or more good GCSEs, including English and Maths.[4] We will come to the reasons for this metamorphosis but I first want to chart London's lead, on an array of school performance indicators.

According to the Social Market Foundation, geography is now more closely attached to school performance than at any moment in recent history. For a child born in 2000, birth-place was a more powerful predictive factor of their success than those born thirty years prior.[5]

The radical divergence of performance based on geography does not occur from the moment that a child steps into school. Children in the North of England perform worse than their peers in London at key stage one level, though the divide is little more than a few percentage points. This gap widens as the school years progress, spurred by the comparative poor performance of the most disadvantaged students.

Statistics from the Children's Commissioner show that a child who qualifies for free school meals in London achieves, on average, half a grade higher in every subject at GCSE than a child on free school meals outside the capital, even if they both start secondary school at the same level of attainment.[6] Children on free school meals in London are 20 per cent less likely to achieve a C or above in Maths and English at GCSE than the national average for all students, while children on free school meals in Northern city regions are 40 per cent less likely to achieve this standard.

This chasm further widens above the age of 16. London-based students on free school meals are slightly more likely to attend university than the national average for all students, whereas those on free school meals in Northern city regions are 50 per cent less likely than the average. In other words: a pupil from London on free school meals is twice as likely to attend university as a child from an equivalent socio-economic background in the North.

'Material poverty threatens your chance of a good start wherever you're born,' notes Anna Round, a senior research fellow at IPPR North, 'but that threat seems to be greater in the North than in the capital.'

Some explanation for this rupture can be found in Ofsted ratings. In the most deprived areas of London, 35 per cent of secondary schools are classified as outstanding and close to 90 per cent are either good or outstanding. In the most deprived areas of the North, less than 10 per cent are rated as outstanding and less than 50 per cent are either good or outstanding – an eye-watering drop in standards compared to the capital.

In terms of standards at least, schools in London exist in a different universe to those elsewhere. Some 50 per cent of all secondary schools in London are rated as outstanding by Ofsted, and 95 per cent are classified as either good or outstanding. In the North, those figures are 30 per cent and 75 per cent respectively.

Thus, a fledgling adult in the London school system is much more likely to attend university than those who've been deprived of the capital's academic booster-shot. A staggering 49 per cent of all London students end up in higher education, compared to 36 per cent in Northern and Southern city regions, and 37 per cent in Midlands city regions.[7]

Raw funding is one factor that has exacerbated these inequalities. In 2016, for example, secondary schools in the North received on average £1,300 less per pupil than schools in London.[8] And while schools in London have been able to rely on donations to compensate for funding shortfalls, charitable gifts have been more constrained in other parts of the country. In 2017–18, the average school in London raised £43,000 from donations while in Yorkshire the equivalent figure was just £13,300. Indeed, the average donations raised by schools in London surpassed the second-placed region, the East of England, by 58 per cent, or nearly £20,000 per school.[9]

Inequalities in the education system are a permanent feature of national life, begrudgingly accepted by most people. But place-based inequalities have added a new dimension to the disparities that mould the British class experience.

From the pageantry of the House of Lords to the twitching moustaches of the military high command, the UK is renowned for its hereditary culture. This lingering world – of lords, ladies, butlers and unearned privilege – is still one of our most lucrative exports, as the producers of *The Crown*, *Downton Abbey* and *Made in Chelsea* will attest. One suspects that the tabloids would struggle to fill their pages without the help of the royal family.

But while the concurrent veneration and exploitation of aristocracy in popular culture has continued apace, politicians have deployed high-minded language about meritocracy and social mobility. In his 2012 Conservative Party conference speech, prime minister and old Etonian David Cameron articulated an idea that is institutionally accepted among major parties: 'It's not where you've come from that counts; it's where you're going.'

Without a shred of self-awareness, the UK has simultaneously flogged its heritage of privilege to Hollywood while in return pilfering the rhetoric of the American dream: the conviction that anyone can succeed merely through hard work and intelligence. As Michael Young says in his 1958 dystopian fiction *The Rise of Meritocracy*, the worthiness of an individual is based on a simple algorithm: IQ + Effort = Merit.[10]

This is a seductive notion, and one that invariably appeals to the people who own and run the country. After all, it takes courage to admit that your privilege is inherited and not in fact a product of your God-given aptitude. However, the formula described by Young does not measure the input of social circumstance. After all, according to the algorithm, 'it's not where you've come from that counts'.

The term 'social mobility' has popularised this suppression of social and economic background. Adopted by the New Labour governments and now broadly uncontested among the establishment left and right, social mobility suggests that people can vault up the social hierarchy and transcend the limitations of their circumstances. It implies that class divisions are perfectly acceptable as long as achievement flows from merit.

Of course, in reality, the aptitude of an individual is dependent on where they were born, which school they attended, the profession and wealth of their parents, and plenty more besides. Flattening these inequalities is the only way to create a more meritorious society; otherwise, the pursuit of meritocracy and social mobility merely reinforces the supremacy of the privileged. Opportunities are offered for a few pioneers to eclipse their background – creating an illusion of fairness while members of the aristocracy continue to enjoy the pre-ordained advantages of their status and wealth, from childhood to death. The divide between London and the rest – how it has emerged and why it is tolerated – can only be properly understood through this myth of meritocracy, whereby the preservation of inequality is garbed in the language of opportunity. As the Sutton Trust and the Social Mobility Commission declared in 2019: 'the latest indications are that social mobility across the UK is low and not improving'.[11]

To summarise, while 7 per cent of children are educated at private school, their graduates represent 29 per cent of MPs, 57 per cent of peers, 44 per cent of newspaper columnists, 59 per cent of civil servant chiefs, 38 per cent of top-selling pop music artists, and 29 per cent of BBC executives.

'The alumni of just nine leading public [i.e. elite independent] schools in Britain are 94 times more likely to reach elite positions than those from other schools,' the report reads, 'and much of that advantage still persists even when they have not attended top universities, suggesting that the old boys networks formed in top private schools play an important role in access to the elite.'

Alan Milburn, a former Cabinet minister under Tony Blair, resigned as the chair of the Social Mobility Commission in 2017 after five years in the post, citing a lack of 'meaningful action' from the Conservative government. 'Whole communities and parts of Britain are being left behind economically and hollowed out socially. The growing sense that we have become an us and them society is deeply corrosive of our cohesion as a nation,' Milburn stated in his resignation letter. 'As the Commission's work has demonstrated, the twentieth century expectation that each generation would do better than the last is no longer being met.'[12]

Traditional critiques have deployed private schooling as a proxy for elitism in Britain, given the direct correlation between someone's social privilege and the price paid for their education. Schooling is also easy to tally and measure, given its universal nature, unlike many other class identifiers.

But using private schooling alone as a surrogate for inequality seems insufficient in the modern era. While paid schooling is a valuable measure of privilege, strong geographic disparities now exist alongside the private–state gulf.

In effect, a new sorting system has emerged whereby kids from one part of the country have a better chance of securing good grades, attending university and opening up the widest range of career paths. This is obviously a different form of privilege to the private school system, which is a crude exchange of money in return for opportunity. The imbalance between London and the rest is not brazenly nepotistic, but it is random. A child in an outstanding London state school derives their opportunities from fate of birth rather than any sort of rational sorting process.

Profound place-based inequalities in our schooling system have emerged under the radar. After all, we supposedly live in a meritocracy. Debates typically revolve around the ownership, management and selective nature of the institutions – free schools, academies, grammar schools, comprehensives, private schools, etc. – rather than where they are located. Equally, therefore, the comeback achieved by London's schools over the last two decades has been little appreciated, purging any lessons that could be applied to the rest of the UK.

Between 2000 and 2013, there was an upward swing of 21 percentage points in the quality of teaching in London secondary schools and a 17 percentage point improvement in their overall effectiveness.[13] From the start of the new millennium to now, London's inner-city schools have been transformed from the worst performing in the country to the best. Between 2003 and 2011, the percentage of primary schools in England that fell below minimum attainment targets showed a slight increase. In London, the number of these poor-performing schools fell by more than a third.[14]

'The day of the bog-standard comprehensive is over,' New Labour spin supremo Alastair Campbell declared in 2001, as the Blair government promised a relentless focus on 'education, education, education'. London's schools matched the rhetoric, evolving from nightmare student to teacher's pet in little over a decade.

The reason for this turnaround is still the subject of academic jostling. London as a city experienced simultaneous demographic, cultural and political revolutions during the New Labour years – changes that invariably seeped into the capital's education system. As one of my former BBC colleagues once remarked, when a younger member of staff expressed anxiety about sending their kids to an inner-city London school: 'Don't be silly. All the mums and dads are intellectuals like you. Half of them are probably journalists.'

However, it is universally accepted that one policy functioned as an academic steroid in London's schools: the London Challenge, that ran from 2003 to 2011. The basic mission of the project was to improve the worst-performing schools, those in disadvantaged areas, while multiplying the number of outstanding institutions.

These objectives are not necessarily unique. Indeed, it would be worrying if any one of these mission statements was absent from a state-backed education agenda. Unlike most government projects, however, the London Challenge delivered objectively exceptional results.

Schools were not offered a special sauce to enhance their performance. There were many, multi-faceted reasons for the success of the London Challenge, exemplified when the government attempted to export the model to other parts of the country. But several key components can be discerned, which illustrate why London went from the runt of the litter to the leader of the pack.

Primarily, the London Challenge had political backing. Education was a policy priority for the Blair government, not simply a rhetorical tool or a snappy slogan. Spending on education during the New Labour years increased in real terms by 78 per cent, and the London Challenge picked the fruits from this tree, boasting a budget of £40 million a year at its peak.[15]

Yet, although the programme was supported by central government, it was run by specialists. Tim Brighouse, a teacher and education policy expert with vast experience in the Oxfordshire and Birmingham school systems, was hired as the Schools Commissioner for London in 2002 and was therefore the de facto chief of the London Challenge.

'The political impetus was immensely important,' Brighouse tells me. 'There was political clout, and we spent a lot of time with the London boroughs and with the local directors of education.'

Now 81 years old, Brighouse is not the project manager that he used to be – apologetically calling an hour after our arranged time. However, his passion for education remains undimmed: when we speak he's working on a book, interviewing past education secretaries.

Brighouse had a constructive relationship with Labour's education team – particularly Estelle Morris, who had served in the Department for Education from 1998 to 2002 and had witnessed Brighouse's work at close quarters in her Birmingham Yardley constituency. 'Estelle was totally persuaded,' he says.

Yet even when Morris left the Cabinet, replaced with new faces and ideas, support for the London Challenge persevered. 'Sponsorship from key policymakers, over many years and across different administrations, was one of the fundamental drivers behind the success of schools in London during the 2000s: allowing reforms to take root and to become established,' concludes the Education Development Trust.[16]

The reason for this durability perhaps relates to the structure of the London Challenge. Rather than dictating policies to schools, the project was designed to foster a network of information-sharing between similar institutions. 'I have never been one for top-down imposition,' Brighouse says. 'The idea was to get schools to learn from each other.'

So, the London Challenge created 'families' of schools with similar characteristics, typically the socio-economic and demographic backgrounds of their students. 'You'd have fifteen or twenty schools in a family, and then you'd show the schools all the data, to get them interested in visiting and understanding each other,' Brighouse explains.

The trick was to match high-performing schools with low-performing partners that shared mutual traits: a high proportion of children with first-generation immigrant parents, for example, or two schools with above-average levels of poverty among their students. This created a twinning relationship whereby the policies of the high-performing school could be adopted by the less successful twin with a high degree of confidence that they would work. The shared circumstances of the two schools also forged mutual trust that could be drawn upon when problems arose.

The London Challenge did not prescribe a firm set of principles or policies for schools to follow, so the project rarely conflicted with the attitudes of ministers. 'The various activities and interventions were characterised by a belief that school-to-school collaboration has a central role to play in school improvement; a recognition of the importance of school leadership; and a data-rich approach to tackling issues and sharing learning,' says an analysis by London Metropolitan University.[17]

But creating a series of interconnected institutions relies heavily on local context. In particular, the idea functions most effectively in areas with a high density and volume of schools, thereby increasing the likelihood that several, proximate institutions will share characteristics.

In many ways, this functions like a dating app. If you're a 23-year-old K-pop enthusiast looking for someone who shares your passion, you're far more likely to find that person in a city of 8 million people than sleepy small-town suburbia. In other words: in London.

'You'd get on the Tube in London and at each stop you'd get kids joining. Kids travel from all over the place in order to get to school. They criss-cross each other,' Brighouse says. The full benefits of this educational agglomeration are only possible in large, interconnected cities, which excludes most places aside from London.

The sole objective of the policy was to improve standards, learning from institutions and teachers that had delivered exceptional results. 'I spent a lot of time in schools trying always to make sure teachers knew they were hugely valued, highlighting successful practice, identifying problems,' Brighouse says.

One of his ideas was to create a new rank among teachers, the Chartered London Teacher, to incentivise higher standards. In exchange for this status, plus a £1,000 cheque, teachers had to demonstrate that they had visited a number of schools, were progressing in their subject knowledge, were working on overcoming barriers to children's progress, and displayed an understanding of equal opportunities.

'That did a lot,' Brighouse says, not least by ensuring that the teaching unions were on board with his reforms – although the charter was ultimately abandoned (recently revived in a different guise) because it was too expensive.

Teach First was also launched in 2002, integrated with the London Challenge until its expansion to Manchester in 2006. The idea behind Teach First was and still is to create an avenue for skilled graduates to enter the teaching profession and spend time working in disadvantaged schools. 'The Teach First programme contributed significantly to a new perception of teaching in London as a high-status profession for both idealistic and talented recruits,' according to the Education Development Trust.[18]

Aside from London's unique ability to foster clusters of knowledge, there is an ongoing academic debate about the extent to which the city's schooling system has pulled ahead due to its ethnic diversity. A minority (44.9 per cent) of London's population identifies as White British, compared to 80.5 per cent among the whole UK,[19] while 37 per cent of Londoners were born in other countries.[20]

Brighouse believes this theory has some credence. 'If you've come from a different part of the world and you've made an emotional and physical journey to get to London, the likelihood is your parents are going to be pretty supportive of what you do.' However, the data shows this was a marginal factor at best, he acknowledges. The performance of all major ethnic groups improved in London between 2005 and 2013, while there is evidence to suggest that non-White ethnic groups outside London did not progress at the same rate as non-White groups in the capital.[21]

Ultimately, the government did attempt to apply the London Challenge formula to other parts of the country – rolling out City Challenge programmes in Greater Manchester and the Black Country in 2008 – though their success was diluted compared to London. The capital managed to close the attainment gap between primary school children on free school meals and their peers by a more substantial margin than in the two other city regions. And only London managed to narrow the gap between secondary school pupils eligible for free school meals and their peers.[22]

A survey conducted by the City Challenge scheme affirmed these findings, showing that London-based headteachers were far more positive about the impact of the scheme than their counterparts in Manchester and the Black Country. Some 67 per cent of surveyed headteachers in London said that the London Challenge had enabled their school to improve more rapidly than would otherwise have been the case, compared to 49 per cent of those surveyed in Greater Manchester and 59 per cent in the Black Country.[23]

The London Challenge programme had of course run for five years prior to the inception of the satellite schemes, inevitably increasing its chances of success. The political impetus for reform had also waned by the twilight of New Labour's time in office, which came to an end in 2010. But Brighouse is still optimistic that similar programmes could be incubated outside London and could mirror the results enjoyed by the capital. Indeed, Liverpool City Region Mayor Steve Rotheram tells me that his team are currently studying the London Challenge, to see how its lessons could be applied to the city.

'I'm not saying you could replicate it all across the country – situations are different,' Brighouse cautions, 'but there are similar ingredients to success: you want the whole system to improve on its previous best, and you want to focus on the things that you can't necessarily measure.'

However, while Brighouse sees no theoretical reason why reforms can't be implemented elsewhere in the country, the Conservative Party has so far blocked the path of progress, he says. To his astonishment, only one Education Secretary has sought Brighouse's advice in the last twelve years. 'The only one who ever did was Damian Hinds,' who served as

Education Secretary from 2018 to 2019, but only 'because he was prompted to by Estelle [Morris]', Brighouse claims.

When I ask him why he thought his advice was not sought, or why the Conservatives ditched his policies, his answer is short and exasperated: 'I don't know.'

'I'm sure you could roll out the approach, subject to context,' he adds, although, 'you must never think that what you do in one place is going to work in another. And that was incidentally the idea of families of schools, because we were trying to put similar schools with each other. The same would be true of communities.'

Blair 'followed through' on his education rhetoric, Brighouse maintains. 'All that has gone,' set alight on the bonfire of David Cameron and George Osborne's austerity agenda, which sought to drastically reduce public spending in the wake of the financial crisis. 'Trying to motivate teachers now is a lot more difficult,' he says.

From 2009/10 to 2018/19, real-terms education spending in England fell by 8.3 per cent while pupil numbers rose by 10.2 per cent.[24] During the same period, annual classroom pay fell by more than £4,000. It's therefore unsurprising that the catch-up effort has stalled outside London in recent years.[25]

There is a cultural dimension to the place-based inequalities that riddle our education system, transcending the policies of any one administration. Namely: an elitist culture within the country's top universities; a palpable awareness that people of certain backgrounds don't really belong there.

The social and racial discrimination present in Britain's leading academic institutions is an uncomfortable bedfellow of our meritocratic ideals. The UK is one of the least discriminatory places on earth, the government itself has claimed, and so anyone who objects to racism, sexism or class discrimination at university is a 'woke snowflake' – someone who peddles a contrived form of victimhood in order to gain sympathy.

It's instructive that the 'anti-woke' mob consists largely of people who benefited from the most expensive schooling available in Britain – who have an interest in ensuring the walls of privilege are not torn down – alongside those who did not attend university at all.

Anyone who has attended a highly selective university from a position of disadvantage is fully aware of the overt and covert forms of social stigma that are embedded in the fabric of these institutions – with people from working-class backgrounds, particularly from geographic hinterlands, relegated to the bottom of the hierarchy.

'The education system is still primarily educating the three social classes separately and for very different social roles and economic outcomes,' says LSE Sociology Professor Diane Reay.[26] Most people are aware of this, even if policymakers feign ignorance. While university students from marginalised backgrounds are exalted by politicians, their experiences expose the meritocratic deceit.

University life is semantically and romantically described as a great levelling experience, where young people from all walks of life can study and mingle together, dedicated to the common pursuits of reading, shagging and drinking. Unfortunately, that's not quite the case.

'I was feeling homesick. And I was like: how can that be possible? I'm literally half an hour away from home.'

Lauren White is a Durham University graduate and someone I have known for a while in the political blogosphere. Lauren was raised in Gateshead, which flanks Newcastle on the South side of the Tyne. Aside from Northumbria,

Newcastle and Sunderland, no university is closer to home than her chosen institution. Both of Lauren's parents dropped out of school at 16, which makes her a beacon of meritocracy.

'At first when they mocked and mimicked my accent, I sort of went along with it, even laughed, but then when I persistently became the butt of jokes about coal mining and started to get called "feral" … it started to feel malicious.'

Riled by these experiences, and isolated in a place so close to home, Lauren wrote an article for the blog NE Beep, entitled, 'Things Posh People Have Said to Me' – in reference to her time at Durham.[27] 'I was made to feel like I was an alien in my own corner of the country. It's not like I'd gone to Exeter. I went 30 minutes down the road,' she wrote.

The article resonated with other students at Durham, who similarly felt like strangers in their own backyard. So Lauren catalogued their testimonies, recording stories that resonated far beyond the North East.

One Durham student who graduated in 2017, originally from Liverpool, described their university experience as 'horrendous': 'I'm from a working-class background. I was reminded of this every single day,' they said.

This same student recalled a common phrase on campus – 'rolling in the muck' – used to describe sleeping with a Northern, working-class person. 'I remember there being nights dedicated to [this], where sports teams or societies would go out to try and get with [i.e. snog] Northern working-class people,' they claimed.

Durham University student ambassador Jack Lines told a similar tale, alleging that he was approached on a night out by a female student who said that she had a 'poverty fetish' and wanted to sleep with him. She then encouraged Lines to start a fight in order to seduce her, because 'that's what you people do, you fight whenever you get drunk'.

Lauren's investigation encouraged others, at different universities, to broadcast their encounters with prejudice. Writing for the *Telegraph*, Jack Rear recounted his experiences at Royal Holloway University in London. He says that a fellow student waved a £50 note in his face and said, 'I bet you'd sleep with me for this, wouldn't you?' simply because Rear had a Northern accent.[28]

Joshua Dexter, the former chair of the Durham University Northern Society, offered an astute analysis of this regional-class bigotry. 'You come to university and expect people to be enlightened and open-minded. It's strange to see people talk articulately with ignorance,' he told me.

I spoke to Josh, and the chair of the Durham Working-Class Association, Jamie Halliwell, because I was intrigued by the existence of their societies. Why have clubs been formed to represent Northerners and the working class? After all, Durham is a former mining town situated just 70 miles south of the Scottish border. Societies premised on geography or ethnicity are typically only required if a group of people feels marginalised and seeks the comfort of their own clan.

'There is a sense of entitlement. The people who study at Durham are used to the locals not being their peers but the people who help or work for them,' Josh says. This sentiment is repeated by Lauren, who tells me that 'the only people with an accent are the people who work [at the university]. The cleaner speaks fluent Geordie, and everyone else will take the mick out of how she speaks.'

Following the publication of her report, Lauren met with the then Vice Chancellor of Durham, who said: 'We believe that everyone has the right to study and work in an environment that is respectful and where people feel comfortable to be themselves and to flourish.'

Yet Durham's entry data shows a stark regional imbalance. Over the last five years, only 7.8 per cent of Durham graduates were drawn from the North East, compared to 23 per cent of Newcastle University graduates.[29]

Durham's record is matched at other elite institutions. Between 2010 and 2015, Northern students received just 15 per cent of Oxford offers and 17 per cent of Cambridge offers. Over the same period, students in London and the South East accounted for 48 per cent of all Oxbridge offers.[30] Ultimately, the rapid expansion of higher education in the UK has masked the fact that elite institutions are still elitist. University attendance rates have risen from 15 per cent in 1988 to 33 per cent in 1994, and now stand at more than 50 per cent.[31] However, many of the country's top institutions still operate like private finishing schools for the hereditary intelligentsia.

In fact, while the structure of the British economy has changed profoundly since the 1980s, the growth of the service sector driving an expansion in higher education, few policies have helped past generations to cope with this new reality. Mass industrial employment has been confined to a bygone era, yet those who lost their jobs have been offered little support through education or retraining. Universities have remained in the clutches of higher social classes, shutting out a lost generation of older, working-class people in small towns who have effectively been consigned to the scrap heap. There has been a 45 per cent decline in funding for adult skills over the last decade, according to the House of Commons Education Committee, which has resulted in adult education participation rates almost halving since 2004.[32]

For many of those who do enter higher education, the experience simply institutionalises the cultural stereotypes about North and South, London and the left-behind, that they have been drip-fed since birth. As the Children's Commissioner notes, young people in the North are acutely aware of the negative clichés associated with Britain's former industrial heartlands. Children 'displayed a nuanced understanding of how crime, lack of opportunity and an undesirable public perception of the North can combine to impact outcomes for young people', reads a report produced by the Commissioner in 2018.[33]

Jamie Halliwell of the Durham Working-Class Association puts it a bit more bluntly: 'There's an assumption that everyone just works in Greggs.'

Young people from unfashionable parts of the country understand how they are perceived. They also know that top academic establishments are the preserve of people from London, the privately educated and nannied. Therefore, they know that attending an elite university will involve suffering from discrimination on the basis of their accent, their culture and their class. This awareness is usually intensified by the physical infrastructure of elite universities – the spires and the portraits that leer disdainfully over pimple-faced undergrads. A general unease and unfamiliarity, combined with the prospect of open hostility, dissuades the state-schooled Barrow boy from applying to join the pageantry of privilege at an elite university – sticking instead to an establishment closer to home, that is more familiar and probably mundane. And so the position of the privileged is preserved; the imperial masonry managing to guard what the upper classes have owned for centuries.

'Accent can become a marker of everything else, a tangible barrier, most of all to the young people themselves, who internalise a sense of social inferiority,' says Sammy Wright, lead commissioner on schools and higher education for the Social Mobility Commission.[34]

I know first-hand about this process of self-limitation. During sixth-form college I applied to four Northern universities and only one in the South – Oxford. I totally botched my interview at Mansfield College, Oxford, and ultimately read History at the University of York.

York is a great university, don't get me wrong, but looking back I can now see how my ambitions were tempered by my background. Why didn't I apply to the London School of Economics (LSE) or University College London (UCL) – both of which were thought of as more prestigious universities than York – even though I would more than likely have been accepted?

I was scared, if I'm being truly honest. Scared of London, a city that I had only visited once before in my life; scared of being judged and taunted for my background or my accent; scared of simply not finding anyone similar to me. So I toned down my ambitions and went to a university that was closer to home and closer to my life experiences. It all worked out in the end and I don't feel as though I missed out, though I could quite easily have been curtailing my life opportunities if things had panned out in a different way. Some of my friends, to provide a point of comparison, couldn't even understand why I was bothering to apply to one elite Southern university, such was their internalised aversion to regional conflict.

This fear of stigma also has an effect after university. If you choose not to apply to an elite university because you don't want to become a social pariah, it's highly unlikely that you will apply to an elite profession. Alternatively, if you did attend an elite university and you were labelled as a pleb for three years, it's probably even less likely that you'll want to join the hordes of former private school boys marching towards the City of London.

Granted, the regional hostility documented by Lauren is not an everyday occurrence. Rather, bias is more commonly exhibited through cultural indifference. 'I remember one girl from London who said if she was going to put Durham on the map she'd put it in the middle of the country,' Lauren recalls.

I encountered the same attitude at university, from people who couldn't locate York even though they were physically inhabiting the city. There was a prevailing attitude, I thought, among people from London and the South East who saw the North as a playground – a three-year escape from their parents and the constraints of their childhood – before they were forced to return to the capital for work. Their life in York was a temporary fling, and anyone who romanticised the North and its culture was seen as a bit silly.

Prejudice and indifference do not just hinder people with regional accents, however. Universities are also forums, show-cases, for other forms of inequality. At half of UK universities, fewer than 5 per cent of students are classified as being from a disadvantaged White background.[35] Meanwhile, only 2 per cent of Black Caribbean and White British boys eligible for free school meals gained entry to highly 'selective' universities in 2020.[36] As recently as 2018/19 there were just 100 Black undergraduates admitted to Cambridge University – a tiny fraction of the student population, albeit a record.[37]

Higher education is the end point for 46 per cent of White British girls in the state system not on free school meals, in contrast to 13 per cent of White British boys on free school meals. And while 48 per cent of White and Black African girls on free school meals reach university, only 28 per cent of their male counterparts do. There are also huge disparities between different non-White ethnic groups. While universities welcome 82 per cent of girls and 74 per cent of boys from

Chinese backgrounds not on free school meals, the equivalent figures are 45 per cent for White and Black Caribbean girls and 33 per cent for boys – the second lowest figures among any ethnic group not on free school meals.[38]

University entry rates among different ethnic groups is a more nuanced issue than it is portrayed in the media – juxtaposing the under-performance of working-class, White boys with the relative success of some non-White groups. This narrative is infused with racist undertones, implying that White people somehow have a greater right to academic success than people from minority ethnic backgrounds. It is striking how many publications, even the BBC, compare the university entry rates of White working-class boys with the performance of non-White students who aren't on free school meals – thus artificially exaggerating the divide.

And although the media lens periodically brings into focus the issue of higher education entry rates, markedly less attention is paid to the performance of these same individuals at university. Statistics from the Office for Students show that roughly one in six (15 per cent) of Black undergraduates drop out of university before completing their course, compared to 9 per cent of White undergraduates. Meanwhile, 82 per cent of White undergraduates achieve a first-class or upper second-class qualification, markedly more than the 60 per cent of Black undergraduates and 72 per cent of Asian undergraduates who achieve the same standard.[39]

The prejudice and elitism that drive hostility towards people who are different can be found in more extreme and troubling forms in the racist incidents that have been seen on campus in recent years. In 2015, the Oxford Union was forced to pass a motion condemning itself as institutionally racist after it advertised a 'colonial comeback' party.[40] The Plymouth University Conservative group was suspended in

2018 after some of its members were seen sporting T-shirts with anti-Semitic and racist messages.[41] In 2019, a Leicester University student was pictured wearing racist slogans at a social event, including one that read, 'Hitler wanted my kind alive.'[42] A year later, some members of the Essex University Conservative Society suggested that coronavirus passing through Black Lives Matter protesters was simply 'natural selection'.[43]

These incidents are not isolated – the government's equality watchdog, the Equality and Human Rights Commission, found that a quarter of university students from minority ethnic backgrounds claim to have experienced racial harassment. This figure rises to almost a third among Black students. Professor Julia Buckingham, President of Universities UK, has called the findings 'sad and shocking'.[44]

One could argue that there has been a concerted effort in recent years to trigger conflict between White working-class boys from 'left-behind' parts of the country and people from minority ethnic backgrounds. This is a faux war, stoked by opportunists who see racial conflict as the vessel for their political ambitions. Ultimately, while the details are multi-dimensional, Brits who are marginalised on the basis of region and race suffer mutually from potent strains of elitism and discrimination in the education system. This manifests at different times and in different ways – overlapping with deep-seated class hierarchies – but social inequality is an ever-present feature of growing up in Britain.

This rigged system is covered up by the rhetoric of 'meritocracy' – the deceit that we live in a country where anyone can succeed, regardless of their background. This principle doesn't stand up to scrutiny, especially in relation to geography. Children in London benefit from an enhanced state school system – largely thanks to the transformative impact of the London Challenge programme – that markedly elevates their attainment and their outcomes. The spectre of social stigma further dissuades students in hinterland Britain from pursuing elite higher education options, while the daily jibes suffered by those who have taken the leap cause them to regret ever having done so.

And that's even before they hit the job market.

2.

CRADLE TO GRAVE

So you've bounced through the education system, made the leap from a neglected region to an elite university and have just about survived the snobbery. You have done everything that teachers, parents and career advisors instructed, even softening your accent in the process. The next step is finding a career.

Yet, as your student housemates make the journey down the M1, back to the capital, you realise that you are not travelling to the same Britain. Your hometown is a graveyard of industry; a place starved of opportunity. So, your only option is to leave.

Research from the Centre for Towns shows that, since 1981, towns and villages in Britain have lost more than 1 million people aged under 25, while gaining more than 2 million over-65s.[1] Accordingly, a quarter of all new graduates from UK universities in 2014 and 2015 were working in London within six months – including 38 per cent of Russell Group graduates with first-class or upper-second degrees.[2]

As North-East local and Durham graduate Lauren White says: 'I either stay here and get a job that frankly, not to be rude, I'm over-qualified for, or I leave all my friends and family, move to London and live by myself. The alternative is to compromise on everything that I've been working for since I was 12.'

But the reality is more complex than troops of be-flat-capped Northerners lining up to board the Hogwarts Express down to King's Cross. The cannibalisation of Britain's regions by London is often experienced most acutely by the places that are trapped in the immediate gravitational pull of the capital. In 2016, 54.9 per cent of graduates in South East England (outside London), 46.6 per cent of graduates in the East and 46.4 per cent of graduates in the South West left their respective regions for employment. This compares to 40.7 per cent of graduates who departed the North East and just 27.3 per cent who left London itself.[3]

The proportion of graduates leaving the capital is comparatively small, and I would bet that it's artificially inflated by the swathe of students who left their hometown to study in London but who now, after graduating, simply can't afford the rent.

Ultimately, if you do manage to stake a claim in the capital – clinging to its underbelly – your career opportunities are vastly enhanced. An audit conducted by the LSE in 2013 found that London and the South East 'feature disproportionately' on the CVs of parliamentarians, which is invariably also the case for other top professions. 'The most striking feature of the employment data ... is the over-representation of London,' the report reads. Of all England-based MPs, 52 per cent worked in London at some point prior to their election. The most common pre-Parliament professions were finance, law, journalism and of course politics – all of which are disproportionately concentrated in London.[4]

'If you're in any of the professions, there's only one destination for you, if you want to advance,' public relations supremo Karl Milner, a former political advisor to Gordon

Brown and Hillary Clinton, tells me. 'And government investment has been a real driver of disparity between London and
everywhere else.'

The problem is summarised by David Goodhart in his
book *Head, Hand, Heart*. Goodhart deploys the term 'heartlands' to describe the neglected, former industrial areas of
many Western nations, originally coined in this context by US
writer Michael Lind. 'The heartlands are particularly
neglected in Britain thanks to an over-mighty capital city,'
Goodhart writes.[5]

But this regional imbalance has not spontaneously morphed
into existence through an act of nature or a rogue SimCity
experiment. This economic consolidation, to the extent that
we see today, has taken place over the last sixty years, spurred
by political choices.

Britain's industrial landscape has undergone a revolution
since the 1950s and 1960s. 'The share of manufacturing
workers in total employment peaked in the 1950s, the absolute number of workers in manufacturing in the 1960s,'
writes pre-eminent historian David Edgerton in *The Rise and
Fall of the British Nation*. 'This was Britain's manufacturing
moment; the moment too of the industrial working class.'[6]

Yet, since the 1980s, traditional industries and the areas
that nourished them have been pillaged by the free market.
The mines and the plants have been sold off for scraps,
replaced with an information economy reliant on the service
sector. At the start of Margaret Thatcher's tenure as prime
minister, thanks to high interest rates and a strong currency,
manufacturing output collapsed by 15 per cent in just two
years. Imperial Chemical Industries (ICI), a firm that
employed several of my family members, lost 30 per cent of
its workforce between 1979 and 1983.[7] And now data has
replaced coal as the key commodity in the British economy,

while the pinstripe suit has supplanted blackened dungarees as the uniform of the worker.

The demonisation of unionised labour and state planning collided with the renewed popularity of libertarian economics, theorised by Milton Friedman and Friedrich Hayek and popularised by Thatcher. The aggressive retrenchment of the state thus had profound regional implications, freeing the market in the wealthiest parts of the country while extracting the industrial lifeblood from its rust belt.

As Thatcher said to journalist Brian Walden in January 1983, epitomising her economic mindset: 'I think we went through a period when too many people began to expect their standard of living to be guaranteed by the state.'[8] So, the Conservative leader pulled the plug on industry, including manufacturing, which relied on government support – and curtailed the boundaries of the state, cutting public spending as a percentage of GDP from 44.6 per cent in 1979 to 39.1 per cent when she left office in 1990.[9]

Britain's once-mighty industrial core was dwindling even before Thatcher. Over the course of the 1960s and 1970s, more than 300,000 coal mining jobs disappeared in the UK.[10] 'By the late 1960s Japanese and German firms were catching up and taking over' in the sectors of manufacturing and engineering, Edgerton observes.[11] However, Thatcher signed the death certificate – reducing the number of coal miners from 230,000 to just 57,000 in ten years. By 2004, only 6,000 were left. In 1984, during the prime minister's bout with Arthur Scargill and the National Union of Mineworkers, a battle over proposed pit closures, the country's unemployment rate stood at 11.9 per cent.[12]

'It's particularly evident to me that in the 1970s and accelerated into the '80s and early '90s, the collapse of traditional industry – and I was living through it – had a profound effect.

Not just in terms of people losing their jobs, but the status of the jobs. The nature of self-identity deteriorated very quickly.'

These are the reflections of former Education and Employment Secretary David Blunkett, who served in Tony Blair's Cabinet from 1997 to 2005. A foot-soldier for South Yorkshire, born and bred in Sheffield, Blunkett was the leader of the city council during much of Thatcher's rule. 'We lost 50,000 jobs in British steel and engineering in just three years,' he says. 'That had a massive knock-on effect on the individuals and their families.'

In 1957, the proportion of workers in industrial employment in the UK stood at 48 per cent. By 1979, this figure had fallen to 38 per cent, declining to 27 per cent by 1998 and just 15 per cent by 2016.[13]

Thatcherite economics assumed that once the umbilical cord was cut – once the heartlands were liberated from dying industries – spare economic capacity would be harnessed by the free market to galvanise new, more prosperous forms of innovation. However, without the guiding role of the state, the free market concentrated economic activity in the places where it could achieve maximum productivity: ergo, in cities such as London, where a nexus of creative, financial and political activity conspired to generate disproportionate opportunities for wealth creation. In contrast, peripheral regions were gutted, and were gradually saddled with the social and cultural problems that accompany persistent levels of unemployment and a diminished collective sense of self-worth.

'While the cities were able to adjust and adapt and started to provide a magnet to other activity – particularly cultural activity – small towns festered, the public sphere deteriorated, and with that the self-belief and the attitude of the people living there,' Blunkett contends.

Ultimately, Britain's industrial heartlands lacked visionaries, Blunkett says, who could have made the case for state-led regeneration and a gradual divestment from declining modes of production. 'The North was caught in a vacuum between two groups – one, the Thatcherites, that thought the government didn't have a role, and the other, the unions, that just wanted to defend what was already there,' he says.

'Back in the 1960s, the Labour government talked about the white heat of technological change, but instead attempted to prop up industries. This wasn't as much about planning for the future as retaining what was already there.'

Libertarians eventually won the political war, carrying out the rapid deindustrialisation and financialisation of the UK economy – simultaneously scaling back the industrial planning functions of the state alongside welfare provision. Pockets of economic heat were incubated – particularly in London – while the industrial North, Midlands, Wales, Scotland and Northern Ireland were kneecapped.

London itself was industrial – indeed it was the trade and manufacturing hub of the Empire. But we don't refer to the capital as 'post-industrial', perhaps because it is one of the few places in the UK that has found a new economic identity in the era after Thatcher. 'For centuries, London has been a world centre of capitalism,' *Guardian* columnist and senior economics commentator Aditya Chakrabortty tells me. 'It was the beating heart of the Empire. It funnelled capital from London to the rest of the world, and it took in goods from the rest of the world and sold it to the rest of Britain.

'But it was also a manufacturing capital of Britain,' he adds. 'The industrial era is everywhere in London, but it's masked by the flat conversions of former industrial sites. It's wrong to think that London was always like it is now – this weird place that sucks in people from the North because they want to get a job in politics or the media or finance. It used to be very different.'

As Alan R. Townsend wrote in the immediate aftermath of the Thatcher years in 1993, the Conservatives encouraged a 'services-led Southern boom'.[14] From 1979 to 1990, the GDP of the South East increased threefold from £57 billion to £170 billion and, in the space of just six years from 1984 to 1990, the GDP of London soared from £38 billion to £71 billion. In the same six-year period, total household income per head in London jumped from £5,543 to £9,897. By the end of the decade, household income in the North lagged behind the capital by 25 per cent.[15]

And while some regions extended their advantage over others, so did the richest individuals over the poorest. While the weekly income of the bottom 10 per cent of families increased by just 4.6 per cent from 1979 to 1990, the income of the top 10 per cent increased by 32 per cent. Considering the era of deindustrialisation as a whole, from 1970 to 2005, the top 0.1 per cent of people – amounting to just 47,000 individuals – saw their average income increase nearly eightfold, from £98,193 to £780,043. The bottom 10 per cent, meanwhile, saw their incomes rise by just 50 per cent, from £11,400 to £16,837.[16]

Extreme inflation during Thatcher's early tenure was a boon for property owners. This process has continued in London ever since, the capital's glass towers acting as a safety deposit box for the world's rich. Labour leader John Smith, who sadly died suddenly in 1994 after taking over from Neil Kinnock in 1992, described this rampant wealth inflation as 'casino economics'. Britain had turned into a 'speculators' paradise', he added.

From 1981 to 1991, the number of households in social housing fell from 5.4 million to 4.5 million as council properties were transferred en masse to private owners. Meanwhile, the average selling price of a house in the UK trebled, from £19,925 in 1979 to £59,785 in 1990. This figure hit £251,634 in 2010, by which time the London market was beginning to detach itself from the rest of the country.[17]

It's worth noting that deindustrialisation did not halt when Labour returned to power in 1997. While London grew exponentially, manufacturing as a share of the economy fell in the thirteen years of New Labour, from 18 per cent to just 10 per cent.[18]

'To be fair, when I look back on it, the last Labour government had half a plan,' former New Labour advisor and minister Andrew Adonis tells me, in a somewhat jumpy Zoom call from his home in Italy. 'We had a public services plan, which did genuinely level up the whole country. But unfortunately, we didn't have a robust enough industrial plan, and we didn't talk overtly enough about industrial policy.

'We were still too much of a Thatcher tribute act,' he says, with refreshing candour. 'We mirrored the false notion that governments shouldn't engage in industrial policy alongside the private sector.'

Greater Manchester Mayor and former Health Secretary Andy Burnham agrees, echoing the remarks of Adonis. 'The government I worked for didn't do enough to rebalance the country,' he tells me.

That said, former prime minister Gordon Brown was at least perceptive enough to diagnose the problem, observing in 2016 that 'economically, Britain is becoming two nations – a prosperous South East and a permanently struggling North – with, at the centre, a London economy which is appearing to decouple from the periphery of the county'.[19]

Thatcher liberated the market, allowing investment to flee from the old economy to the new, simultaneously removing barriers to mass unemployment and deprivation. The wealth of the nation migrated from the sites of industrialised, unionised labour to the places that housed the service sector, financial and property markets. In other words: from industrial heartlands to the capital.

'In a way it is even humiliating to watch coal-miners working. It raises you a momentary doubt about your own status as an "intellectual" and a superior person generally. For it is brought home to you, at least while you are watching, that it is only because miners sweat their guts out that superior persons can remain superior.'

George Orwell, *The Road to Wigan Pier*

It takes just two and a half hours to travel from London to Port Talbot in South Wales, but the contrast in the landscape can only be measured in decades. The journey starts in Paddington, the place elevated to international fame by a small imaginary creature. And while Paddington Bear is a figment of the imagination, so too is the city he inhabits. The story conjures up an image of London as a neighbourly, charming, eccentric place – an idealised version of the city in 1958, when the tale was originally conceived.

If the story were rewritten today, it might feature Lamborghinis roaring through the streets of Bayswater, the vacant rows of stucco mansions providing a summer playground for the preened heirs to foreign fortunes. In the shadows and in the gutters, meanwhile, hollow souls lumber their duvets to the nearest begging spot, hoping to be showered with some new money.

But on the other side of the tracks, Port Talbot has also been captured by mythology. Once the site of the largest steelworks in Europe, the town's industrial glory has faded, its proud heritage now laced with regret at how quickly the country and the world have left it behind.

Indeed, Port Talbot and its neighbours in South Wales embody the struggle between the old economy and the new – and the extent to which former heartlands, the furnace of Britain, now trail behind London.

While Port Talbot is famed for its steelmaking, the South Wales landscape, its places and its people have been moulded by the mining industry. Prior to the First World War, Barry was the largest coal exporting port in Britain, possibly even the world.[20] By the end of the war, South Wales accounted for more than 20 per cent of the nation's employment and economic output, while 250,000 miners worked in Wales. It's estimated that between 1851 and 1911, 366,000 people moved to South Wales to take advantage of the opportunities presented by the coal mining industry, its economic pull extending to England, Ireland and even continental Europe. The population of the two Rhondda valleys stood at 1,998 in 1851. By 1911 it had risen to 152,781.[21]

However, in 1984, the Thatcher government accepted a commission report recommending that twenty-seven of the thirty-three remaining collieries in South Wales should be closed, and that an embargo should be placed on the hiring of new staff. The region fell to Thatcher's axe, and the newly redundant labourers suffered the double indignity of being instructed by Employment Secretary Norman Tebbit to follow the example of his father by getting 'on their bike' to find work.

But the invisible hand of the free market did not rescue the people of South Wales. In Swansea, for example, a comparatively prosperous city on the south coast, gross disposable household income per head was £15,755 in 2018 – 7.9 per cent below the Wales average and 25.4 per cent below the overall UK average – while median weekly household earnings lagged 8.1 per cent behind the national average. These statistics are matched by overall productivity in Swansea, measured by Gross Value Added (GVA), standing at 23.1 per cent below the national average.[22]

In 2018, gross disposable household income per head in London was £29,362, while in Port Talbot it was £16,535.[23] For every minute on the train from Paddington to South Wales, income falls by £85. Statistics produced by the ONS in 2020 suggest that of the fifty places with the highest disposable incomes in England and Wales, forty-one were in London. The same data shows that 28 per cent of all local areas in Wales were among the poorest 10 per cent of areas before housing costs, a higher proportion than any other part of Britain.[24]

The evaporation of wealth, the stagnation of wages and an exodus of opportunity has a profound effect on the material and mental wellbeing of a place. 'Frankly, the high street is dying on its feet,' Port Talbot postman Mark told me a couple of years ago, when I was making a BBC documentary. Mark had been on the beat for thirty years, having been born and raised in the town. He had witnessed its glory days, and its abandonment by successive governments.

While the local steelworks used to provide reliable, well-paid employment in Port Talbot, there has been a persistent sense of doom in recent years. The Tata-owned plant has ricocheted from crisis to crisis, perpetually on the brink of collapse. Lots of people rely on the steel works, Mark says, not just for employment, but for the retail spending provided by its workers. There is consequently a lingering atmosphere of trepidation in the town. The steel works is not just Port Talbot's major employer but also its most visible landmark.

Its looming presence on the West Glamorgan dunes, over-looking the Bristol channel, is a constant reminder of the town's uncertain future.

Wealth and health are also intimately linked, and a profile of the local area conducted by the council in 2009 found that each ward 'suffers from some aspect of deprivation, with health deprivation being a particular issue for most wards'.[25]

The current generation of young people in Port Talbot therefore have no other choice but to leave the town – moving to Cardiff or London in search of opportunities. A generation ago, 95 per cent of people who were born in Port Talbot chose to stay there, Mark estimates. Now, he says, that figure is probably below 50 per cent.

To people living in London, or other big cities, this may not seem like a big deal. London is a city in permanent flux, constantly regenerating. But this is not the norm in Port Talbot. There is a strong sense of local community and shared history. Mark claims that his family has lived in the area for ten or eleven generations, and that he only proposed to his wife on the proviso that she would move to the town from her native Shrewsbury. In your worldview, this may be archaic or overly sentimental, but it's an unavoidable reality of Britain's heartlands, where identity is rooted in local pride. 'I couldn't move anywhere else,' Mark says.

In recent years, however, the economic landscape has started to change in South Wales. New factories pepper the skyline, bedecked with the smirking logo of America's tech-retail giant, Amazon. In 2013, the *Independent* reported that Amazon's fulfilment centre situated between Swansea and Port Talbot was the company's second largest in the UK,[26] the whole site employing 1,200 people as of May 2019.[27] While Tata Steel employs roughly 8,000 people in the UK, Amazon's national workforce has burgeoned from 6,000 in 2013 to approximately 30,000 today. Thanks to booming online sales during the Pandemic, the firm announced in May 2021 that it planned to boost its UK workforce by another 10,000.[28]

This is the next phase of economic evolution in many of Britain's industrial heartlands – a big tech revolution that is providing a new era of factory floor employment. But this fourth industrial revolution has created its own unique swathe of challenges. As James Bloodworth's book *Hired* reveals in graphic detail, factory labour in the tech industry is plagued by insecurity, low pay and poor conditions.[29]

It would be naïve to imply that working down a pit was easy. As George Orwell writes in *The Road to Wigan Pier*, 'Most of the things one imagines in hell are there – heat, noise, confusion, darkness, foul air, and, above all, unbearably cramped space.'[30] But it's undeniable that Thatcher's successful attempt to dismantle unionised labour precipitated a recession of workers' rights that is being suffered in factories today. The futurists of the 1970s foretold an age of post-industrial abundance and leisure; the immediate reality for vast swathes of workers has been 'a move to harder, longer, less-well-paid work', says Edgerton.[31]

Amazon is also in a minority. It's one of the few monoliths of the modern economy that requires factory hands to work alongside computer science nerds. Other tech giants, like Facebook and Twitter, largely exist in the ether. Technology is most likely destroying high street jobs more rapidly than it is replacing them. High street retail employment fell in more than three-quarters of local authorities between 2015 and 2018,[32] while thirty-two major retailers went bust from 2008 to 2019 – with the loss of 115,000 jobs.[33] The collapse of Arcadia and Debenhams during the 2020/21 Christmas period put a reported 25,000 jobs at risk – more than the number employed in the entire UK fishing industry.[34]

What's more, there's uncertainty about how long these new factory jobs will last. Amazon evidently has the incentive and the ability to automate vast numbers of factory jobs in the coming years, substituting expensive, unreliable humans with infinitely more efficient robots. According to Scott Anderson, Amazon's director of robotics fulfilment, fully automated factories are 'at least' ten years away, a length of time that's not as reassuring as Anderson seems to think it is.[35]

'Frankly it's looking like George Orwell's *1984*, where I could be replaced by a robot or a drone,' postman Mark gravely predicts. 'Any community spirit that's left is going to be eaten away, if the worst-case scenario does happen and all these jobs are thrown on the scrapheap and replaced by robots.'

Moreover, successive governments have struggled to ensure regional redistribution through the tax system, given the uncanny ability of big tech companies to shield their profits from Europe's debt collectors.[36] This contributes to a stubborn and malignant perception in former industrial areas that the fruits of their labour are being poached, both by corporate suits and by the nation's capital.

'The majority of participants from all types of places, bar core cities, bemoan that big businesses work to overall remove money from the local economy,' says a survey conducted by the UK in a Changing Europe and the Joseph Rowntree Foundation in 2019.[37] 'The bulk of revenues and high-skilled employees are perceived to be funnelled away to more prosperous parts of the country, predominantly London, leaving their local areas seldom better off for having big businesses in the area … Across locations, participants spoke of a London-centric economy in which other areas of the UK are forgotten.'

This economic system is a hangover of imperialism, says Labour MP Clive Lewis. The nature of British capitalism was created to 'extract wealth from the countries within the British empire, which has now been enshrined in corporate law and how the neo-liberal economic system functions'. However, now that Britain has lost its empire, 'these same laws and principles have been used to extract wealth domestically'.

To feed London's insatiable appetite, international imperialism has been replaced by regional imperialism.

The antagonism that much of the country harbours towards London may seem like petty jealousy – an older sibling holding a distasteful grudge towards their more successful brother or sister.

This fuels hostility from the capital towards Britain's regions, couched in the dangerous belief that different regions compete against one another in a meritocracy of geography. You cannot blame London for being more productive and prosperous than the rest of the country, it is suggested. In fact, poorer regions should be grateful that tax revenues raised in London are redistributed across the country to prop up their failing local economies. This attitude has emanated most strongly from the Left in recent times – a peculiarity that is explored in Chapter 4.

However, the United Kingdom is (for now) still united. We have not fragmented into a Darwinist competition between different regions, with the strongest and richest purging the weak. The essential purpose of the nation is to ensure the safety and prosperity of all its citizens, not solely property-owners in the capital.

Yet, over recent decades, regional economic inequality has been an uncontested feature of the nation, actively pursued by the government. Productivity in London, measured in terms of GVA, is 30 per cent above the England-wide average, and

40 per cent above the lowest-performing regions. Indeed, economic under-performance is the norm throughout the country. London and the South East are the only regions that are more productive than the UK average.[38]

If we deconstruct the data on a more granular level, the disparities are even more absurd. According to the Industrial Strategy Council, the country's most productive region, West inner London, has an income per hour that is 70 per cent higher than Northumberland's.[39] For context, there is a similar percentage gap between the GDP of Ireland and the GDP of Iraq.

Average gross weekly earnings in London are 20 per cent higher than the England average among full-time employees, and more than 30 per cent higher the average in the North East.[40] Even after housing costs are taken into account, between 2014 and 2017 household income in London was greater than in the East Midlands, Yorkshire, Northern Ireland, the North West, the West Midlands, the North East, and Wales.[41]

This is a bleak picture. After a period of convergence during the middle of the twentieth century, regional fluctuations in incomes now match the disparities seen in 1901.[42] Meanwhile, Scotland is the only area of the UK that has experienced an improvement in its relative productivity since the latter decades of the twentieth century, now the third most productive area of the UK, behind the South East and London.

And while Scotland is making up ground, many cities in the North of England are still on a downward spiral. Ten of the twelve cities that are suffering the worst levels of relative decline are in the North of England, according to a 2016 report by the Joseph Rowntree Foundation, namely: Rochdale, Burnley, Bolton, Blackburn, Hull, Grimsby,

Middlesbrough, Bradford, Blackpool and Wigan. All of these areas voted for Brexit. In contrast, the South of England doesn't feature among the top twenty-five declining cities.[43]

The performance of regional economies relates directly to their composition, with London hoarding all the best cards. Ever since Thatcher set the bailiffs loose on Britain's industries in the 1980s, the service sector has gained a monopoly – now representing 75 per cent of the economy – with London eclipsing the rest.[44]

As of 2018, London accounted for 30 per cent of all private sector employment in the UK, despite its population representing roughly 15 per cent of the national total. Meanwhile, regions that lost a relatively large proportion of their public sector jobs after the 2008 financial crash and the subsequent years of austerity – such as the North East, North West and Yorkshire – have only gained private sector jobs at approximately half the rate of the capital since that time.[45]

Financial services contributed £132 billion to the UK economy in 2019, up from £33.5 billion in 1990, alongside 1.1 million jobs. Yet 49 per cent of the sector is holed up in London's money factories, comprising 15 per cent of regional output. The place with the UK's second highest endowment of financial services is Scotland, with just 9 per cent of the national total.[46]

Legal services contributed £60 billion to the UK economy in 2018 and in 2017 employed 338,000 people,[47] a third of whom plied their trade in London, compared to just 13,000 in second-placed Manchester.[48] Of the top law firms in the country by revenue, at the time of writing, more than half are based in London.[49]

'When I qualified as a lawyer, the impression I was left with, by everyone I spoke to, was that in order to progress at speed and to have the greatest opportunities, I had to be in

London,' Nazir Afzal tells me. He grew up in Small Heath in Birmingham, eventually becoming Chief Crown Prosecutor for North West England following years of working in the capital.

Afzal says that moving to London was 'the best thing that ever happened to me', exposing him to high-profile cases in the nerve centre of the legal profession. 'Within a couple of years, I was working on the cases of serial killers,' he says.

'But the fact was that I had no other option – I had to leave Birmingham. All the main barristers' chambers are in London – and certainly in the 1990s, if you didn't work in London, people didn't think you were good enough.'

He points out that there is, in effect, only one Crown Court in England – based in London. Therefore, all the highest-profile cases are tried in the capital, even if the crimes were committed elsewhere. The trial of the Yorkshire Ripper took place at the Old Bailey in St Paul's, for example.

'The Crown Prosecution Service is based down there, the Royal Courts of Justice are all down there, the senior judiciary are all based down there, all the major government departments related to law are down there,' Afzal laments. 'London remains the epicentre. If I were to give advice to any budding lawyer right now, I'd tell them they need to be in London at some point in their career.'

The UK is also home to some of the world's largest consultancy firms – amorphous institutions that provide all manner of accountancy, legal and advisory services to companies and governments. In 2018, the UK consulting market grew by 5.6 per cent to £8.2 billion, representing one of the largest market shares in Europe.[50] It's estimated that the sector grew by another 8 per cent in 2019, after which the consultancy giants were embedded in the UK's response to the Pandemic.[51] At the time of writing, McKinsey – nicknamed 'the firm' by its staff – is advertising for jobs in nine different locations in Germany but only one UK city: London. Deloitte, which basically acted as a surrogate for the civil service during the Pandemic, meanwhile appears to have six offices in London, and only three in the entire North of England.

'In many ways, the economic geography of the UK is reminiscent of a much poorer country at an earlier stage of economic development.' This is the view of Professor Philip McCann, who works at the University of Sheffield and studies regional inequality. He maintains that the UK's place-based divides are regional, more so than the recently popularised contrast between towns and cities. He also says that the UK is an international outlier. Using several different methodologies, McCann calculates that regional inequality in the UK is more extreme than in any of the other twenty-eight advanced OECD countries.[52]

This may be embarrassing for the UK, but the ultimate cost is not to our collective ego but to the people who have suffered from the unremitting deterioration and neglect of their areas. People like Les, a former mining engineer who now stacks shelves at his local supermarket, alongside running a working men's club in Dewsbury.

'I was a skilled worker; had been for 25 years,' Les told me. 'But when the pits closed, there was nowhere else for me to work. I'm not proud of working at a supermarket – it's dull as hell. I have to take orders from a jobsworth. But, to be honest mate, I have no other options. Some of my mates never found work again.'

These people have been pummelled by the political and economic shocks of the past forty years, fostering a deep-seated loathing towards those in power – something that motivated Les to vote for Brexit. In this sense, the EU Referendum was a basic equation: do you want fewer politicians governing you?

In the context of government-imposed deindustrialisation, austerity, inequality – and the accompanying side effects of declining health and rising crime – the result can be easily explained.

This is a point acknowledged by Blunkett, a self-professed Eurosceptic who backed the Remain campaign. 'The losers have always been the same people' since the 1980s. On the EU's own measurements, the number of struggling regions has burgeoned in the UK over the last decade, from three in 2008 to seven in 2017, latterly including southern Scotland, West Wales, Cornwall and the Isles of Scilly, Lincolnshire, Tees Valley and Durham, South Yorkshire and outer London (East and North East).[53]

The regional Darwinism project of the last fifty years has particularly afflicted coastal towns, once the beneficiaries of rapidly swelling consumer income during the middle of the twentieth century. From Blackpool in the North West to Rochester in the South East, coastal communities exhibit low productivity, high poverty and complex health needs as their greying populations steadily expand.

According to the local Joint Strategic Needs Assessment, Blackpool is the most deprived local authority area in England, with all measures of deprivation having increased since 2007. In 2016, 26.2 per cent of children in the seaside town were in relative poverty, the fourteenth highest level of child poverty in the country, compared to an England-wide average of 17 per cent.[54]

But this is not a North–South divide. The Industrial Strategy Council suggests that Cornwall is the UK's least productive region, while an annual influx of holiday-goers, bankers and Bentleys distracts from the intense poverty that can be found in this corner of the country.[55]

On a recent visit to Cornwall, the similarities with South Wales were immediately apparent. Off the tourist track, you notice that the villages are forged out of stoic, workmanlike stone terraces or modest, mid-century council-built properties. The vacant petrol stations and the rugged country pubs give an impression of dislocation – one that has prevented the area from claiming a place in the modern economy.

While London consumes much of the private sector and professional services, areas outside the capital rely on the foundational economy: the basic requirements of life for all citizens irrespective of their income and location. This includes infrastructure – such as systems for water, electricity and transport – as well as primary services like education, health and social care. Since March 2020 and the onset of COVID, the people working in the foundational economy have been affectionately called 'key workers' – a belated tribute to the efforts of these public servants who prop up the country.

The book *Foundational Economy* suggests that key workers constitute 43.8 per cent of the UK's workforce. This figure is lowest in London, at 35 per cent, while the proportion of key workers in all other nations and regions surpasses 40 per cent. In the North East, 50 per cent of the workforce is foundational.[56]

There appears to be a pretty even split in the number of key workers employed by the state and the private sector. As of June 2020, there were 5.5 million public sector workers in the UK, the majority of whom worked in health and education, representing 16.7 per cent of all people in employment.[57]

Karl Milner has first-hand experience of regional cleavage in private sector employment. After applying his trade in

London for many years, Karl decided to move home in the late 2000s, escaping back to the North.

'There wasn't a PR market in the North of England – it just wasn't there,' he tells me over the phone from his base in Leeds. 'When I came North, everything in the Northern economy revolved around anchor institutions – things like the utilities and the hospitals – which is the route I ultimately took. If you were going to earn a decent wage, that's what you did. To an extent you can still track most economic activity back to those big anchor institutions.'

However, though key workers have been venerated during the Pandemic, the state was not so generous prior to this moment of national crisis. The government has actively encouraged a briefcase mafia of lawyers, bankers and venture capitalists to overrun the capital. Yet, when the Jenga tower collapsed – via an economic crash birthed by Wall Street and their underlings in Canary Wharf – the Conservative government was quick to shift the blame to the public sector and its improvident spending on key workers.

As Professor John Tomaney wrote in 2018 for the LSE Review of Books: 'Orthodox thinking is fixated on the contribution of hi-tech, knowledge-based industries and property-led regeneration to increases in GDP.' This has neglected the backbone of the economy: key workers, who predominate outside the capital.[58]

It would be a mistake to believe that all areas outside London have experienced the same economic changes over the last forty years. 'The model is failing – but it is important to recognise that it is failing in different ways in different places,' says Aditya Chakrabortty. However, there are common trends that underpin the lives of people across different regions, he says.

'Working life for people who aren't lucky enough to make it into the higher-earning sectors of the economy has been pretty poor for quite some time. It's a fact that working life is now less unionised, more temporary, more precarious and lower paid. That is true across the board; across the country.'

This has been a process both actively encouraged and quietly accepted by successive governments. The creation of a Yuppie paradise in London during the 1980s, propelled by the banking boom of the 2000s and preserved by the property bubble of the 2010s, is the source of the capital's hegemony in the post-industrial, post-imperial era. However, rather than using its vast resources as a counterweight – rebalancing the economy away from a swollen capital city – the state has more often done the exact opposite.

One of the great myths of twentieth-century British political history is that Margaret Thatcher was a small-state prime minister. As described above, Thatcher certainly believed in the morality and efficiency of market forces, rather than the auspices of technocratic state planning, but her methods for carrying out this economic revolution were heavy-handed. She deployed the full weight of her office to crush the miners, to change the composition of the economy and flog state assets. Thatcher was an activist prime minister who capsized industries and the places they resided while implementing a ruthless libertarian agenda.

It's crucial to remember, although surprisingly easy to forget, that cities are human and political constructions. Places may exhibit favourable topographical or geological features that make them more conducive to trade or settlement, but no place is preordained with prosperity. North Korea is abundant in metals and coal, for example, yet its towns and cities remain desperately poor.

'Capitals and other leading cities and regions might attract and then gain further from market activities, but it was rarely the market that provided the foundations of their success,' says the sociologist Colin Crouch. 'Capital cities in particular have been public projects, often being built up over centuries to be worthy seats of monarchs and later governments.'[59]

The Thatcher era redrew the UK's regional architecture, to which future governments have only made marginal adjustments. The New Labour governments spent record amounts of money on the foundational economy – investing heavily in education and health – reversing Thatcher's record of public sector privation that was suffered most acutely outside the financial metropolis. Yet Blair and Brown accepted the general composition of the economy they had inherited from Thatcher. London continued to outperform other regions during the New Labour years, spurred by the financial sector, almost doubling its contribution to the UK economy from 1990 to 2009.[60]

This is a source of grief for fellow New Labour ringleader Blunkett, who laments that, 'even with thirteen years of a Labour government, and even with obvious changes in their lives: the change in the whole nature of their local schools, new sixth-form colleges, a complete transformation of primary care and their hospital, the minimum wage,' people in former industrial areas still did not feel as though their lives had measurably improved.

This, perhaps, was because New Labour accepted the terrain of Thatcherism and explicitly pursued evolution not revolution. Whereas political contests in the twentieth century revolved around the structure of the economy – the ownership of infrastructure and the pattern of industry – there is now a post-Thatcher consensus in which the pendulum only swings back and forth between 'spend more on public services' and 'spend less on public services'.

The former policy raises the tide for all regions when government generosity abounds, as during the Blair and Brown years, but it doesn't alter the fact that London owns a yacht whereas much of the rest of the country bobs around in dinghies.

David Cameron's Conservative government espoused austerity from 2010 to 2016, effectively draining the ocean. Local government budgets in England were cut by more than half between 2009/10 and 2015/16. The budget of the Department of Work and Pensions – the body responsible for administering benefits – was cut by nearly 60 per cent, the Justice budget by almost 40 per cent, the Defence budget by 20 per cent and the Transport budget by only marginally less.[61]

Seven of the ten cities that experienced the largest spending cuts from 2009/10 to 2017/18 were located in the North East, the North West or Yorkshire. On average, cities in the North suffered spending cuts of 20 per cent, compared to cuts of 9 per cent in the East, South East (excluding London) and South West.[62]

Saddled with a 40 per cent reduction in day-to-day spending on public services, Barnsley was the city hardest hit by austerity – experiencing a reduction in funding of around £145 million, or £688 for every resident. On a per capita basis, Liverpool was the worst affected, its £441 million spending cut equating to £816 for every person in the city. Elsewhere, Doncaster saw its public funding slashed by 30.6 per cent, Wakefield by 30.1 per cent, Newcastle by 26.6 per cent, Huddersfield by 23 per cent and Sheffield by 22.4 per cent.[63]

This public sector belt-tightening extended to pay, frozen between 2011 and 2013, after which increases were capped at

1 per cent until 2018. As the Pandemic struck, Chancellor Rishi Sunak followed the example of his predecessors by enforcing a public sector pay freeze for non-NHS workers and those earning more than £24,000 a year. From 2010 to 2020, meanwhile, the basic annual pay for Members of Parliament increased from £65,738 to £81,932.

In sum, during the peak years of Conservative austerity, the number of public sector jobs in the UK fell by 1.1 million, or 17 per cent, although this reduction can be attributed in part to the reclassification of some public sector jobs as existing in the private sector.[64] In 2019, IPPR North reported that the North East had 72,000 fewer public sector workers than a decade prior – a fall of 24 per cent – constituting the highest proportion of lost jobs in any English region. London, by comparison, saw a fall in public sector employment of just 9 per cent.[65]

The Cameron government was renowned for its vacuous slogans, primary among which was its purported support for 'hardworking families'. Yet low-income working families were punished by austerity. By 2017/18, the proportion of children in relative poverty who lived in working families hit 70 per cent, a jump of 20 per cent from 2009/10.[66] As of April 2020, more than one in three (38 per cent) of people said that, at least once a year, they run out of money before their next pay cheque.[67]

Yet the financiers and property speculators who trashed the economy in the first place were unlikely to be among this group. From 2012 to 2013, weekly earnings rose by more than 11 per cent in the finance, insurance and real estate industry.[68] Average weekly earnings (including bonuses) in the 'finance and business services' sector rose from £1,004 in March 2015 to £1,121 in March 2020 – an increase of more than 10 per cent.[69]

Austerity was flogged to the nation using the same credit-card economics that Thatcher marshalled with such mendacious ingenuity – namely the idea that Britain had 'maxed out' its account before the 2008 crash. This is a simple idea for people to understand, as it relates to their own personal finances, but it has very little basis in real-world economics. In particular, Cameron and Osborne emphasised the supposed burden of public sector workers, purportedly overpaid and overly comfortable. The Labour Party created a 'public sector boom and a private sector bust', Cameron claimed in a speech on austerity in 2010.[70]

This encapsulated the basic dichotomy – the hero–villain axis – on which austerity was manufactured. A reliance on the state, in whatever form, was suddenly portrayed as a financial burden to the country and therefore morally questionable. Given the schism between the North and the South, in terms of the distribution of private and public sector employment, the demonisation of the state had obvious geographical implications.

'Strivers' and 'shirkers' was another Orwellian doctrine deployed to justify the parsimony of Cameron's state. 'Where is the fairness for the shift-worker, leaving home in the dark hours of the early morning, who looks up at the closed blinds of their next-door neighbour sleeping off a life on benefits?' Osborne asked at the 2012 Conservative Party Conference.[71] Yet, once again, this potent allegory was estranged from reality. More than a third of Universal Credit claimants – the flagship benefits system conceived by the Cameron government – are in employment,[72] rising to 40 per cent in Scotland.[73]

Osborne pledged to cut welfare by £12 billion and by 2016 claimed to have achieved this ambition – while his government infamously cut the tax rate for the highest earners and corporations. Speaking to BBC Newsnight in 2018, Osborne said that giving tax breaks to wealthy individuals and businesses 'created jobs at a time when people thought there was going to be mass unemployment'.[74] The same logic was not applied to the millions of public sector workers – themselves consumers – whose incomes were concurrently squeezed by the Lego-haired Chancellor.

Boris Johnson's administration has subsequently nudged the pendulum in the opposite direction, promising more money for public services – primarily for the health service and for police recruitment. However, like Blair and Brown, the prime minister has not envisioned a fundamentally different economy. He has taken the easy option, instructing Whitehall to turn on the taps, rather than attempting to reverse London's conquest of modern industry.

If anything, Johnson's mode of public investment has aided the cause of commerce and its refuge, London. The private and public sectors have fused during the Pandemic, as corporations have been tasked with providing personal protective equipment and COVID tests, alongside the basic management of the 'test and trace' system. As of July 2021, the government had outsourced COVID contracts worth £54.2 billion to some 1,600 firms, equivalent to the GDP of 140 countries and territories.[75] Deals worth at least £3 billion have been granted to companies owned by Conservative donors and associates.[76]

An analysis of public contracts by the *i* newspaper found that, in 2021, 70 per cent of all central government contracts and 63 per cent of all local government contracts were won by firms based in the South of England. Contracts worth millions of pounds, designed to help peripheral areas of the country to formulate and deliver 'levelling up' policies, have also been handed to London-based management consultants.

This public–private merger cannot be disentangled from the government's growing intoxication with high-tech, speculative investments – encouraged by Johnson's former chief aide, Barnard Castle enthusiast Dominic Cummings. The flagship project in this techno-nationalist delusion is the Advanced Research and Invention Agency (ARIA), an £800 million fund to provide 'high risk, high reward' rapid funding for UK inventors and researchers. At the same time, the government has been accused of blowing hundreds of millions on space research.[77] I highly doubt that the Vote Leave campaign – run by Cummings – would have won the 2016 EU Referendum if its slogan had been: 'Let's spend £350m a week on lunar transport.'

The government should be investing in the future of industry, and particularly the implications of artificial intelligence, says Blunkett. However, unless the funding is directed towards the North, he says, 'and unless it's the Northern universities that get the research funding, it'll all go into Imperial, Oxford and Cambridge. And then you reinforce all the existing inequalities and things will get worse.'

These are sentiments shared by Blunkett's former colleague Andrew Adonis. 'It's obviously the case that when it comes to state-led industrial sponsorship that a sensible policy will seek to intelligently locate new and growing industries – particularly green industries – in the Midlands and the North,' he says.

Public services may well improve exponentially when we develop the tools to map genomes, predict the spread of diseases and create vast databases of information and knowledge. But, at the present moment, this seems like a Devil's bargain whereby the core facets of the state are being consumed by the market; by consultants and tech pioneers operating out of London, Silicon Valley and New York. An army of misfits and weirdos are thus being awarded lucrative public contracts, while the government equivocates about whether to award nurses a paltry pay rise. The Johnsonian ethos ultimately treats public services as enterprises, not as human ecosystems. As Karl Milner puts it to me: the government needs 'to realise that value comes from more than just pound notes'.

In fact, even when government investment in public services and its workers has been forthcoming, it has too often been funnelled towards London and the South. 'Public policy has often followed the market, intensifying problems of geographical inequality. In Britain, large sums of public money are spent to sustain London and the South East as economic powerhouses and attractive places in which to live, while proposals to revive the declining towns of the North and Midlands are met with criticism and scepticism,' writes Colin Crouch.[78]

This balance of power is best epitomised by the Pacer train, retired from service in November 2020.[79] The Pacer train was born in the 1980s by literally hitching the chassis of a train to a bus carriage. They were slow, noisy, unreliable, and were deployed widely across the North, Midlands and Wales for forty years – double their intended lifespan. If anything symbolises the second-class treatment of people outside London, especially the heartlands, it's the Pacer train.

Meanwhile, as Owen Hatherley writes in *Red Metropolis*, 'London has the only public transport system in Britain that can be compared with any other in Europe without embarrassment.'[80]

In 2017/18, the capital accounted for 54.2 per cent of the UK government's annual transport spending, while other regions hoovered up the dregs. Yorkshire and the Humber, by contrast, accounted for just 3.2 per cent of total spending.[81] According to an analysis by the renowned public health academic Sir Michael Marmot, the wealthiest 10 per cent of people in England receive almost four times as much public spending on their transport needs as the poorest 10 cent.[82]

Transport may not be the sexiest policy area, but it is one of the most universal. Even private car users come into frequent contact with the ramifications of public transport decisions; moaning about potholes is practically a national hobby. Consequently, people are very aware that London has been showered with new transport projects – Crossrail, HS2 and the Elizabeth Tube line all elicit varying degrees of rage – while local services are left to visibly decay.

'Fundamentally, everyone believed that HS2's aim had been to enable spoiled Londoners to move around the country with greater ease,' writes Deborah Mattinson in *Beyond the Red Wall*.[83] It's predicted that HS2 – a new high speed rail line connecting London to Birmingham – will cost at least £100 billion, compared to the £70 billion spent by the government on the furlough scheme and the £4.2 billion that Johnson has pledged to fix local bus and train services.[84]

The debate rages over HS2, though the person who first conceived of the scheme, Andrew Adonis, still believes that it will change Britain's economic landscape. It will be impossible to fragment and redistribute the financial and professional services that have resided in London for centuries, he says. Therefore, 'levelling up' will require better inter-city transport infrastructure, to bring otherwise peripheral places into closer contact with the almighty capital.

'The closer the economic relationship between London, the South East and the other provinces, the more likely they are to level up,' he tells me. 'This was a dominant part of my thinking in developing HS2. In England, almost without exception, the places with the highest income per head are within an hour's commuting distance from London. Unless the large conurbations of the Midlands and the North come into closer proximity to London, they will remain a world apart and will probably continue to diverge.'

In particular, he says, it would be a disaster if the HS2 project splinters, with the routes to Birmingham and Manchester completed while the eastern leg is cancelled. In such a scenario, travelling times to London from the West would be slashed, but eastern towns and cities would continue to be ostracised from the capital. After the construction of HS2, a journey from Manchester to London is expected to take one hour, while travelling to the capital from Leeds would take twice as long. This would add an East–West dimension to the UK's already multifaceted regional inequalities.

Regardless of your thoughts on HS2, it's self-evidently true that public spending has been shovelled into the capital over recent decades. The Green Book, the Treasury's criteria for investment, has ranked projects based on value for money – creating a bias towards affluent, densely populated areas of the country.

'The more people felt their own prosperity required them to move South, the more public investment followed them, in terms of the need for schools, the need for roads, the need for hospitals, the need for public transport – justified by the Treasury model. Therefore, it was almost sucking the life out of the North,' says Blunkett.

Mary Creagh, the Labour MP for Wakefield from 2005 to 2019, puts it differently. 'There has been a lot of structural violence' carried out by recent governments against communities such as her former constituency, she says. 'Some of the violence happens in plain sight, when you cut funding for bus services and indirectly tell a young person that their future doesn't matter. It also happens when you cut the funding for childcare so that the girl who has a baby at 16 or at 18 and who wants to go back to college, to study and to learn, has her progress curtailed.'

As part of the government's 'levelling up' agenda, which promises to jump-start the UK's left-behind regions, Chancellor Rishi Sunak has pledged to rewrite the terms of the Green Book, so that it no longer prejudices areas outside London and the South East.

'Levelling up' has been a key rhetorical instrument in Johnson's campaign to capture and retain so-called 'Red Wall' seats that are shedding their Labour loyalties. A master of oratory over reality, Johnson's words hold great promises. 'For too many people geography turns out to be destiny,' Johnson said in a flagship levelling-up speech in July 2021. 'This country is not only one of the most imbalanced in the developed world, it is also one of the most centralised – and those two defects are obviously connected,' he said, adding that Britain was only 'firing on one cylinder'.[85]

However, there is little reason to believe that Johnson's agenda will be any less vapid than its predecessor – the 'Northern powerhouse' launched by Osborne in 2014. Indeed, despite Johnson's flowery rhetoric, it was reported in January 2021 that Transport for the North's budget had been slashed by 40 per cent.[86]

'The government's commitment is there, but it hasn't yet been delivered upon,' said Henri Murison, director of the Northern Powerhouse Partnership, in 2019. 'The idea it's just a hobby-horse project for chucking in initiatives across the government rather than a serious attempt to rebalance the economy is a real fear to me.'[87]

So too has the levelling-up project been accused of empty promises, serving as the basis for shameless electioneering. When the Chancellor announced an initial £1 billion fund to boost struggling towns, it was calculated that the vast majority of the cash would be invested in Conservative constituencies.[88] In an attempt to prove its conviction, the government has announced that 400 Treasury staff will move to Darlington – a seat won by the Tories in 2019 – while 500 staff from the Ministry of Housing, Communities and Local Government will be sent to Wolverhampton, a city that saw two Conservative gains at the same election.

'The government is evidently letting politics drive levelling up,' Burnham says – who notes that, since the Conservative Party's loss at the Chesham and Amersham by-election in June 2021, the government has stretched the scope of 'levelling up' beyond the Red Wall – increasingly applying the term to the South as well as the North.

'Without being cynical, levelling up is the right theme – but it has got to be done in the right places and in the right way – and not so broad that it becomes meaningless,' he tells me. 'If anything, we're in retreat from where Johnson was a couple of years ago. The question is how far in retreat.'

Indeed, the direction of travel is not encouraging. Since 2014, transport spending has risen by more than twice as much per person in London as in the North, in real terms. And from 2014 to 2019, the number of children in the North living in a poor household increased by 200,000 – taking the total figure to 800,000. Over the same period, weekly pay increased by only 2.4 per cent in the North versus 3.5 per cent nationally.[89]

Similarly, there's little evidence that the levelling-up agenda will compensate for the spending cuts imposed on disadvantaged areas of the country during the austerity era. In his 2021 budget, for example, Sunak announced the first batch of spending on his 'Levelling Up Fund' – which ultimately intends to invest £4.8 billion in left-behind communities.

However, the fifty-nine English local authorities that won £1.25 billion in levelling-up funds had seen their spending power reduced by some £25.5 billion from 2010 to 2018. Calderdale in Yorkshire, for example, lost £259 million in spending power between 2010 and 2018 – only to receive £12.2 million for a swimming pool in Halifax through the Levelling Up Fund.[90]

Notably, the Levelling Up White Paper – released belatedly in February 2022 – offered grand rhetoric about the scale of the UK's regional divides, but failed to match this rhetoric with government funding. In fact, according to the Northern Powerhouse Partnership, Johnson plans to spend less on English regional development than either Theresa May or David Cameron.

And these circumstances are only set to deteriorate further. An energy crisis blowing from the East is dragging more people into the cyclone of inflation and poverty. It has been estimated by the Fuel Poverty Coalition that, as of April 2022, more than 2.2 million households with children will struggle to pay their electricity and gas – a rise of 74 per cent from 2019 when around 1.2 million children were living in fuel poverty.

This is all a far cry from Johnson's 2021 Conservative Party conference speech, in which he promised the return of a 'high-wage, high-skill, high-productivity economy'. In reality, it appears as though he is overseeing a new, sustained period of economic discontent – invariably suffered most acutely by the most disadvantaged.

What's more, the current government's levelling-up vision is ill-conceived, concentrating on small-scale infrastructure projects that look good on the leaflets of local candidates – the regeneration of a town centre or the improvement of a train station – but have comparatively little economic impact.

Indeed, the National Audit Office (NAO) – the independent public spending watchdog – says that the sort of infrastructure projects funded under the levelling-up agenda 'do not usually drive significant growth'.

This is despite the need for intelligent, generous investment being more urgent than ever. As a result of austerity, the circumstances of former industrial seats have deteriorated since 2010. Child poverty, for example, increased by 16 per cent in the Red Wall from 2014/15 to 2019/20 – double the England-wide average. Child poverty in the North East increased from 26 per cent to 36.9 per cent in this period, while it fell in the South East, from 24 per cent to 23.8 per cent, and only marginally increased in the South West – from 26 per cent to 26.1 per cent.[91]

Yet, the Chancellor announced a new fiscal rule in his 2021 budget: the government will only borrow to invest in capital projects (i.e. infrastructure), while day-to-day spending should be met exclusively through tax revenues.

Sunak and Johnson can therefore invest in headline-grabbing infrastructure schemes, while restricting the amount of support provided to local authorities for basic services. This may be designed to give the appearance of 'levelling up' even as the government upholds its general antipathy to state spending.

As Marcus Johns of IPPR North said in response to Sunak's announcements: '[It] looks like this Budget is going to be capital intense and revenue light, and the Chancellor's new fiscal rules could lock in austerity in public services and local government while central government points to new infra-structure projects as levelling up.'

Ultimately, says Chakrabortty, 'Levelling up has always been an electoral strategy, rather than an economic strategy. This is not a deeply held conviction that flows through Johnson's bloodstream. It's completely for show. Frankly, austerity is going to stop, but it's not going to be reversed by this government.'

The finer details of public policy are also inseparable from structural, seismic political shifts. While official estimates suggest that London will be able to navigate the economic aftershocks of Brexit – an internal Conservative Party psychodrama that has spilled into national politics – regions outside the capital are likely to be more severely affected.[92]

Evidently, the Northern Powerhouse agenda has aided more devolution to nations and regions, which should be celebrated, even if the scope and form of this devolution is the subject of scrutiny. However, devolution aside, recent regional redistribution campaigns have been uninspiring, ineffective and brazenly opportunistic.

Granted, when a single urban centre gains a vast commercial advantage over a period of decades, it's difficult to reverse the process. London is the land of opportunity – a harbinger of capitalism with unyielding forward momentum. Yet this climate has been created by a state which has invested disproportionately in the capital for decades, and now pursues a great regional rebalancing in rhetoric only.

3.

CAPITAL IN
THE CAPITAL

If you live in London, searching for a property is soul-sapping
– an eternal struggle between your bank account and your
landlord – an unfair fight with only one inevitable winner.

The London property market has assumed comedy status
in recent years; laughter being the only recourse for desperate
tenants and buyers, their anger and bewilderment expended
long ago.

It's not just the extremes of the London property bubble
that are absurd. The market has failed, from root to branch,
as millions of us are forced to pump more and more money
into the pockets of landlords and lenders in a seemingly
never-ending public bailout.

In large part, this is a symptom of the economic clustering
described in the previous chapter. London has cornered the
job market, particularly high-end private sector employment,
but simply doesn't have the accommodation for this volume
of workers. Mass cramming has therefore caused three
phenomena to occur in conjunction, none of which are
particularly healthy: hyperinflation, property speculation, and
a deterioration in both the size and the quality of homes.

London's bloated property prices are a physical barrier to
opportunity in Britain. Young people from peripheral regions

– potential prodigies and innovators – are obstructed by a financial roadblock when they try to pursue their dreams in the only place available: London. Any illusion of fairness in Britain is dismantled by the entry fee demanded from outsiders to access the job opportunities that the capital holds in its custody.

However, people from outside London do not exclusively suffer from this worst excess of the capital. Indeed, a smugness emanates from those who have seceded from the rat race, whenever property prices are discussed. Inflation only benefits those who own property, punishing the millions of Londoners who have no capital in the capital. In this regard, London needs to be saved from itself.

The absurdity of the London housing market has been catalogued online for some time. VICE's Joel Golby has been running a 'London rental opportunity of the week' blog since 2015, highlighting some of the more ballsy/ridiculous/exploitative (delete to preference) attempts to rip off tenants.[1] Golby's work should eventually be put into print form and archived in the British Library so that future generations can study how exactly we were enslaved by a new era of feudalism, 350 years after the system allegedly ended.

Over the years, the Golby Files have featured some corkers, not least a glorified rabbit hutch in someone's lounge, that they attempted to rent out for £530 a month;[2] a mattress in a cupboard under some stairs, Harry Potter style, that someone was flogging for £350 a month;[3] a makeshift 'bedroom' formed from an Argos partition screen and a ladder leading to a diminutive attic in someone's front room, for a cool £665 a month;[4] a garage fitted out with a camp bed, all yours for £750 a month.[5] And these are just appetisers.

As a yardstick, in the space of two minutes on Rightmove I have found several perfectly nice one-bedroom properties in

York for no more than £750 a month that don't pose the risk of asbestosis or the indignity of sleeping in someone's garden shed.

London is not the most expensive city in the world, nor does it have the worst housing problems. But our capital city has a unique monopoly over the domestic economy. By combining a housing affordability crisis with an internationally unparalleled concentration of jobs in one city, the UK has produced a rigged social system.

That's not to say you can't find a job in finance, law, journalism, the arts or politics elsewhere in the country – you obviously can. But your chances of reaching the top of these professions are hamstrung if you want to live and work outside London.

As Danny Dorling writes in *Inequality and the 1%*: 'London is where financial deregulation began in the 1980s. It is London that benefited most ... London is home to most of the 1 per cent, most of the rest of whom live just a short distance away.'[6]

Pursuing a career in the capital incurs a London tax that largely manifests in the form of property costs. It has been estimated by Loughborough University that it costs between 15 per cent and 58 per cent more to live in London than in the rest of the UK, depending on household composition. Either you pay this tax, or you downgrade, downsize and accept a smaller existence. According to the Loughborough report, 41 per cent of Londoners have an income below what is needed for a minimum standard of living.[7]

In terms of housing, the capital is an outlier of extreme proportions. In 2020, the average house price in London stood at £497,000 – almost double the England-wide average of £262,000.[8] In Yorkshire, the figure was £175,000, in the North West £177,000, and £275,000 in the South West.

Mirroring the economy, there are even wilder divergences at a local level. The average house price in Kensington and Chelsea in March 2020 was £1.4 million, in Islington it was £632,000 and in Southwark it was £489,000.[9] This compares to £200,000 in Manchester,[10] £220,000 in Leeds[11] and just £165,000 in Durham.[12]

At the time of writing, a £500,000 war-chest purchases a comfortable, five-bed detached house in Durham, or a one-bedroom flat in Islington, North London.

It's estimated that the average price of a London home will be £1 million by 2030,[13] while the average price of a detached property has almost reached this mark already, standing at £971,000 – almost three times as much as in Birmingham (£371,000) and Manchester (£350,000).[14]

These figures have been propelled by four decades of hyper-inflation in the capital, hitting more than 200 per cent in the 1980s, more than 100 per cent in the 2000s and more than 60 per cent in the 2010s. Thus, if someone bought a property in London during the 1980s for £50,000, it's likely to be worth some £770,000 today. A £50,000 foray into Yorkshire's housing market in the 1980s, by contrast, will have yielded a property value of £380,000 today.[15]

This farce is summed up neatly by Anna Minton in *Big Capital*, who points out 'If food prices had tracked house price inflation, in London a chicken would [now] cost £100.'[16]

There is an obvious problem, and one that has repeated throughout history, when prices outstrip wages: the goods or services in question – in this case housing – transform into a luxury enjoyed by an economic elite.

This is increasingly the case in London, as spiralling property prices transform the capital into an enclave for the rich. In Islington, for example, a hipster enclave, the typical cost of a two-bed home is more than twelve times the average income.[17] Meaning, if a couple who both earn the average wage want to purchase this sort of property, they would need at least three mortgages. Or they would need to earn three times the average salary to secure just one mortgage for a relatively small home – certainly not one in which they could comfortably raise children. This is the case across London, not just in the vegan-bourgeois parts of the city.

People are therefore trapped in rental accommodation, exposed to the impulses of their landlords and the ever-present threat of price hikes. Defying examples from the continent, notably Germany, the UK has very few legal protections for tenants. Short tenancy periods are the norm, incentivising owners to ramp up the rental value at the end of each contract period, maximising their profits and creating an inherently unstable market for the capital's burgeoning body of renters. Over the last twenty years, from 1997/98 to 2018/19, the number of people in private rented accommodation in the UK has more than doubled, from 5 million to 12.9 million.[18] And the rental market has not just captured young graduates – the number of private rented households with dependent children increased by 37 per cent, or 1.1 million, between 2010/11 and 2017/18.[19] This trend has been suffered most acutely in London.

This creates a form of servitude – facilitated by the government – whereby a property-owning aristocracy occupies the market, drives up the cost of purchasing a home, artificially enlarges the rental market, and hoovers up the profits. Indeed, since 2010, average private rental prices in London have grown at five times the rate of average earnings,[20] the former now representing 41 per cent of the latter.[21] The average rent for a one-bed home in the capital is more than it would cost on average for a three-bed place in every other English region.[22]

In a twisted irony, aspiring property owners have also been stymied by the aftershocks of the 2008 financial crash, causing a much more conservative attitude from banks towards mortgage lending. An incongruous situation has thus unfolded whereby someone can be paying £1,200 a month on rent – and could have done so for years – yet in the eyes of the bank they can't afford an £800 a month mortgage.

Karl Milner, who contributes to his daughter's rent in London, has seen this impact his own bank account. 'We are subsidising her rent so that someone else gets fatter and fatter down there, sucking the money I would be spending in my local economy into London,' he tells me.

With no shackles on the market, London property is a safe bet for investors who seek regular income and an above-inflation appreciation of their assets. At the behest of the government, making virtually no effort to deter this frenzy of predatory capitalism, London has been colonised by development companies and professional landlords – both domestic and foreign.

'Many London homes are not bought to be used as a primary residence by their owners, but rather as either a store of wealth, a vehicle to deliver capital appreciation, a source of rental income – or a combination of the three,' says the campaign group Action on Empty Homes.[23]

As Minton adds, the 'use value' of property in London is now completely divorced from its 'exchange value' – i.e. the amount of value derived from living in a property versus the amount of money that the home is traded for.[24] This is because property is now treated by the market and by the government as a financial commodity rather than a human asset. Homes are bartered like stocks, with little appreciation for how this warped game ends up ruining lives.

'Let me give you my vision: a man's right to work as he will, to spend what he earns, to own property, to have the state as servant and not as master – these are the British inheritance. They are the essence of a free country and on that freedom all our other freedoms depend,' Margaret Thatcher said in her first speech as Conservative Party leader in 1975.[25]

London's property market violates this ideal. The 'property-owning democracy' preached by Thatcher is now only fulfilled ironically, in the fact that our democratically elected representatives benefit substantially from property ownership. Indeed, a quarter of sitting Conservative Party MPs are landlords, accruing wealth from the property bubble that Parliament has failed to pop.[26]

For professional property owners, this is easy money. The government has calculated that landlords receive more than 40 per cent of their total income from their rental properties. More than half of landlords own several properties and the total equity of UK landlords more than doubled from 2004 to 2014, from £384 billion to £818 billion.[27] Owning properties is a highly lucrative hobby. For the country, however, London's housing market is a breeding ground for regional inequality, transgressing the meritocratic ideals that underpin our national sense of fair play.

One of the guiding principles of meritocracy is equality of opportunity: the conviction that everyone should be provided with a fair chance to grab life's riches. The alternative doctrine is the supremacy of a hereditary elite whose wealth and status are derived directly from family members. The London housing bubble is rebuilding these walls of privilege.

London has a monopoly on the commercial, financial, intellectual and technological professions that hold court in the post-Thatcher economy. Thus, to access these professions, you must plunge into the capital.

Except, the majority of these professions require their young staff to work for free, or virtually for free, through one or several unpaid internships, before progressing to low-paid freelance work. This system excludes graduates outside London, whose parents don't live in the orbit of the capital and who lack the means (or the appetite) to fund a £700-a-month cupboard in Walthamstow. These young people must either live in squalor or find a job closer to home.

Try telling your parents, who have a deep-seated distrust of London, that you plan on moving to a glorified squat in the city rather than living close to home. Trust me, it's not a fun conversation – and it's one that prevents many young people from trying their hand in the capital. 'You shouldn't have to pay for the privilege of living there,' is a phrase that I heard countless times from family members during my own journey South.

Meanwhile, the other half – the ones who can bunker with parents in London – enjoy enhanced prospects. London is their home, their playground and their provider. Whereas those outside the capital have to virtually sell organs to pay rent, London graduates typically have minimal bills to pay while they're living at home.

This has a liberating effect on their career chances. Subject to the approval of their parents and the limits of their sanity, they can take an internship tour of the capital, they can accept the short-term, poorly paid gigs that act as a bridge to better work, and they can generally elevate the health of their career above all short-term financial considerations.

In 2018, the monthly cost of an internship in London was estimated to be at least £1,100 – while 70 per cent of all internships are unpaid.[28] 'Nearly half of top graduate employers report that candidates who have not gained work experience through an internship will have little or no chance of receiving a job offer for their organisations' graduate programmes, regardless of academic qualifications,' reports the Sutton Trust. And yet, the majority (58 per cent) of advertised internships are in London, while research carried out by the Trades Union Congress found that 78 per cent of 18- to 24-year-olds could not afford to live away from home, in London, for an unpaid internship.[29]

Unpaid internships are basically illegal. For an unpaid internship to be legal, the intern is not allowed to do any work, rendering the whole process useless. Yet, in 2017, the government admitted that no firms had been prosecuted for the offence.[30]

'The high cost of living in London is likely to be pricing out young people from families on low and middle incomes, especially those living outside of the South East, or those whose families cannot offer them a room for free,' the Sutton Trust concludes.

'In London, there's the sense that you're told: "Yes, you can do this." And you can afford it, because you can move back in with your parents for a year and save up your money,' says Durham student Jamie Halliwell, whose family lives in Liverpool. 'For me, if I wanted to move to London after uni, it would be awful, because the rent's so expensive. You can't just get your degree and go to London and see what presents itself. Students from outside London have to tune down their aspirations. You don't have the opportunity to dream as big.'

I know several Londoners who have lived at home throughout their twenties, harvesting opportunities that others simply can't afford. This decision is entirely rational and I don't hold a grudge against these people for bathing in the fountain of privilege – as long as they recognise that it's not a pool open to everyone.

These early-career opportunities also create a snowball effect. Living at home allows Londoners to feed their bank accounts rather than a landlord – in the process building up a healthy slush fund that can be deployed as a house deposit at some point down the road. And early-career opportunities soon manifest into fully ripened forms of employment, accompanied by greater financial rewards. If you have climbed the career ladder early, it's easy to keep climbing.

Now, you may argue that the Pandemic has to some extent severed the link between work and geography – unlocking opportunities in London to those who don't live here. I am sceptical of this argument. For starters, consider this: the economic downturn caused by the Pandemic has disproportionately clobbered young people. As the Institute for Fiscal Studies (IFS) has calculated, workers under the age of 25 are two and a half times more likely to work in sectors that have been closed down, compared to those over the age of 25.[31] In March 2021, ONS figures suggested that two-thirds of people who lost their jobs during the Pandemic were under the age of 25.[32]

This fits the pattern usually seen during economic downturns. Evidence from the last three recessions suggests that young people are on average 7 per cent less likely to be in paid employment a year after entering the labour market. Those who graduated after the 2008 recession had a 30 per cent higher chance of working in a low-paid 'non-graduate' job a year after leaving university, while the median earnings of graduates in their late twenties fell by nearly 20 per cent between 2008 and 2013.[33] Echoing this adversity, in August 2020 it was reported that 60 per cent fewer graduate jobs were being advertised than at the same time in 2019. The number of applications per job had also increased by 47 per cent.[34]

Do you think this scenario – one in which opportunities are rationed – acts to the advantage of those with greater access to professional work, by virtue of their proximity to the London job market, or those with comparatively limited access?

An answer is provided by the Office for Students (OfS), the independent regulator of higher education in England. The OfS admits that graduates in certain areas of the country will suffer more severely than others. 'Current graduate employment prospects are extremely uncertain. COVID and lockdowns have resulted in a severe economic contraction. Many businesses have gone into administration and many more have instigated a hiring freeze. The impact is likely to be geographically uneven and long-lasting,' it wrote in December 2020.[35]

Life in London is often assessed on the basis of raw survival – whether people can afford to both live in the capital and put food on the table. In one of the richest countries in the world, in its most prosperous city, it should be possible for the overwhelming majority of people to meet this threshold. It should be a source of national humiliation that a disproportionate number of people do not.

The normalisation of extortion in London means that people are prevented from enjoying aspects of life that are basic human rights in other parts of the country. In London, a home within 500 metres of an outstanding primary school will set you back an average of £685,000 – a premium of £93,000 versus a home in close proximity to a 'good' school and £196,000 more, on average, than a home in the catchment of a school that 'requires improvement'.[36] Thanks to its warped property market, the capital's state schools are now a market commodity, offering access on the basis of wealth.

'There are still often competitive bidding wars near good schools,' says Philip Eastwood, partner at property agency The Buying Solution.

This postcode lottery exists across the country, of course. But upgrading to a better schooling area outside the capital requires a much smaller investment and is far less restrictive. In the North East, the school housing premium was equivalent to 14 per cent of local property prices, or £18,200, in 2017.[37] The premium paid in London, meanwhile, can hit 40 per cent of already hyper-inflated local prices.[38]

The quality of education enjoyed by children in the London state school system is therefore dependent on income – a clandestine cash-for-access scheme that affords the best schooling to those who can afford the housing costs. This also fuels the more blatantly elitist private school system. After all, a £100,000 state school housing premium is equivalent to several years of private fees. In this environment, it makes perverse economic sense to send your kids to a private school rather than buying a property in the catchment of an outstanding state institution.

The only hindrance might be the competition for private school places created by London's thriving oligarch class. Trevor Abrahamson of the estate agency Glentree International told City AM that oligarchs pay 'ludicrous' house prices in an attempt to secure a place for their children at the top-rated Highgate School, 'so that at the interview with the school they can claim they own a piece of Highgate, thinking that will help demonstrate their qualifications for entry'.[39]

However, elitism is expected in the private sector, which unashamedly supplies opportunities to those who can afford it. This process is altogether more insidious when it extends to the state school system, which is ostensibly supposed to offer a good standard of education to all, regardless of background or wealth.

Yet, according to researchers from LSE, London risks creating a self-perpetuating elite based on 'selection by mortgage of the richest and brightest children into the best schools. This process reinforces school segregation and inequalities in performance and achievement, and reduces social mobility across the generations,' they say.[40] A survey by Santander Mortgages likewise found that a third of parents in London had bought or rented a particular property because of the local schools, compared to a quarter nationally.[41]

Parents make superhuman efforts to ensure that their children succeed. Nothing can be done to prevent this instinct; it is a core part of human nature. Rather, the fundamental moral and political dilemma is this: how much freedom should be accorded to parents, by the state, to boost the chances of their own children at the expense of fairness and equal opportunity?

Through the London housing market, I fear we have sown the seeds of extreme regional-generational inequality, by allowing the vast concentration of unearned wealth among a London-based elite.

The 'bank of mum and dad' – the money handed from parents to children for housing costs – is now the UK's sixth largest lender, according to the Family Building Society.[42] In 2019, family and friends lent £6.3 billion, while 45 per cent of first-time buyers now rely on a gift, a loan or inheritance.[43] Modelling from the Council of Mortgage Lenders has suggested that the proportion of first-time buyers able to purchase without the help of their parents fell sharply from 70 per cent in 2005 to 40 per cent in 2011 – and, by 2017, 62 per cent of under-35s had received some financial help in the property market.[44]

These statistics are exaggerated in London. The percentage of first-time buyers in the capital receiving parental help has fluctuated in recent years between 25 per cent and 40 per cent

– consistently 10 percentage points higher than the rest of England.[45]

As noted earlier, a couple in London who bought a property in the 1980s worth £80,000 will have accumulated, on average, £390,000 more than an equivalent couple who bought a property worth exactly the same amount, at the same time, in Yorkshire. This wealth is unearned; it has accrued not due to merit or hard work, but through the random fortune of owning a property in a particular city. It is the definition of a postcode lottery.

Consequently, this asset acts as a trust fund for future generations, providing a crash pad for children when they chase opportunities in the capital, before eventually delivering a sizable financial endowment with which their progeny can buy a place of their own in the capital, perpetuating the cycle of regional inequality.

'Inequality between the older and younger population is widening over time, partly as a result of the gap in housing wealth,' says the Social Market Foundation. 'In turn, the subsequent distribution of this wealth downwards through bequests and the "bank of mum and dad" exacerbates wealth inequalities within the younger cohort.'[46]

Indeed, there's growing evidence to suggest that home ownership is no longer a democratic right, at least for young people, but is instead a minority privilege. The proportion of homeowners among the 20 to 24 age group fell from 40 per cent to just 13 per cent from 1990 to 2010, while for 25- to 29-year-olds it slumped from 63 per cent to 31 per cent.[47]

Owning property in London provides a wealth fund for its members, an access card to the elite. Savills, the property agency, recently released figures showing that the total property equity in London and the South East amounts to £1.53

trillion, versus £533 billion in the North.[48] Homeowners in the capital are therefore the beneficiaries of a colossal property reserve, which will be endowed to the next generation, compounding the inequalities between London and everywhere else.

Several governments around the world have trialled the idea of sovereign wealth funds, whereby state resources are invested in commercial ventures. Norway is a pioneer, investing oil revenues in real estate, companies and bonds, with the proceeds helping to fund the welfare state. The Norwegian fund owns roughly 1.4 per cent of all the world's listed companies and, since 1998, has averaged a 6.3 per cent annual growth rate, at the time of writing.[49] London's wealth fund is not so well orchestrated, nor so progressive. Unlike the Norwegian system, which delivers equal profits to all the country's citizens, London bestows privileges to a regional minority with the richest gaining the most.

London is the silent patron of all its citizens: it supplies a well-funded school, a place at university, open access to prestigious internships and entry-level jobs, career opportunities in high-wage sectors, and – if you're having a lucky life – an inherited property fortune.

Whereas in the past, privilege has poured down through the generations through land ownership and aristocratic titles, it seems that acquiring a slice of London now has the same effect. Meanwhile, those outside the gilded club, who want to live a comfortable life, own a home and have a family, must carry these dreams – the basic promises of British life – somewhere else.

Ironically, plenty of people have taken the decision to flee the capital during the course of the Pandemic. Liberated from the tyranny of the commute, many Londoners have opted to swap their overpriced hamster cages for veritable palaces elsewhere in the country.

In 2020, Londoners bought homes outside the city worth some £27.6 billion amid repeated lockdowns and the normalisation of working in your underpants, on your sofa.[50] There have been some indications that working from home may break the stranglehold of office micro-management. The outsourcing giant Capita plans to close a third of its 250 offices, after concluding that staff work just as efficiently from home,[51] defying the comments of former Mayor of London Boris Johnson in 2012, who branded working from home 'an excuse for general malingering'. Johnson said that working for home basically involved 'wondering whether to go down to the fridge to hack off that bit of cheese before checking your emails again'.[52] Perhaps he was speaking from personal experience.

Some 92 per cent of surveyed London companies told Gerald Eve, a property consultancy, that they were considering reducing their office space requirements as a result of the Pandemic.[53] The City of London, the command post of global capitalism with its glass crypts and suspicious-looking investment firms, now symbolises a rich man's tribute to the death of the high street. As in small-town Britain, the City has rows of boarded-up betting shops, attached to the placards of hopeful estate agents.

At the end of 2020, the year-on-year growth in UK house prices had hit 8.5 per cent, a six-year peak, while detached properties had inflated by 10 per cent.[54] This surge was stoked by Chancellor Rishi Sunak's decision to suspend stamp duty – the tax on property purchases – for first-time homes worth less than £500,000. The North West recorded the highest regional annual growth in house prices in England, 11.2 per cent, while London recorded the smallest rise, 3.5 per cent. This was not driven by a surge from urban to rural environments, either. Leeds logged property inflation of 11.3 per cent and Newcastle 6.6 per cent in 2020.[55]

At the same time, rents collapsed in many cities in the year up to February 2021, led by London. Average rents in the capital fell by 12.4 per cent, in Edinburgh by 10 per cent and in Manchester by 5.3 per cent.[56] This all suggests that London experienced an exodus, supported by an IFS study finding that a higher proportion of Londoners are able to work from home than people in any other region.[57]

However, the extent of this Pandemic-driven exodus is uncertain, alongside its potential to rebalance regional disparities in the UK. For starters, rents in London are set to rebound. While the Pandemic provided the impetus for some Londoners to desert the capital, the falling cost of renting has prompted a new surge of inward migration. The number of new leases agreed in prime central London in the three months to February 2021 was 17 per cent higher than during the same period a year earlier, according to the property network LonRes.[58] This will inevitably put upward pressure on rent prices, though I hope my landlord continues to believe the opposite.

What's more, when the particles settle, I suspect that a large proportion of firms will opt for hybrid working – asking staff to ditch their pyjamas for two or three days a week. This is the ideal scenario for many firms, allowing them to reduce their office space and cut costs at a time of economic turbulence, while maintaining some collaborative working. Importantly, though, hybrid working demands that staff live within a commutable distance to the office. Londoners may choose to relocate to a more affordable suburb, perhaps one that offers more outside space or the opportunities for a better family life, but they won't be able to escape the clutches of the capital entirely.

'The overwhelming feedback we had during the course of last year was that how we have worked in the past is not how our colleagues want to work in the future,' a Metro Bank spokesperson told Sky News in February 2021. 'We developed our future working plans in response, and when we return to the office we will move from being in the office full time to a hybrid model where colleagues split their time between working from home and working in the office.'[59]

The data also doesn't show a once-in-a-generation migration event. People leaving London bought 73,950 homes outside the capital in 2020, the largest exodus in four years, according to the estate agency Hamptons.[60] This is a large figure, but I wouldn't be jumping out of my armchair to cover this modest stampede, if I were Sir David Attenborough.

The Pandemic has evidently made a dent in London rental prices, though the longevity of this trend is still uncertain. Purchasing prices, meanwhile, continue their inexorable rise – even if growth has been more muted in the capital than in recent history.

Embedded within the COVID Pandemic, however, has been the illumination and exacerbation of other housing inequalities. Primarily, we have been forced into a closer relationship with the spaces and places that we inhabit. London is cramped, with the co-occupation of housing the only option for many people. There is nowhere in the UK that one has a closer and more awkward relationship with human saliva than its capital. This has created fertile conditions for an infectious disease to germinate – one reason for London's comparatively high case rates at various stages of the Pandemic.

These are also sub-optimal conditions for home working. I have rented places in the past, like many people in the city, that are intended and designed for little more than sleeping and occasionally eating. Before COVID, I spent the vast majority of the day either commuting, working or in the pub, and so a larger flat was an indulgence (not that I could afford more room). These are the circumstances that people, predominantly young people and those on low incomes, have been forced to endure during the Pandemic – shoehorning makeshift desks into windowless corners.

Moving out of the capital has been a necessity for many people, not an indulgence. The upshot, however, has been the transfer of London's rampant property inflation to areas of the country that don't boast the capital's buoyant wages.

This was already an issue prior to the Pandemic. As the London commuter belt has expanded, its Southern reaches extending to parts of the South coast, property values have risen steeply. More and more places have become feeder towns to the big city, thus pricing out home buyers who don't draw their cheques from London. As of May 2020, the worst affordability crises in Britain were suffered by Oxford, Cambridge, Brighton, Chichester, Bath, St Albans and Chelmsford – all boasting average house prices that exceed the affordable level for the local area by more than 59 per cent, and all of which are just a ninety-minute train ride or less to the capital.[61]

It's of little surprise that similar satellite towns and cities have seen the largest influx of Londoners during the Pandemic. The local authorities with the largest year-on-year increase in the share of homes bought by Londoners in 2020 were Sevenoaks, Windsor, Maidenhead, Oxford, Rushmoor, Eastbourne, Wokingham, Stevenage and Luton.[62] All of these places are within reaching distance of the capital. Londoners are generally not scattering to all corners of the country – and the number of people moving to London-adjacent areas could imminently spark a series of new housing crises. Sevenoaks alone experienced a 39 per cent increase in London movers compared to the previous year.

To put it bluntly, many London property owners are using this opportunity to liquidate their assets, accrued from living in the capital, buying bigger homes in neighbouring places and elevating prices for everyone else. You can see why this is appealing for city-dwellers who've been caged in overpriced, overcrowded accommodation, but you can also see why the residents of these new London feeder towns would be seriously narked.

The shockwaves can even be felt in Birmingham. HS2 has promised to reduce commuting times from Birmingham to London – incentivising a migration of people to the Midlands during the Pandemic. 'When I sold my house and when my mother-in-law sold her house recently, everyone who came to look around was from London,' Birmingham Yardley MP Jess Phillips tells me. 'What's more – they come and they live mortgage free. A friend of mine is a midwife, she's not a wealthy woman but she happened to buy a house in London in the early 1990s. She managed to buy a seven-bedroom house in the poshest part of Birmingham without a mortgage.'

To anticipate how this situation may evolve, the example of Cornwall is instructive. Roughly a quarter of the properties in St Ives, a popular beach town nestled on the south-westerly tip of the British Isles, are second homes or holiday lets. In 2020, the largest inflow of newcomers to Cornwall was from London, outstripping third-placed Bristol by 360 per cent.[63]

In 2016, the average house price in St Ives was £324,000, reported the *Guardian*, eighteen times the typical local salary.[64] Cornwall is a honeypot for tourism, its rum-and-sand spirit appealing to our inner voyager. But, as a result, the area has a high proportion of seasonal, low-paid, hospitality jobs. A part of the country with a strong sense of local pride has been ostracised from itself, due to the growth of property prices and the stagnation of wages.

'I am 44 years old and I have probably lived in thirty-five different rental and social properties,' due to the prohibitive cost of buying a home, Kate Ewert tells me. Ewert is a Labour councillor for Rame and St Germans in East Cornwall, a short distance from Plymouth, separated by the southern contortion of the River Tamar.

'You've got such heat in the Cornwall property market for both rentals and for purchasing, but that heat isn't coming from Cornwall – it's coming from outside the area, from people in Bristol and London, who are selling their £750,000 houses and are rushing down here, cash rich, and are gazump-ing local people. Second homes and holiday lets are killing our coastal communities,' she says.

The rental market, an inherently fickle system in the UK, is further destabilised in Cornwall by the summer demand for holiday accommodation. 'I've got people in my area who are living in cars because they've been booted out of their houses so that the landlords can put them on Airbnb over the summer,' Ewert says. 'It's heart-breaking. These are people who just want to live in the community where they were born. They want to live close to their mum and their gran, but they're being told they basically can't live here.'

Cornwall hasn't experienced this trend alone. In 2018, average house prices in Bath and North-East Somerset were fourteen times the local average earnings – a disparity that has trebled since 1999.[65]

So, in 2016, St Ives voted to stop local properties from being purchased as second homes. In July 2019, the price of new homes in the town was 13 per cent below what it other-wise would have been if the previous rate of inflation had continued, *The Economist* reported.[66] But the St Ives model hasn't taken hold in the rest of the region, and Cornwall was caught in the updraft of rapidly rising house prices during the Pandemic, experiencing a 9 per cent increase in the year to May 2021. In the first half of the year, 44 per cent of buyers were from outside Cornwall.[67]

Yet, the government has actively provided support for the owners of holiday homes in the area. Figures uncovered by Labour councillor Cornelius Olivier showed that £50 million of grants had been claimed by the owners of holiday lets in Cornwall, under the government's scheme to assist small businesses hit by the Pandemic.[68]

London's COVID evacuation, to the extent that it has occurred, will not flatten regional inequalities. The capital's money trail has reached surrounding areas, saddling low-wage towns and cities with property prices that most cannot afford.

It is entirely rational for Londoners to flee the capital during a Pandemic. I don't blame them for acting in their own self-interest. We all have some level of collective and individual responsibility for the inequalities that exist in our country, and for fixing them, but there's a reason we elect 650 people to the House of Commons every few years – to implement change on our behalf. It's up to them, not us.

I'm not trying to vilify Londoners, nor am I suggesting that London should somehow be dismantled and its treasures redistributed. London is an iconic city, an all-night rave comprising a thousand different cultures, cuisines and currencies. It should be a beacon of progress and human accomplishment, a model to the rest of the UK and the world. But, currently, London does not live up to its own myth, and the capital's unconditional advocates guard the gates of poverty, predatory capitalism and intense inequality.

Living in London is not easy for an overwhelming number of its inhabitants. In fact, for many, it is exhausting; a perpetual struggle for sleep, sanity and survival. It's not easy for the butchers on Rye Lane, Peckham, who don their aprons at dawn and deal hunks of meat like blackjack cards for hours amid the tang of fermenting carcasses. It's not easy for the cockney cabbies whose industry has been invaded by low-wage gig firms. Vast internal inequalities of wealth are brewed by our hegemonic capital city, poisoning London and left-behind regions alike.

To a large extent, the London property market is now a nesting place for billionaires and foreign capital, that treat the city's homes as assets in an investment portfolio. Meanwhile, poor Londoners are driven into expensive rental accommodation, forced out of their communities and gradually purged from the city.

As of April 2021, 19 per cent of Londoners had been forced to borrow money to pay their rent or mortgage in the previous six months, according to the housing charity Shelter.[69] Currently, the London market is split, with roughly 50 per cent of households owning a property and 50 per cent renting.[70] In England, 63 per cent of households owned their own homes from 2016 to 2018.

If you were living in London in 1981, you were more likely to be in social rented housing than any other form of accommodation. Spurred by Thatcher's housing reforms of the 1980s, however, social rented housing is the least typical avenue for Londoners now, constituting just 20 per cent of households. The market rented sector, meanwhile, has boomed – its share increasing from roughly 10 per cent in the late 1980s to nearly 30 per cent today.[71]

In this regard, young people are suffering more than most. In 1990, 25 per cent of people aged 16 to 24 owned their own home in London, falling to 7 per cent by 2018, correlating with a fall in the 25–34 age bracket from 57 per cent to 34 per cent over the same period. Yet, ownership rates among those aged 55 to 64 have remained relatively stable, and ownership among those aged over 65 has actually increased by 20 per cent.[72] The makeup of the new proletariat is young and poor.

The recent distortions of the London housing market cannot be separated from the city's open-arms attitude to foreign wealth. London's prime real estate, and even its landmarks, are increasingly being purchased as foreign assets. The Shard, the tallest freestanding structure in the city and the second tallest in the country (behind Emley Moor Mast), is owned by the state of Qatar. It is effectively a glass temple to an offshore elite that has quietly occupied the capital. The Gherkin, the Shard's phallic rival, is owned by a Brazilian conglomerate; the 'Walkie Talkie' is owned by a Hong Kong company best known for its Chinese-style food sauces.

This investor's paradise comes into full view when you walk over Vauxhall Bridge and gaze eastwards. The stretch of the Thames from the US Embassy to Battersea Park is a tower block dystopia – akin to a scene from Ridley Scott's *Blade Runner* – the area occupied by a hundred looming glass statues. At the centre of this citadel is the Sky Pool, reportedly the world's first pool bridge, suspended 82 feet in the air between two luxury apartment blocks. The development is owned by a Malaysian property company, which is flogging two-bed apartments in the complex for between £1 million and £1.7 million. At the time of writing, the most expensive property is selling for £1,700 per square foot.

An apt representation of London's property dysmorphia is Battersea Power Station. Once a coal-fired power station, generating 20 per cent of London's electricity supply at its peak, the landmark has been developed into flats, commercial and leisure space – sold to the Malaysian sovereign wealth fund and the Employees Provident Fund of Malaysia for £1.6 billion in 2019.[73] A three-bed apartment in the power station, with 2,600 sq ft of internal space and an eleventh-floor 1,200 sq ft roof terrace, will set you back £8.45 million, at the time of writing. The cheapest property on the market is a 429 sq ft studio apartment, priced at a cool £610,000. A property of equivalent size in the building is being rented out for roughly £1,900 a month – providing a six-year return on investment for buy-to-let owners. The engine of industry in twentieth-century London has mutated into the epicentre of the capital's new economy: property speculation.

As Simon Jenkins wrote in 2020 for the *Guardian*: 'To own land in a city is to be part of that city's lifecycle. Yet one of the reasons foreign buyers prefer tower blocks is that they evoke no such concern. They are locked away, anonymous, the antithesis of what an urban community should be like … A city is not an object, let alone a bank account. Those who own it should commit to it.'[74]

London, on the other hand, has been partitioned and sold to the highest bidder. This process has occurred under the radar – masked by complex commercial structures, agreed through handshakes in exclusive Mayfair clubs. Many of the buildings haven't changed, they haven't been lassoed by a crane and shipped overseas. But, to all intents and purposes, they no longer belong to London – or the country at large.

There are some similarities here with the rest of the UK – and in particular the North of England – even if the scale of London's property inflation defies comparison. 'You've got large chunks of Northern towns in the hands of absent land-lords who actually face minimal regulation,' Greater Manchester Mayor Andy Burnham tells me. 'A really powerful policy for parts of the North would be requiring landlords to maintain their homes to a decent homes standard, or face compulsory purchase, or be disqualified from any form of housing benefit. Really strong policies on intervening to improve the quality of the housing stock would have a big impact on large parts of the North.'

Indeed, this may well be a point of consensus for those who seek to bridge Labour's divide, between its former industrial heartlands and its new metropolitan strongholds. Burnham agrees. 'There is a sense that Londoners need to be saved from London. If we had a very different country, and if we were to intervene in the housing market, it would help people who are hit by the never-ending inflation of London housing. London doesn't work for the people who live there either, does it?'

I am an internationalist – I believe in the basic common humanity of all people and am instinctively dubious of nationalist symbols and cults that serve to classify people. However, to a large extent there is a two-tier system of globalisation in the modern world. While ordinary immigrants are maligned, and countries erect walls to keep them out, the free movement of the oligarch class continues unencumbered. This is perverse, but it suits the agenda of conservatives and those who advocate on behalf of corporate interests. The average immigrant wants to build a life in Britain – to work, study, pay taxes and raise a family. The property speculator, meanwhile, has already achieved his wildest dreams; he already has more money than he needs, and owns more homes than he can ever inhabit. His rapacious greed therefore offers little to the country.

This is not conjecture: it's the lived reality of the 'buy to leave' property market in present-day London. In the bourgeois neighbourhoods of Knightsbridge and Belgravia, 25 per cent of residential properties are empty most of the time, rising to 40 per cent in the West End.[75] This isn't difficult to imagine, when you wander through an area like Earl's Court, the buffer between Kensington and Chelsea. Many properties are unkempt, their front patios invaded by weeds, paint flaking off imposing front doors that open onto deserted streets.

Almost 25,000 London homes were left unoccupied in 2020 – the highest figure since 2012 – at an estimated total worth of £11 billion.[76] Some 11,000 people sleep rough on the streets of the capital every year,[77] while homelessness and rough sleeping rates rose by 165 per cent in England between 2010 and 2018.[78] Councils are now permitted to charge a council tax premium on vacant properties, up to 200 per cent, though only on homes that are left empty for longer than five years.

Meanwhile, 'those on low incomes are being shunted into low quality and relatively high-cost private accommodation,' according to Action on Empty Homes – in many cases encouraged by councils that have decideed to flog their properties for huge profits.[79] Between 2005 and 2015, fifty council estates in London with a population of 30,000 or more were subject to 'estate regeneration', increasing the number of private homes on the estates tenfold and cutting the stock of social homes by 8,000, according to Owen Hatherley in *Red Metropolis*.[80]

Transparency International has calculated that at least £6.7 billion worth of property in the UK has been bought with suspicious wealth since 2016 – more than 80 per cent purchased in London. Out of the £6.7 billion, £1.5 billion has been bought by Russians accused of corruption or links to the Kremlin, with these individuals favouring the City of Westminster (accounting for £430 million, or 28.3 per cent) and Kensington and Chelsea (£283 million or 18.8 per cent).

In the throng of the city, rich and poor often live cheek by jowl – wrestling on a daily basis with gentrification, displacement and inter-community tension. This was exposed to the nation and the world in the early hours of 14 June 2017. Grenfell Tower, a block of flats in North Kensington, was engulfed by a fire that raged for several hours. At least seventy-two people died in the blaze, stranded in smoke-filled stairwells or trapped in their flats. Eyewitnesses reported seeing several people jumping from windows, and four victims were later found to have died from 'injuries consistent with falling from a height'.[81]

The fire was spread by the cladding that had been installed on the tower in 2015 and 2016, designed in part to improve the 'environmental performance of the building and its physical appearance'. It was therefore inferred that dozens of people had been killed partly because the council, representing one of the richest areas in London, sought to stop the tower block from being an eyesore.[82]

The inhabitants of Grenfell Tower were a microcosm of London's forgotten poor. I have spoken to a number of survivors and their relatives – people with broken English, physical and mental health problems, who exist in the margins of society. Years after the fire, abandoned by central government and in permanent conflict with a council that is the subject of manslaughter charges, they are still treated like second-class citizens.

'England is supposed to be the fairest country in the world, but here I have no rights. I feel like a slave, because a slave has no rights,' Maryam, a survivor, told me. Within walking distance of luxury and royalty, Grenfell Tower is situated in one of the most deprived areas of England.

In 2016, Public Health England reported that life expectancy is some sixteen years lower for men in the most deprived areas of Kensington and Chelsea than in the least deprived areas.[83] Statutory homelessness is also significantly worse than the England average, as is child poverty – in an area that holds close to £300 million in reserves and has offered tax rebates to its wealthiest residents.[84]

'Within a fifteen-minute bus ride we've got the Sultan of Brunei and people who can't afford to put food on the table – literally,' former local Labour MP Emma Dent Coad tells me. Dent Coad served the area from 2017 to 2019 and currently sits as a local councillor. 'During the Pandemic, my colleagues were running around with hot food for people who couldn't afford to buy any.'

However, there has been a concerted attempt to shield this desperation and poverty from the eyes of wealthier residents, Dent Coad claims. 'The difference between poverty in Kensington and Chelsea and poverty elsewhere is that the council could afford to fix it and they have chosen not to – unlike many other areas. The poverty is also sanitised. The trees are pruned and the streets are swept, but behind that façade people are kept in really poor circumstances,' she says. 'I find it despicable.'

This was the underlying reason for the fatal facelift of Grenfell Tower, motivated by a 'disdain for social tenants', Dent Coad claims. 'They're seen as sub-human. Some of it is racism and some of it is just blatant class snobbery – I see it all the time.'

This intimacy of poverty and over-abundance is not unique to Kensington. The poorest 50 per cent of Londoners hold just 6.8 per cent of the capital's wealth, while the top 10 per cent retain 42.5 per cent.[85]

As of 2020, 28 per cent of people in London were living in poverty, after housing costs, compared to 22 per cent in the UK as a whole.[86] The number of people suffering from poverty in the capital – 2.5 million – is only marginally less than the total population of Greater Manchester. Mirroring the UK population, poverty in London is not restricted to those out of work. Some 74 per cent of impoverished adults in the capital are in working families, up from 62 per cent a decade ago. In the three years to 2016, 39 per cent of private renters and 46 per cent of social renters were in poverty, falling to 12 per cent among owner-occupiers.[87]

The wealth disparities between different parts of the city are also vast: 57 per cent of children in Tower Hamlets are in poverty and the overall poverty rate in the borough was 39 per cent in 2013/14, compared to 15 per cent in leafy Richmond.[88] As the IFS states: 'Inequality is far higher within London than in any other part of the UK.'[89] Londoners are not immune to the inequalities that have been cultivated in the capital.

This materialised on the city's streets in August 2011. The London Riots have been systematically suppressed in public dialogue over the last ten years. It's highly unusual to find any reference to the looting, violence and arson in current political debate. The riots and the Grenfell fire violated the romanticised identities of Britain and London – a diverse, liberal, prosperous city and a 'great' nation governed by the rule of law and the basic equality of all citizens. A nation that views itself as a good chap playing by the rules couldn't explain a state-sanctioned atrocity or widespread anti-establishment social unrest, so their memory has been expunged from popular consciousness.

What's more, the anger expressed on the streets of London in August 2011 is radically different to popular conceptions of the city today. A decade ago, the streets played host to fierce racial grievances, with disadvantaged, disenfranchised Londoners seemingly lashing out at a system that had both routinely ignored and methodically demonised their communities. Ten years later, the same city – in which socio-economic inequalities have continued to fester – is allegedly a model of liberal racial harmony and progress.

'While London is not a dangerous city by global standards, it is hard to overstate just what a scary place London is to be a working-class Black male teenager. You are in one of the wealthiest cities ever built, yet the vast majority of your friends and family live in some of the worst poverty in Europe,' writes the renowned author and rapper Akala in *Natives*.[90] The city experienced by forgotten Londoners is very different to the one documented in high-minded periodicals.

Not least, the sourdough columnists portray London as a rich haven of opportunity and freedom, thus overlooking the financial and psychological barriers that are imposed on its inhabitants. In real-life London, an ordinary, middle-class existence requires deep pockets – inhibiting those who were born into nothing.

The metropolis is hardly an oasis of freedom either, despite the tantalising promises that emanate from Soho's bars. London is subservient to rampant corporate landlords; a new age of feudalism in which freedom is throttled by extortionate housing costs, the threat of eviction and perpetual insecurity. Our masters are the property-owning gentry, and they decide our career choices, relationships and purchasing habits, even if only subliminally. Our 4 a.m. warehouse blowouts are just a coping mechanism; solace found through the illusion of liberty.

In real-life London, there is an overwhelming financial incentive for young Londoners to remain in their family home and avoid landlord servitude. From 1996–98 to 2014–15, the capital saw a 41 per cent increase in young people living with their parents.[91] This may keep the rent-seekers from their door and markedly increase their career opportunities (as described earlier in this chapter), but it's also claustrophobic. Their experiences are akin to a teenager whose mum has taken them out shopping. They feel stifled and awkward, but there's a bitter acceptance that reaching the shopping centre would be impossible if they didn't hitch a lift in mum's car.

The alternative, if you're not a member of the bank of mum and dad, is to limit your freedom in other ways. There doesn't seem much freedom in cohabiting an overpriced, grotty flat in Hackney with an upsetting array of suspicious odours. Most private renters in London bounce from property to property, convincing themselves it's a free-spirited adventure and not something that's being imposed on them by insecure employment, extortionate rents and exploitative landlords. As Ryan Bassil wrote for VICE in 2020 about his experiences of renting in London: 'I was a voyeur in everyone else's lavish life.'[92]

London's toxic hegemony – its monopoly over key sectors of the economy, its collusion with extractors of economic and human wealth, and its carnivorous property market – has nurtured harmful disparities between regions, and between its own inhabitants.

However, despite embodying and perpetuating glaring inequalities, the city retains a positive image among left-wing figures – the very people who rightfully rage against other forms of inequality and discrimination.

4.

LEFT BEHIND?

If London is a fortress, its mercenaries are left-wing. After years of sustained attack from assorted Conservative and pro-Brexit forces, who have branded the capital as a bastion of the 'metropolitan elite', London is now a safe haven for progressive groups.

This is not merely a physical process, though London does harbour a larger number of Labour MPs than anywhere else in the country. The capital is also a metaphor for many groups on the left: a symbol of their values, seemingly signifying diversity, tolerance and social justice.

'The only bad thing about London is the rent and cost of living. That's it. It's a diverse, safe and fascinating city,' says Aaron Bastani, co-founder of the influential left-wing outlet Novara Media. He was responding to a Twitter post from his colleague Ash Sarkar, who said that she was sick 'of London slander from pricks' – though she did acknowledge that 'there are lots of shit things about living in London'.

London is a city of nearly 10 million people – it can and does represent a multiplicity of different values, cultures and tax brackets. London is not a homogenous blob, either culturally or ideologically. Yet, this nuance has not proliferated among the Left. There is a collective, borderline-religious faith towards London from the leaders of the progressive movement, who have in turn abandoned the cause of regional equality. This is jarring.

The Left ostensibly claims to believe in greater equality, yet the extreme disparities within and between different parts of the UK, epitomised by the supremacy of London and its property-owning oligarchy, have been ignored and even belittled.

There is an ideological and rhetorical inconsistency between the grand proclamations of left-wing voices about social injustice, and their fortification of the capital. They are of course right to celebrate the generally progressive attitude of Londoners towards race, sexuality, religion – the conviction that no one should be judged for their identity. But this social liberalism is accompanied by a malignant concentration of power, wealth and opportunity in London, of the sort that should offend anyone of a progressive mindset.

There is a rough analogy in recent political history. David Cameron's Conservative-led coalition government passed gay marriage into law – a welcome and long-awaited affirmation of social equality. However, neither Cameron nor his administration are regarded as progressive, because they implemented a litany of other policies that cut welfare spending, demonised the poor, incapacitated state services and advanced the interests of the rich.

Online debate may condition us to view politics as a contest between heroes and villains, the universally righteous versus the eternally depraved. But, in reality, every political actor – whether that is a place or a person – is composed of a complex blend of good values and bad. We therefore must assess whether, on balance, they conform to our beliefs or not. The perplexing question is why there is an enduring consensus that London is a beacon of progress, among those on the Left, when so much evidence points to the contrary.

To evaluate this question – especially for those who aren't immersed in the psychodramas of the Labour movement – it's worth mapping the different groups involved and their attitudes to regional affairs.

Let's begin at the socialist end of the Labour movement and drift towards the centre – as tends to happen in the lifecycle of the party.

There are of course many sub-genres within this strand of left-wing politics – Marxists, Trotskyists, Stalinists, Militants, internationalists, anarchists, single-state socialists – each more self-impressed than the last. To save your sanity and mine, I'm simplifying this group to those who broadly supported Jeremy Corbyn's leadership of the Labour Party from 2015 to 2019, which encompasses the majority of the aforementioned.

Corbyn managed to accommodate all of these acolytes without too much civil warfare – at least to the extent that is common on the Hard Left. As Katrina Forrester of Harvard University says: 'Corbynism is best understood as the name for a period of left unity, at a time of disunity within the larger Labour Party.' Corbyn was the messiah of the movement, its prophet and commander, and his own personal identity is important if we are to understand the people he attracted to the cause, and how he moulded their agenda.

Corbyn was elected as the Labour MP for Islington North in 1983, having previously served as a councillor in Haringey, which neighbours Islington, since 1974. His political alliances, and his attitudes, reflect an international class struggle whereby the concerns of Cuban workers are of equal importance to those in Castleford. Broadly unpopular within the

Parliamentary Labour Party (PLP), Corbyn retained friend-ships among a core group of like-minded London-based MPs.

As Owen Hatherley acknowledges in *Red Metropolis*, figures associated with the Greater London Council (GLC) – the administrative body for the capital from 1965 to 1986 – had 'taken over the leadership of the Labour Party' under Corbyn. Diane Abbott, the Shadow Home Secretary and MP for Hackney North and Stoke Newington, was formerly the GLC's press officer. John McDonnell, Shadow Chancellor and MP for Hayes and Harlington, was at one time its second-in-command and finance minister.[1]

The Corbyn-sympathetic left is deeply embedded in the politics of the capital. They form some of London's highest-ranking and longest-serving representatives; people who have spent decades advocating for the city and its people. Their blindness to London's corrupting influence is therefore some-what unavoidable. If you have spent a lifetime in the furnace, you eventually forget about the heat.

Corbyn came of political age during the social struggles of the late 1960s and the frenzied debates over the threat of nuclear weapons. His parents were peace campaigners with an internationalist tilt – Corbyn's mother and father first met at an event in relation to the Spanish Civil War of the 1930s.[2] Corbyn joined the Campaign for Nuclear Disarmament while he was still at school and protested against the Vietnam War. This foregrounding, his ideological pubescence, has perme-ated Corbyn's entire political career, including his time as Labour leader.

These themes were reflected in his 2016 speech to the Labour Party Conference. In that address, Corbyn apologised for the last Labour government's involvement in the Iraq War, paying tribute to the peace process in Colombia, denouncing UK government arms sales to Saudi Arabia, and calling for action to end the war in Yemen. Corbyn only briefly mentioned the plight of Britain's abandoned heartlands, specifically in the context of Brexit. He claimed that these areas have been 'left behind by years of neglect, under-investment and deindustrialisation,' and said that the EU Referendum result should be respected, though he refrained from developing his regional agenda any further.[3]

This remained the case throughout Corbyn's leadership, including his 2019 swansong campaign. Confronted by a reincarnation of the Vote Leave Referendum campaign – Boris Johnson again masterminded by Dominic Cummings – Labour's offering was lame. The Conservatives pitched a combination of flag-waving, Trump-lite nationalism and state-led 'levelling up' investment, served alongside a suppos-edly 'oven-ready' Brexit deal. Yet Labour failed to develop a slogan to rival Johnson's Robin Hood routine. The Conservative campaign was a fable, of course, but it was a potent story sold to the nation by a world-class performer and clown. Labour's pitch, meanwhile, was vacuous.

The contrast is illuminated through Labour's election mani-festo. Instructively, the first picture embossed in the document shows Corbyn flanked by his Shadow Foreign Secretary, Emily Thornberry.[4] I am not suggesting that millions of people read Labour's manifesto, so I'm keen not to overstate its impor-tance, but this image does epitomise the Corbyn movement's tin-eared attitude to its former industrial heartlands. Thornberry, a supremely talented orator and a fierce political competitor, was dumped by Ed Miliband from his shadow cabinet in 2014 after seeming to mock someone for hanging an England flag outside their home. Thornberry, MP for Islington South and Finsbury, was accused of snobbery and a disdain for the symbols of national pride. A few years later, she was the poster politician of the 2019 Labour manifesto.

Optics aside, the manifesto featured an entire chapter on 'A New Internationalism', but not even a subchapter on the issue of regional rebalancing. Instead, various devolution and regional growth policies were embedded within other, adjacent sections of the document.

Jobs created through Labour's so-called 'Green Industrial Revolution', for example, would be distributed to the areas that had suffered from deindustrialisation during the second half of the twentieth century. 'Many parts of Britain would need this investment even without a climate and environmental emergency. Years of under-investment and neglect by Westminster have left too many communities feeling powerless and too many areas left behind with low-quality jobs, weak productivity and slow growth,' the manifesto said.

The policy is a reasonable one, though it is politically and rhetorically incoherent. Labour was promising imaginary jobs in an imaginary green economy, as opposed to the Conservative pledge of more nurses and police officers. Labour's language was also problematic, exposing its awkwardness towards regional inequality. The language quoted above was impersonal and wonkish, using vague concepts such as 'productivity' and 'growth'. It was abstract, referring to 'left-behind' areas in a way that one might describe a distant moon, rather than presenting them as a core part of Labour Britain. And it even managed to be condescending, claiming that people work in 'low-quality jobs'. If they were asked to name the lowest-quality job in Britain, I'd bet that 'Labour Party leader' would be mentioned frequently by voters in left-behind areas.

The 2017 general election demonstrated a more inclusive form of Corbynism – weaving economic populism with fiscal responsibility and Brexit pragmatism. People justifiably criticised the Corbyn movement for being too inward-looking – focusing on internal Labour campaigns rather than the country at large. But the 2017 election was the moment at which Labour, under Corbyn, most clearly aligned its agenda with the attitudes of the people.

Circumstances aided this process, of course. If Theresa May had not malfunctioned – steering towards a hard Brexit and promising what became known as a 'dementia tax' – the polls promised to deliver a Johnson-esque majority. Corbyn, actually a relatively unknown figure to the wider public, also benefited from cascading public opinion – much in the same way as Johnson in 2019.

For once, Corbyn's internal Labour popularity was an electoral asset, with the BBC broadcasting crowds of adoring supporters at rallies across the country. Many people seemed to support Corbyn because other people supported him – a ripple effect that knocked the Conservatives off their perch. 'If the campaign had been a couple of weeks longer, we would have secured a majority,' McDonnell said after the result.

However, for whatever reason, the Labour leadership retreated to familiar terrain after 2017 – to London and a pseudo-intellectual agenda premised on green industrial reform, large-scale public ownership and complex Brexit prevarication.

Faced with scathing attacks from inside and outside the Labour Party, this was perhaps a way that its leaders sought political and personal comfort – picking up the ideological weapons that they had relied on for decades before.

Ultimately, Corbyn was and is more occupied by global social justice than regional inequality – further evidenced by his post-2019 career. After resigning as leader, Corbyn launched a 'Peace and Justice' project – aiming to address 'economic security, global justice, a democratic society, and climate justice'.[5] Regional disparities are once again confined to the margins.

'Jeremy [Corbyn] has no empathy or understanding of the Midlands or the North,' contends former New Labour advisor and minister Andrew Adonis – an ardent critic of the former Labour leader. 'He is an Islington man.'

The excommunication of regional issues from modern socialist politics has its roots in a Marxist instinct that reduces all economic concerns to the issue of class. As left-wing activist and commentator Owen Jones wrote in 2014 for the *Guardian*: 'Though saying so may seem disloyal to my Northern homeland, the North–South divide is just another dangerous distraction.' In this worldview, 'there is one division that matters: those who have wealth and power, and those who do not'.[6]

This is a strange hypothesis, given that the unequal distribution of wealth and power unfolds in various ways, not simply through traditional class warfare. The disproportionate use of 'stop and search' police powers on Black and minority ethnic people is a manifestation of racial hierarchies laced with class assumptions. The abuse of female assistants by Hollywood actors and directors also evidently relates to power and wealth in the context of gender.

In a video about the performance of school students, attempting to address the claim that the Left has 'abandoned' White working-class boys in favour of minority ethnic groups, Novara's Ash Sarkar tried to correct the record, saying that the underperformance of this demographic is due to both 'race *and* class'.

Aside from the fact that gender is also evidently a factor, this statement shows how some parts of the Left have tempered their Marxist impulses in recent times, adopting 'intersectionality' as a guiding ethos. This term describes the interconnected nature of social identities, particularly race and class, and the inequalities that stem from their interactions. Ergo, 4 per cent of White people were unemployed in 2019, a figure that doubled among Black, Bangladeshi and Pakistani people – the causes of which relate to both class and racial identity (and likely more besides).[7]

'Somebody who is LGBT is going to experience the world differently than somebody who's straight. Somebody who's LGBT and African American is going to experience the world differently than somebody who's LGBT and Latina. It's sort of this commonsense notion that different categories of people have different kinds of experience,' says American lawyer and civil rights activist Kimberlé Crenshaw, who coined the term in 1989.[8]

However, the British Left's application of intersectionality doesn't currently extend to geography. The movement is justifiably critical of exploitative labour practices, vast inequalities of wealth, and interlaced forms of identity-based discrimination – but this rarely intersects region. Differences in school performance evidently relate to geography, with children in some places performing markedly better than others. But this belief is almost entirely absent from the Left. Redistribution is one of the core tenets of the Left, yet regional redistribution isn't part of this agenda.

Increasingly, the only left-wing forum that articulates the politics of place in a nuanced (and occasionally abrasive) manner is a breakaway movement called the Northern Independence Party (NIP). The party was founded by academic Philip Proudfoot, a former Labour member who supported Corbyn's leadership. The party controversially stood former Labour MP Thelma Walker in the May 2021 Hartlepool by-election, another brick in the Red Wall that fell into Johnson's wheelbarrow.

Regional inequality is 'the biggest development challenge the country faces – we basically have a partition that has emerged even without a war – but it's never been front-and-centre of Labour Party policy,' Proudfood told me, not long before the Hartlepool ballot. 'There has to be a democratic socialist voice arguing that the North–South divide is a major issue and can only be addressed through serious progressive policies, not just a few hundred Treasury jobs moving to Darlington, as the Tories are doing, or waving the Union Jack in the desperate hope that people will start voting for you again.'

This latter comment relates to a report, commissioned by Labour and leaked to the *Guardian* in February 2021, that called on Keir Starmer to deploy the Union Jack and more overt forms of patriotism to win back voters in 'Red Wall' seats.[9]

'It's patronising,' Proudfoot says, adding that Labour must resist projecting an image of the North that has been manufactured by reactionaries. 'For a long time, Nigel Farage was the media substitute for an authentic Northerner – even though he's very much not ... Even lefty London figures parrot this myth of the North as a place populated by bigots who wear flat caps and drink gravy. We call it "the fictional Northerner" because it's a caricature that doesn't exist.'

Indeed, as Byline Times polling by Omnisis shows, people in the North are more likely to say that the Conservative Party's immigration policies are 'unfair', compared to those in the South.[10]

Yet, an ignorance towards London's monopolisation of the nation is not reserved to the Corbyn-adjacent left.

In particular, the Blair and Brown administrations institutionalised the idea that politics and economics were becoming more globalised, more interconnected and more mobile. Therefore, by implication, place-based pride was naïve, and an attachment to past sources of local industry overly senti-mental: a blockade to progress.

'I hear people say we have to stop and debate globalisa-tion,' Blair told the 2005 Labour Party Conference. 'You might as well debate whether autumn should follow summer,' he said, wryly.

Globalisation would be disruptive, and some may be left behind, but our 'changing world' was 'replete with opportu-nities' that are awarded 'to those swift to adapt' and 'slow to complain', Blair said.[11]

As the New Labour years progressed, there was a growing sense that, although Blair and Brown had transformed public services, they had accepted Thatcher's belief in the 'managed decline' of former industrial heartlands.

This perception was buttressed later when Labour once again entered opposition. The leaders of New Labour had a significant input into the Referendum debate, spearheaded by former European Trade Commissioner and 'Prince of Darkness' Peter Mandelson. Ultimately, the Vote Leave campaign better understood and articulated the sense of ostracisation, disadvantage and disillusionment harboured by many areas of the North, Midlands and Wales. This was captured through the derision of a distant 'metropolitan elite' in London kowtowing to bureaucrats in Brussels.

And although I'm thoroughly sick of the notion that being opposed to Brexit is a 'betrayal' of the Red Wall, the metro-politan attitudes of the centre-left help to explain why the Remain campaign lost the argument.

As Deborah Mattinson writes in *Beyond the Red Wall*, recounting her conversations with former Labour voters who switched to the Conservatives in 2019: 'When some talked about the North–South divide, they talked as though they were witnessing a theft ... Funds were being taken away from them and transferred to wealthier parts of the country, places where the political sun had been shining – London came in for special mention again and again.'[12]

Brexit will disproportionately afflict peripheral regions, as the government's own models have predicted. It will torpedo the fishing industry, after promising to be its saviour, and it will almost certainly fail to reduce overall levels of immigration. Brexit is an elaborate and pernicious fallacy that will damage areas that have already experienced decades of decline. Opposing Brexit, in my opinion, is not some form of treason – if it rests on the conviction that Britain's nations and regions will suffer from its sordid side-effects.

However, the Referendum result buttressed the sentiment among some London-based Remainer progressives that London is enlightened, and the Brexit-voting regions are both stupid and bigoted. London voted Remain by 60 per cent to 40 per cent, though it delivered roughly the same total number of Leave votes as Yorkshire and the Humber. Therefore, rather than seeing London as part of the problem, these progressives maintain that the rest of the country should replicate the capital and its ideologies. London's supremacy is seen as a reason why Brexit was nearly avoided, rather than why it occurred at all.

One of the spiritual leaders of the London-Remain coalition prior to the 2019 general election was Holborn and St Pancras MP Sir Keir Starmer, Labour's shadow Brexit secretary and a keen second-referendum proponent. Starmer used this anti-Brexit clamour to launch a successful takeover of the Labour Party, easily winning its post-Corbyn leadership contest.

However, under the weight of electoral necessity, Starmer has turned his gaze to the heartlands, voyaging out of his

London comfort zone and directing his cavalry to the Red Wall. Mattinson has been hired as Labour's head of strategy, joining head of policy Claire Ainsley whose 2018 book *The New Working Class* observes that, 'There is a significant disparity between economic opportunities in London and the South East and the rest of the UK, despite the fact that three-quarters of the British population do not live there.'[13]

Foreseeing the popularity of Johnson's 'levelling up' pitch, Ainsley predicted that, 'There is a significant political gain for the party that can convince the new working class in constituencies all across the UK that their employment and earnings potential will be best served by a party that can lead national efforts to drive inward investment into the regions of the UK.'[14]

While there is a growing panic within the Labour Party leadership about the dissipation of the Red Wall, leading to a belated appreciation of local circumstances and grievances, Starmer's crude flag-waving campaign shows this is unfamiliar terrain. 'I'm afraid that I think Keir [Starmer] is in many ways a continuation of Corbyn,' says Adonis. 'He's a London-based MP and his roots are firmly in the South and in the capital.'

Indeed, while Starmer evidently sits on a different wing of the party to Corbyn, they appear to share an enthusiasm for vague, abstract ideas – a form of cliché politics that predominates on the Left. Both Corbyn's Green Industrial Revolution and Starmer's flag-waving campaign are performative; they are detached from the language and the values that people use to describe their lives and the changes they seek.

Labour should 'start by asking what people want out of their economy', says Aditya Chakrabortty of the *Guardian*. 'In London, that would be the desire to live in an affordable home without cockroaches and damp. In other parts of the country, it would be the ability to get to church on Sunday without having to wait three hours for the bus.'

However, while the priorities of people vary between places, absolutely no one talks about wanting Britain to be a 'winner in the global race against China and India', Chakrabortty says – or that we should be 'world-beating in bio-technology'.

Both wings of the Labour Party have forgotten how to speak to the concerns of ordinary people in words and concepts that resonate with their lives – seemingly confirming the idea that Labour is now a party of the metropolitan middle classes.

It has been suggested in some quarters that Starmer is veering towards Blue Labour, a strain of alternative thought on the Left that has morphed in recent times into a form of experimental provocation.

Theorised by the political scientist Adrian Pabst, Blue Labour is a counterweight to Blairite liberalism, advocating instead the merits of place, faith and stability. Blue Labour's foundational ideas relate quite closely to the conservative disposition described by Michael Oakeshott as 'to prefer the familiar to the unknown, to prefer the tried to the untried, fact to mystery, the actual to the possible, the limited to the unbounded, the near to the distant, the sufficient to the super-abundant, the convenient to the perfect, present laughter to utopian bliss'.[15]

'The trouble for Labour is that the rest of Britain is not going London's way,' Pabst argued in a compendium of ideas on Blue Labour, published in 2015. 'Never mind the wealth gap, it is the deepening divide along cultural lines – between a more liberal-cosmopolitan and a more conservative-communitarian outlook – that the party has ignored for far too long.'[16]

The book featured endorsements from anti-Brexit *Guardian* columnist Rafael Behr, right-leaning journalist Peter Oborne and rabid reactionary Rod Liddle. It included chapters from individuals who landed on different sides of the Brexit war, David Lammy and Tom Watson in the Remain camp and Frank Field in the Leave. All made thoughtful contributions, unpicking Labour's metropolitan mindset and the recent evolution of the party.

This cross-ideological collaboration has been expunged from Blue Labour, perhaps as a consequence of a Brexit campaign that created a bitter, simplified, polarised divide between two deeply entrenched groups – an infantilisation of politics that suited Boris Johnson and rendered constructive debate politically dangerous.

In this two-tone political environment, Blue Labour has embraced its blue streak, seemingly swallowing Johnson's soup of anti-woke nationalist nostalgia. Blue Labour's advocates, led by London-born reactionary Paul Embery, are afforded regular right-wing media slots through the likes of UnHerd and GB News, and could now more accurately be described as Labour-inclined Conservative shock-agitators than Conservative-inclined Labour intellectuals.

'The [Labour] party had been swallowed by a poisonous brew of social and economic liberalism,' Embery writes in his book, *Despised*, about the party's recent history.[17] Embery even chooses to malign the liberating reforms of the 1960s, which included Harold Wilson's near abolition of capital punishment, the decriminalisation of sex between men in private, the liberalisation of abortion laws and the abolition of theatre censorship. In a sermon that could feasibly have been delivered by Mary Whitehouse or Margaret Thatcher, Embery writes: 'Though the '60s were plainly not all bad, it is hard to imagine that we would have experienced to the same degree such problems as family breakdown and father-lessness, atomisation and loneliness, teenage pregnancy, widespread drug abuse, social exclusion, an abject lack of discipline in the education system, and the steady drip of lawlessness and disorder on our streets, if we had not chosen quite the path we did back then.'

Therefore, while Blue Labour may criticise London and claim to care about regional equality, these arguments are hardly derived from left-wing principles. 'What is amazing about [Blue Labour's] current trajectory is how willing they are to discard the core values of any progressive movement – liberty, equality and solidarity – and the speed with which they have moved to become fellow-travellers of the national-ist right,' wrote Jon Bloomfield of the University of Birmingham in 2019.[18]

Finally, and perhaps most significantly, Labour still retains an extensive network of local and regional leaders – the nerve-system of the party that far outnumbers its Westminster contingent (there are more than 5,000 Labour councillors in the UK and fewer than 200 Labour MPs at the time of writ-ing).

The figurehead of this town hall infantry is Andy Burnham, Mayor of Greater Manchester and de facto 'King of the North'. Since leaving Westminster in 2017, Burnham has been warring against the regional imbalances that plague the Labour Party and the country at large. Immediately following the 2021 local council elections and Labour's loss in Hartlepool, Burnham called for a culture change in the upper ranks of the party. 'I'm getting a bit fed up with saying this to them, but now they really do need to listen ... and end the London-centric Labour Party that I have been in all my life,' he said.[19]

And yet, for a party that preaches progress, Labour is remarkably slow to adapt. 'The elected Labour Party politicians who have the most influence over people's lives are city-region mayors, and yet they're invisible in the structures of the Labour Party,' former Labour MP for Wakefield Mary Creagh laments. 'There's a kind of blindness from Westminster to these really important, really powerful politicians who are showing how Labour can lead the way.'

Indeed, no Labour mayor was allowed a main-stage speech at the party's 2021 conference – a fact that riled Burnham. 'Get Northern voices talking to Northern voters, is what I would say. We have the first woman metro mayor [West Yorkshire Mayor Tracy Brabin]. Why she didn't have a main stage speech lord only knows,' he tells me, a few weeks after the conference. 'Use devolved leaders and build from there. We are in power – we are actually doing things now. It's as though the party doesn't notice that or doesn't want to promote it.'

Burnham included, there are currently eight regional Labour mayors governing 19.5 million people. However, due to their distance from Westminster and the nexus of the Labour movement, they are often sidelined from discussions about the direction and evolution of the party. This is ironic, considering Labour's relative success in devolved elections outside Scotland. The party holds all but two regional mayor positions in England and delivered a convincing victory in the 2021 Senedd election in Wales – increasing both its number of seats and its share of the vote. There are lessons to be gleaned from these campaigns, and the policies that have consequently been implemented. But, instead, Labour is stuck in a London loop that continues to administer ever-greater electoral setbacks.

'I've not had a conversation with anyone in the Labour Party, I don't think, about regional inequality – what we want to say about it and what we want to do about it,' says Sheffield-based Labour campaigns consultant Mike Buckley, who formerly served as the director of Labour for a People's Vote.

One reason for this regional ignorance, it seems, is that the national Labour movement has not just intellectually clustered around London – it now also physically occupies the capital. Indeed, it's difficult for Labour to hear the pleas and the proposals of regional representatives when the party's trend-setters have flocked to the superpower city.

Traditional routes into the Labour movement have been curtailed, Westminster being the only available finishing school for future left-wing leaders. The highest-ranking advisors, politicians, union leaders, media outlets, campaign groups and think tanks have amassed in London, recruiting from the pool of people who are able to live and work in the city. This filters through to social media, the debating chamber of Labour politics. London-based influencers set the agenda that is aggressively kicked around by activists online.

Previous avenues into the party have fallen into disrepair, including the trail leading through the trade union movement, which used to be an important sponsor of regional interests in the Labour Party. Local union branches are no longer the epicentre of political action on the Left and have instead been supplanted by academic and pseudo-academic, London-based forums.

'The institutional and cultural bonds that linked many voters to Labour have become weaker and weaker over time,' said a post-mortem report from the group Labour Together after the 2019 general election. 'From the loss of local Labour clubs to declining Trade Union membership, Labour has lost many of the institutional roots it had within communities, resulting in disconnection.'[20]

The Fabian Society, Momentum, Progress, the *Guardian*, LSE, UCL, IPPR and Novara form the crux of the Labour movement, supplanting the trade union officer or the local council leader. 'The entirety of our political, journalistic, intellectual classes are all London-centric,' says Proudfoot of the Northern Independence Party. 'I went to LSE, I moved down from the North East and then I gradually saw myself becoming part of the London-centric hive mind, before realising the problems created by that sort of system.'

Even the headquarters of the unions are now clustered in London. Unite, the second largest union in the UK and a major source of funding for the Labour Party, is a twenty-minute walk from the *Guardian*'s offices in North London – the squatting place for various left-wing interests – and just a ten-minute stroll away from Channel 4.

'The strength of the trade unions in the 1960s and 1970s meant a production line of talent from the regions being supported to enter local government and then into Parliament,' Burnham tells me. 'And I think in the era that I entered politics, that had really changed. We were looking much more at a metropolitan class that knew how to navigate the system.'

Burnham recalls his conversations with David Blunkett, who warned that regional accents often damaged the political prospects of MPs, even in the Labour Party. 'And he was right,' Burnham reflects. 'I remember sharing an office with James Purnell when we were the up-and-coming backbenchers, and if a big issue was breaking in the media, Radio 4 would always call James and 5 Live would always call me.'

This state of affairs has persevered throughout Labour's modern history. 'Instead of drawing its political class from trade unions and professionals, it attracted the professionalised millennial precariat,' writes Harvard assistant professor Forrester, about the new influx of members spurred by Corbyn's leadership of the party.

London is the site of Labour politics – the prism through which its agenda is calibrated and its policies formulated. Protest marches take place in Parliament Square, events are hosted in Parliament's committee rooms, interviews are conducted in Portcullis House – sheltering the offices of MPs – or in Millbank Studios just a short walk away. London's concentration of power, journalism, commerce, culture and academia has enticed the Labour movement into the capital, and its leading figures and groups haven't resisted the trend. Few have spoken out about the regional distortion of influence within Labour politics.

This capital clustering has a measurable effect on the Labour movement. For one, its thought-leaders are extracted from the body of people who can afford to live in London; namely, people who have family members in the capital or those who have lived in the city for many years. These people are likely to be reverent towards London, skewing their outlook towards the supremacy of the city and the inequalities suffered by the rest of the country.

Due to their proximity to the nexus of the Labour movement and the media, London-based MPs also have more opportunities to bask in the limelight. The fountains of fame are more easily accessible to MPs with constituencies in the capital – via interviews and speeches – while their liberal, metropolitan values are likely to chime with the attitudes of other left-wing luminaries, buttressing their mutual influence. Meanwhile, as London offers a stage for left-wing politics, participants are deterred from denouncing the platform. Criticising London in a London-based forum, likely with a

London-based audience, is akin to scorning your gran for making a crap Sunday lunch while being sat at her table.

This trend has undoubtedly been accelerated by Labour's rapid demise in Scotland since 2010. At the 2019 UK general election, the Labour Party won a solitary seat in Scotland, Edinburgh South, and 18.6 per cent of the national vote. 'The Labour Party assumed that it would always win elections in Scotland,' Scottish National Party MP Owen Thompson tells me from his constituency office in Midlothian. 'They took the people of Scotland for granted.'

In 2005, Labour had won forty-one of the fifty-nine available seats in Scotland and 39.5 per cent of the vote share. Labour's collapse was dramatic, precipitated and exploited by the Scottish National Party (SNP), which further shifted the locus of Labour politics to Westminster and London. It seems as though this complacency north of the border presaged Labour's crisis in the Red Wall years later.

'The party has entirely failed to adjust to changes in Scotland,' says Buckley. 'Labour lost Scotland in 2015 and then just didn't know what to do about it so didn't do anything at all. For the past five or six years the party has basically just shrugged its shoulders at the fact we lost Scotland.'

At the time of writing, forty-eight of Labour's 199 MPs – 24 per cent of the total – represent a London constituency.[21] This physical and intellectual clustering will only intensify if Labour continues to concentrate its support in metropolitan areas, as seems to be the trend.

Thanks to the complicity of Nick Clegg in David Cameron's austerity government, the Liberal Democrat vote collapsed after 2010 – much of it dispersed to the Labour Party. By 2014, more than half of the most liberal voters who previously supported the Liberal Democrats in 2010 had switched to Labour.[22] Holding the view that Clegg was an accessory to Cameron's various crimes, a wave of defections consolidated Labour's support among well-educated voters, often in metropolitan hubs, with liberal views on issues such as immigration.

As described by Maria Sobolewska and Rob Ford in *Brexitland*, by 2015 Labour represented sixty-seven of the seventy-five seats in England and Wales where the White population share was below 75 per cent. These MPs also carried overwhelming local support, boasting an average majority of 30 per cent. The 2015 election was the first in which liberal identity groups outnumbered conservative identity groups among Labour voters – signalling the direction of travel within the party towards a more urban composition and outlook.[23]

At the same time, as has been well documented, Labour has been decaying in small towns, rural areas and former industrial seats. Part of the reason for this, says PR consultant and former New Labour advisor Karl Milner, has been the party's inclination to parachute candidates from London to the North.

'The Labour Party made UKIP happen,' he says, referring to the emergence of the anti-EU, anti-immigration party led by Nigel Farage in the run-up to the 2016 Referendum: 'It all started in that period when we parachuted clever, erudite lawyers into the North to take parliamentary seats. They should have been getting seats in London – not up here. That's why the system has to change. The Labour Party doesn't promote good candidates from the North. In the past, those sorts of people did make their way in the party. Northern people aren't allowed to stand now, or to develop the networks. It's extraordinary. It's almost by design.'

Milner's political journey began in Wales, he says, but his career thrived after moving to the capital. 'I got a job in London working for Harriet Harman, and from that moment on you're swimming – you meet the right people and you do the right things and all of a sudden your career takes off. That's the way politics works. But can kids now do what I did? Because in those days I could sofa-surf, and I basically spent a year sofa-surfing. I don't think that would be possible now.'

Milner seems to be describing a self-fulfilling prophecy. As Labour entrenches its support in cities, particularly in London, the party has retreated to this comfort zone – causing a cultural and ideological disconnect from non-metropolitan seats and exacerbating its electoral problems in these areas of the country.

As the Fabians pointed out in a 2018 report, 61 per cent of surveyed people in rural England and Wales say that Labour does not understand people who live in the local area, compared to 45 per cent in 'town and fringe' areas and 39 per cent in urban Britain. At the time of the report's release, Labour led the Conservatives by 46 per cent to 37 per cent in urban areas, while the Tories were trouncing Labour by 54 per cent to 31 per cent in rural constituencies. 'Labour's association with the cities leads to an association of Labour with urban snobbery towards rural areas – a sentiment that was shared almost unanimously by participants in all focus groups,' the report says.[24]

An electorally successful strategy for Labour will harvest more votes in peripheral Britain, among those with a more socially conservative disposition, while retaining the support of liberal urbanites. Faced with the prospect of walking this tightrope, and the distinct possibility that it may lead to an embarrassing fall, it is perhaps little wonder that Labour leaders have sought safer ground.

Thus, Labour's gatekeepers are not just detached from ordinary voters on regional issues; it also appears as though they are out of sync with party members. Since the surge in membership that corresponded with Jeremy Corbyn's election as party leader in 2015, a stereotype of the typical Labour member has been constructed by the media. They are supposedly liberal, young, well-educated and urban, probably based in London or the South East, and more likely to belong to a Black and minority ethnic group than the population at large.

As with most clichés, this one is part truth and majority myth. Labour members are, for example, drawn heavily from the well-educated middle classes – 77 per cent belonging to the highest ABC1 social group, according to a 2018 QMU-Mile Institute report.[25] However, after this point, the typecast disintegrates.

Labour members are 96 per cent White – far ahead of the overall UK population – and are more likely to be older than the average Brit. Some 16 per cent of Labour members are under the age of 35, while 56 per cent are over the age of 55. Labour members are also less likely to be London-based than Liberal Democrats, with 12 per cent and 15 per cent of party members based in the capital respectively. And while the leaders of the Labour movement have migrated to London, Labour still retains a considerable body of ordinary members in the North – 29 per cent of total party members, compared to 19 per cent of Conservative members, and 18 per cent of card-carrying Liberal Democrats.[26]

Labour members skew heavily towards more liberal beliefs. On a range of social and moral questions – topics such as capital punishment, censorship and equal rights – Labour members are among the most liberal people in politics, even marginally more liberal than Liberal Democrat members. According to the QMU-Mile Institute report, 85 per cent of Labour members approve of gay marriage, for example, compared to 81 per cent of Liberal Democrat members.[27]

Yet, Labour members defy the instincts of the party's London-based orchestrators by merging this social liberalism with a concern for regional inequality. In a survey conducted by King's College London (KCL), Labour members were asked to select the most serious forms of inequality in modern Britain. Income and wealth came out top, selected by 72 per cent of those surveyed, closely followed by the disparities between more and less deprived areas, selected by 67 per cent of people. Regional inequality was ranked above the disparities between racial or ethnic groups, selected by 62 per cent, differences in educational outcomes between children (47 per cent) and inequalities between men and women (30 per cent).[28]

What's more, contrary to the stereotype, Labour voters who voted Remain are most likely to say that inequalities between more and less deprived areas are a key concern – 70 per cent of Labour Remainers selecting this as a serious form of inequality, versus 61 per cent of Labour Leavers.[29]

Place-based inequalities also concern Labour Remainers more than Conservative Remainers and Conservative Leavers. Asked to imagine a hypothetical scenario in which 'the gap in incomes between areas increases', 62 per cent of Labour Remainers said this would be a 'very big problem', matched by 51 per cent of Labour Leavers, 30 per cent of Conservative Remainers and just 25 per cent of Conservative Leavers.[30]

Labour's gatekeepers are evidently out of step with party members on regional inequality. There is a more balanced dispersal of ordinary Labour members across the country than in the higher ranks of the party – the latter accumulating in the capital. Emancipated from a pathological attachment to London, lay members show that it is perfectly possible to combine social liberalism with a belief in regional redistribution.

Yet, instead, the Labour movement is ruled by multiple groups that have relegated regional inequality to the margin of their worldview – vacating the terrain to those who claim that greater geographical equality can only be achieved through a pseudo-erotic obsession with 1950s social dogma and the implosive economics flogged by Brexit.

I distinctly remember the night of the 2012 US presidential election. I was at university, lounging in my room with a few flatmates, drinking, tweeting and occasionally napping until the early hours of the morning as incumbent Democratic President Barack Obama bulldozed his Republican challenger Mitt Romney.

Though I've pulled plenty of election all-nighters since, this was the first time that I had paid close attention to a political contest – and it was one held in an entirely different continent, never mind my own country.

This isn't unusual. There is a fascination with American politics in Britain that captures both obsessives and casual onlookers. This is partly due to the pageantry of American elections. In the UK, politicians can struggle to attract a few dozen people to a village hall event – a warm-up act to the bingo – half of the audience members barely awake and the other half primed with anger, poised for a brawl at the Q&A. This is very different to the outpouring of adoration, and the mass delirium, that are witnessed during US elections – when the candidates are treated like grey-suited rock stars.

Some of this stardust invariably sails across the Atlantic, consumed rabidly by those who wish our politics was infused with more celebrity, glamour and money. This is aided and abetted by Hollywood, which seems to have a mutually reinforcing relationship with American politics. We watch the political concoctions of screenwriters, only to find that their depraved, mythical candidates have been replicated in real life. It's difficult not to be infatuated.

Britain's fascination with American politics is not reserved to one political faction. It spans Left and Right, moulding the attitudes of both. A raging Atlanticism is palpable among those who led the Brexit campaign, for example. There was a cross-fertilisation between the individuals and ideas associated with the campaign to leave the EU and Donald Trump's bid for the presidency in 2016.[31] Nigel Farage stumped for the orange-faced megalomaniac in 2016 – receiving the honour of being the first foreign politician to meet Trump after his shock victory against Hillary Clinton – and toured the States during his re-election bid in 2020.

The barely veiled ambition of Brexit has been to align Britain more closely with America. Its proponents seek to cut regulation, lower taxes, and roll back the frontiers of the so-called 'nanny state' – creating an American annex on the shores of Europe. As Owen Polley wrote for *The Article* in November 2020: 'It is an unhappy paradox that some of the people who were keenest to see the UK assert its independence from the EU also seem happiest to accept US dominance.'[32]

The British right has also been on a crash course in the 'Culture War', provided by their American cousins. Various pejoratives have been imported from America by Farage and his fellow travellers, most of which have little or no basis in reality. The supposed scourge of campus censorship, the threat of 'woke' warriors and the pervasive influence of 'critical race theory' are all American-made bogeymen, shipped across the Atlantic in an effort to portray the Left as radical and treasonous, regardless of the facts.

A similar process has occurred in a parallel and reverse fashion on the Left – though grounded in legitimate protest against a tyrannical leader of the 'free world'. Opposition to Trump was a focal point for the Left after 2016, reaching a high point through the Trump Baby – a twenty-foot homage to the President that was launched into London's skies during his visit to the UK in July 2018, and subsequently acquired by the Museum of London.

However, the Left's political exchange programme with America has also distorted the priorities of the Labour movement. Primarily, the British Left has absorbed the cultural attitudes of American progressives – premised on personal and particularly racial identity – which are responses to a very different social and political ecosystem.

Undoubtedly, there are similarities between America and Britain – culturally, historically, economically and demographically – that have created shared forms of injustice. The wealth of both nations is a product of conquest and exploitation – of the poor, and of foreign peoples – while there has been a mutual economic shift in recent years towards finance, technology and deindustrialisation, fostering resentment towards both professional politics and the masters of the new economy. We share a language, cultural idols, TV programmes and fast-food chains – nurturing the idea that we are more similar nations than is actually the case.

Indeed, simply transplanting American political campaigns and applying them wholesale to the UK risks overlooking issues that are unique to this country. Roughly 40 per cent of America's population is non-Hispanic White, and it's estimated that non-White voters will represent a majority by 2045.[33] In contrast, some 20 per cent of people in the UK do not identify as White British.[34]

In fact, demographically, there is a lot in common between London and the US – perhaps explaining why the Left, concentrated in the capital, has borrowed from the rhetoric of

American social justice campaigns. Only 44.9 per cent of London's population identifies as White British, while 37 per cent were born abroad.[35] Yet our capital is an outlier. The second most diverse region in England, the West Midlands, has a White British population of 79.2 per cent. The West Midlands also has the second largest Black population outside London, constituting 3.3 per cent of the regional total. London's Black population represents 13.3 per cent of the capital's total.[36]

This is not to deny the presence of racism in the UK or the harm it causes. Structural racism is embedded in many powerful British institutions – politics, the police and academia, to name just a few. This discrimination systematically diminishes the life chances of people from minority backgrounds and preserves an insidious racial hierarchy that often manifests through overt racism and abuse. Racially and religiously motivated hate crimes hit a new high across England and Wales in 2020, government data shows.[37]

Boris Johnson has compared women wearing the burqa to bank robbers and letterboxes; the former leader of the United States has effectively called Mexicans entering the immigration ballot 'rapists'. However, while there are similarities between the two countries, the form and intensity of prejudice is different in the UK and America. Simply reproducing American political campaigns is not a fair reflection of the intense and unique racial inequalities that ravage the United States, to the extent that 200 Black people are shot to death by the police every year; nor does it give fair weight to the unique forms of inequality suffered by people in the UK.[38]

What's more, the nature of the American political system is very different to ours. Regional interests are represented through powerful state legislatures that can prescribe policies on commerce, taxation, healthcare, education and much more besides. The UK's devolution settlement, in contrast, is weak. The devolved nations have comparatively greater powers, though their capacity to intervene in the realms of business, taxation and welfare is notably limited. Regional devolved governments, meanwhile, are more restricted – their core powers largely extending to transport – while the implementation of the devolution settlement has been patchy at best. Some areas, notably London, have gained more significant powers; others none at all.

We are captivated by the US presidential cycle, but our attention drops off precipitously when it comes to state-level elections. We therefore have an incomplete understanding of regional powers in the United States and our comparative deficiencies. We prefer to focus on the ubiquitous, nationwide issues that dominate presidential elections, before using them as a catalyst for spin-off campaigns in the UK.

The concept of a 'Green New Deal' was formulated in the US by Democratic upstart Alexandria Ocasio-Cortez before gaining a foothold in domestic politics (rebranded as the 'Green Industrial Revolution'), and Black Lives Matter entered the British political lexicon after the murder of George Floyd in Minneapolis. To repeat, there's no denying that such ideas are important in a British context. They are relevant, they are certainly not dangerous – as some right-wing commentators maintain – and they have evolved the cause of social justice in meaningful ways. The question is simply whether they should receive the same relative prominence in the domestic left-wing agenda as in the United States.

Additionally, while America has suffered similar industrial changes to the UK, regional inequalities are very different in the two countries. Parallel processes of automation, globalisation and neoliberalism may have caused a mutual manufacturing crisis – percolating through to politics in 2016 when the disillusionment of older, left-behind voters led to a populist earthquake on both sides of the Atlantic. However, while the UK has one, all-powerful urban centre, the United States is a loose, collaborative alliance of dozens. One city has not captured the intellectual and material wealth of the nation in the same way that London has in the UK.

That is why the British Left needs to develop a new, distinct agenda that is orientated more firmly towards geographical equality, while of course retaining a vigorous campaign for racial, social and climate justice. The two are not mutually exclusive.

If this doesn't happen, Labour risks repeating the humiliation of its 2019 general election performance, served up by the very areas that once acted as the breeding grounds of the movement.

5.

RED WALL

'There are too many people in the Labour Party who still want to live in the world of the 1970s, when the working class voted Labour and the middle class voted Tory – because that's the world they're comfortable in emotionally,' says Labour campaigns consultant and writer Mike Buckley.

This mirage collapsed on 13 December 2019. The bitter winter frost cut particularly deep in the Labour Party, as its supporters awoke to a landslide election defeat. It was the party's worst performance since 1935, the newspapers reported. Labour lost 60 seats, a quarter of its total, as Boris Johnson's Conservatives amassed an 80-seat majority.

To raise a point of order on behalf of Clement Attlee, who led Labour's 1935 campaign and whose moustache would undoubtedly be twitching with annoyance at the unfair comparison, Labour did gain more than 100 seats in that election – a markedly better outcome than in 2019. The latter was more comparable to the 1931 election, when Labour lost all but 52 of its seats.

The axis of Labour's defeat in 2019 was the so-called 'Red Wall' – a body of formerly staunch Labour seats spanning across Northern England, the Midlands and Wales that fell to the Conservatives, many for the first time in decades. Such a cataclysmic election defeat naturally had multiple inputs, but the fall of the Red Wall was one of the most consequential. The scale of the desertion among these formerly proud Labour territories has triggered an identity crisis among the movement – one that is inseparable from regional politics.

When Conservative pollster James Kanagasooriam conceived of the 'Red Wall' insignia in August 2019, he was describing a group of constituencies 'stretching from [North] Wales into Merseyside, Warrington, Wigan, Manchester, Oldham, Barnsley, Nottingham and Doncaster'. These seats could be 'launchpads' for a Conservative victory in the upcoming election, he said, if the party could 'detoxify' its image. The demographics of these constituencies were favourable to the Conservatives, Kanagasooriam said, but a cultural attachment to Labour and an ingrained hostility towards the Tories had kept them aligned to the former. The Red Wall therefore not only describes a physical bloc of constituencies, but also a psychological barrier that, before 2019, had prevented the seats from flipping to the Conservatives.

The Red Wall label has been met with some scepticism, founded on the claim that it amalgamates a number of seats that display very different characteristics – flattening the contours of the UK's complex political geography. However, elections are won or lost on the basis of trends that transcend local factors. The trends that have the most merit explain a large number of constituency-level election results without crumbling under the weight of seat-specific circumstances or competing factors.

In this regard, the Red Wall hypothesis is persuasive. According to an analysis by Sebastian Payne in *Broken Heartlands*, Labour lost thirty-three of its forty-three English Red Wall seats in 2019 – half of its total losses in the election. Writing for the *Financial Times*, Kanagasooriam says that

Labour lost 20 per cent of its total 2017 support in the Red Wall.[1]

These fallen heartlands were previously linchpins of the Labour bloc. The party lost seats represented in bygone eras by Tony Blair (Sedgefield), Andy Burnham (Leigh) and the 'Beast of Bolsover' Dennis Skinner. These three seats alone span three different regions, each with unique histories and cultures. Yet, there are undoubtedly common experiences that cut across these geographies, namely: economic stagnation, the deterioration of their local spaces and services – epitomised by the death of the high street – and a greying population with fewer educational qualifications than people in urban areas.

These experiences have triggered a sense of diminished former glory – a perception that their town is on a downward spiral, while other places bask in extreme wealth. Deborah Mattinson describes this common feeling in her book, *Behind the Red Wall*, when she asks Red Wall voters to imagine an 'ideal' political party and to draft its slogan. 'Let's Make Britain Great Again' was the consensus among the participants, evoking Donald Trump's strapline from the 2016 presidential election. A spontaneous chant of 'Let's build a wall' broke out among the group, Mattinson says. When she asked where the wall should be built, 'London!' was the cry from one member, 'and everyone cheered'.[2]

'They could not have been clearer: keeping Londoners in their place would be a very desirable outcome indeed,' Mattinson says.

There is a regional consciousness among Red Wall areas. The disadvantages and inequalities they suffer are firmly understood within a geographical context – premised on the belief that their areas are prejudiced while others are prioritised.

I asked my friends at the polling company Omnisis to ask a few questions about regional inequality to a representative sample of the population. An overwhelming 70 per cent of respondents said that London has been given preferential treatment by governments since 2005 – rising to 78 per cent among Northerners – while only 5 per cent disagreed with this assertion. Even 59 per cent of Londoners agree that the capital has been prioritised at the expense of other regions.

On the flip side, 70 per cent of people said that the government has not done enough to invest in their area since 2005. This figure was highest among Northerners, 82 per cent, and lowest among those living in the capital – 52 per cent.[3]

This explodes the residual conviction on the Left that British politics still aligns to class boundaries. Indeed, Brexit forged a new coalition drawn from middle-class shire Tories and the ex-industrial, coastal working classes, particularly in rural areas and small towns. Brexit was a regional convulsion.

Labour has been slow to observe this new vista, given its historical attachment to the struggle of the proletariat against the profit class. The rest of Britain's political machine has reprogrammed to a new, post-Brexit reality – cultural warfare packaged in local and national perceptions of decline – while Labour's hard-drive is still slowly updating.

This failure to adapt – the party of progress living in the past – allowed the Conservatives to ransack Labour. But while the outcome was bad for Jeremy Corbyn's party, it could have been even worse. Barnsley Central probably would have fallen to the Tories if Nigel Farage's Brexit Party had withdrawn from the contest – along with Ed Miliband's Doncaster North seat, which he won by 14,000 votes in 2017 but just 2,500 in 2019. Even the media hyperbole that has surrounded Labour's collapse doesn't truly reflect the scale of its demise.

This sense of crisis has been intensified by the fact that Red Wall seats, although they weren't classified under this label, represented Labour's home turf in the second half of the twentieth century. Bolsover had been retained by Labour since its creation in 1950, when the party won 80 per cent of the local vote. Presuming these seats were safe, the bedrock of the party, Labour's prodigal leaders were parachuted in as MPs – exposing a complacency within the party that released its payload during the 2019 general election.

Red Wall seats have experienced extreme stagnation. This lack of change was easy to miss, especially among MPs who were occupied with running a government department, and who maintained no previous connection to the area. However, for voters, this steady decline of prestige was a revolution – a reversal of fortunes that should never have been accepted by those in power. As prosperity grew in urban areas, particularly the capital, people elsewhere became aware of their relative disadvantages. Red Wall voters may clamour for a return to the past, which could be seen as a reactionary impulse. But, equally, they are calling for change and progress. Above all else, they are rebelling against the status quo.

'People watch TV and travel – and they see that places have got better, not just in London but in the city centres of Leeds, Manchester and Liverpool,' says Labour campaigner Buckley. 'Money has been invested, but their local area has barely changed – and they still have to get two buses or the same crap train as two decades ago, that's leaky, cold and doesn't always turn up – if they want to hang out in the city centre.'

Meanwhile, the Labour Party has decoupled from its heartlands. Its pulse is set in London, physically and politically detached from the Red Wall strongholds that sustained the party throughout much of the twentieth century. Labour now speaks the language of distant intellectuals – using slogans such as 'the hourglass economy' and 'predistribution' – rather than rooting its messages in places, services and people.

This was a long process of detachment and was only fully realised when Boris Johnson's masterful sloganeering collided with a Brexit impasse, a misjudged Labour agenda and an unpopular leader. As in all aspects of politics, this is not the end point – it is entirely possible that Labour will reverse its current malaise. It is equally likely, however, that Labour will continue to plunge further down its death spiral.

'The suffocating stupidity of left-wing propaganda had frightened away whole classes of necessary people, factory managers, airmen, naval officers, farmers, white-collar workers, shopkeepers, policemen. All of these people had been taught to think of socialism as something which menaced their livelihood, or as something seditious, alien, "anti-British" as they would have called it. Only the intellectuals, the least useful section of the middle class, gravitated towards the movement.'

This is a passage from *The Lion and the Unicorn*, George Orwell's wartime reflection on politics and patriotism, published in 1941.[4] The same could have been written in 2019.

Wakefield was one of the seats lost in this election, a place not too far from my hometown. My dad worked in Wakefield throughout my childhood, though it wasn't somewhere we visited for any other reason. The city, one of the larger settlements in West Yorkshire, seems to lack purpose. It has everything essential that you need – a cinema, some fast-food joints, pubs, supermarkets, shops and relatively cheap housing – but nothing that you want. Wakefield has no unique selling point; nothing to elevate it above the rest.

An important market centre during the industrial revolution, nestled in the throng of the wool industry and coal mining towns, the city has been saddled with second-class status in the modern era – seen as the unpopular cousin of Leeds and Huddersfield, both university hubs. The constituency had largely traded between the Conservatives and the Liberals from 1832 until 1932, when it was won by Labour's Arthur Greenwood, who became leader of the opposition during World War Two. The seat remained solidly Labour from Greenwood's victory until 2019, swept to the other side of the aisle by Boris Johnson's blue tidal wave.

This process was incremental. The dam broke in 2019, but the water levels had been rising for two decades. In 1997, the year of New Labour's first general election victory – a landslide – the party's majority in Wakefield was 29.9 per cent. From this high point, however, Labour steadily descended – logging a majority of 19.3 per cent in 2001 and 11.8 per cent in 2005, when the area welcomed a new representative, Coventry-born Mary Creagh, who had stepped down as the Labour leader of Islington Borough Council the year prior. Support for the party tumbled in 2010, Creagh registering a majority of just 3.7 per cent, recovering to 6.1 per cent in 2015 by virtue of a strong UKIP performance that split the right-wing vote. Labour's majority fell once again to 4.7 per cent in 2017 and, two years later, the Conservative Party won Wakefield by a comfortable margin of 7.5 per cent. This was despite having to replace its candidate at the start of the contest in a racism row.

Wakefield is a model Red Wall seat. Although it has history with the Labour Party, a residual loyalty that kept the seat red for the best part of 100 years, its head has been turning for some time. This wavering fealty can be explained by the changing makeup of voters in the city, corresponding more and more closely with the sort of people who vote Conservative.

The fault lines of modern British politics are captured by a demographic comparison between Wakefield and neighbouring Leeds. Some 5.4 per cent of people living in Wakefield were born outside the UK, compared with 11.5 per cent in Leeds. Wakefield is an ageing city, 46.2 per cent of people aged over 45, versus 38 per cent in Leeds.[5] From 2016 to 2026, the population of Wakefield is anticipated to have aged significantly; the number of people aged between 65 and 79 up by 16 per cent, and the number of people aged over 80 by 38 per cent. In the same time, the working-age population is only expected to have seen an increase of 1 per cent.[6] Average weekly earnings are 5 per cent (or £30) lower in Wakefield than in Leeds, while the proportion of the population with a qualification of NVQ 4 level or above is considerably higher in Leeds – 40.1 per cent versus 27.6 per cent in Wakefield.[7]

In short: Wakefield is less ethnically diverse, older and less well educated than Leeds, though income levels are broadly comparable. Given these differences, and despite occupying territory barely eight miles apart, the political outlook of the two cities has diverged radically in recent years. In the EU Referendum, Leeds backed Remain and Wakefield supported Leave – the latter voting in favour of Brexit by 66.4 per cent to 33.6 per cent.[8] And though Wakefield flipped to the Tories in 2019, Labour has retained clear majorities in its five central Leeds constituencies.

'When I arrived in 2004, it was almost as though Leeds was seen as a completely different country,' says Creagh. 'There were people who had never left Wakefield or Yorkshire – particularly in the former mining communities. And if you've never left, it's easy to think that other places are dangerous or different.'

Creagh is keen to stress, however, a unique factor in Labour's 2019 collapse: Jeremy Corbyn. 'People despised him,' she says. 'We became the nasty party. The stuff around the Salisbury poisonings and our failure to support the armed forces made us look like we're not patriots. If you designed a deliberate strategy to make the electorate of Wakefield hate you, it would be impossible to do it any better.'

To understand the outcome of the 2019 general election, and the Labour Party's retreat from the Red Wall, it's important to consider three factors: conditions, values and triggers.

Conditions are the underlying demographic, economic and social circumstances in particular constituencies – such as those described above in the case of Wakefield.

The values of voters are subsequently derived from these conditions. For example, an older population is more likely to display traditional, conservative attitudes towards law and order, while younger voters are generally relaxed about issues of identity and immigration.

Triggers are the events, policies, personalities and slogans that signal the values of political parties. Weighing up these triggers, voters come to a conclusion about which party corresponds with their values, and therefore who they will vote for.

Political triggers are not always stark. They don't always indicate to voters, unequivocally, which party they should opt for. The modern political environment is saturated with static noise. The frenzy of politics, fuelled by parties that make often spurious and sometimes openly mendacious promises, can be a confusing climate in which to make decisions. Deep-seated, historical (often entirely rational) prejudices also colour the attitudes of voters, causing voting patterns that deviate from the expected norm.

In this respect, however, the 2019 election was different. The triggers of the election exposed two parties with radically different priorities. On the main issue of the day, Brexit, there was a gulf between Labour and the Conservatives. In the 2017 election campaign, both parties supported the implementation of Brexit, and the premature development of negotiations with the EU helped Labour to offer a softer alternative to Theresa May's hard Brexit.

By 2019, with the public thoroughly sick of the endless wrangling, Labour's offer to haggle even more with the EU – on the basis of a vague soft Brexit agenda – was repellent to voters. It was particularly off-putting to those who had voted for Brexit in the first place, who were being offered a 'ready-made' deal by the incumbent prime minister. And so, in 2019, Labour lost 25 per cent of those who had voted for Brexit in 2016 after voting for Labour in 2010.[9]

Corbyn's personal image was also divisive. 'Concerns about Labour's leadership were a significant factor in our election loss in 2019,' says a post-mortem of the election compiled by senior figures from across the Labour movement. The impulse to stop Corbyn 'was a major driver of the Conservatives' success across all their key groups including previous non-voters, and among all the swing voters Labour lost to the Tories,' the Labour Together analysis says.[10] Less than a month before the election, Corbyn's approval rating stood at minus fifty-five, according to YouGov.[11]

Labour's suite of policies, viewed as too radical and too fanciful, likewise ran contrary to the Tory pitch – the latter being a short statement of intent, dedicated to unblocking the Brexit impasse and investing in public services.

In the past, the significance of triggers – the routine events that occur along the political cycle – has been stymied by party loyalty. The equivalent would be if you saw a top-notch

advert for a new brand of cereal. If you had a strong attachment to a different cereal – if your family had eaten a
particular cereal for generations, and if you had an instinctive
aversion to other types of cereal – it's less likely that you
would be persuaded to buy the new cereal, even if it corresponded more closely with your tastes. If your loyalty to any
one brand of cereal was weak, however, you'd be far more
likely to pluck the new cereal from the shelf.

The data shows that political disloyalty has grown steadily
over recent decades – increasing the importance of triggers.
Between 2010 and 2017, for example, more than 30 per cent
of voters switched their party allegiance at each election.[12] A
general inflation in political apathy has also created a new
and significant constituent of people – those who don't vote.
These voters propelled the campaign to leave the EU, as well
as the 2019 Conservative victory. Some 4 million voters
turned out in 2019 who had not voted two years earlier, and
the result was an unmitigated disaster for the Labour Party.[13]

For those who plumped for Labour in 2019, and who
opposed Brexit three years earlier, recent elections have
prompted mass bewilderment. For many, it is impossible to
comprehend why people would have opted for Brexit – and
then Boris Johnson as prime minister. This attitude has
prevailed in the left-wing media, leading to a widespread
ignorance about the unique social circumstances and political
events that caused these upsets.

The new state of play is summed up by the Labour Together
report: 'Age, education and place are the new electoral divides
even more than traditional conceptions of class. Labour's vote
share declined most in small, medium, and large towns, but
consolidated in cities.'[14]

First: age. Since 2010, and particularly since 2016, the UK
has experienced an extreme political polarisation of younger

and older voters – each general election more polarised than the last. In 2019, 62 per cent of 18–24-year-olds and 51 per cent of 25–34-year-olds opted for the Labour Party. On the flip side of the age spectrum, the Conservatives won comfortably more than 60 per cent of the 65+ vote, and 50 per cent of the vote among 55–64-year-olds.[15]

This extreme age cleavage was similarly apparent during the EU Referendum – a watershed election that crystallised the values of certain demographic groups, eroding traditional political loyalties. Some 72 per cent of 18–24-year-olds voted Remain, versus 40 per cent of the over-65s. All cohorts over the age of 45 were more likely to vote Leave than Remain; all cohorts under this bracket were more likely to vote Remain.[16]

This polarisation has not been experienced evenly by all parts of the UK, however. Political partitions based on age – and education – are important because of their interaction with geography. This can be seen in Hartlepool, a seat that flipped from Labour to the Conservatives in May 2021. From 1981 to 2011, the number of people in Hartlepool aged between 16 and 24 fell by 24.5 per cent, while the 45–64 cohort increased by 14.8 per cent and the number of those aged 65+ rose by 26.9 per cent.[17] This has been a mutually occurring process in many Red Wall seats, while the opposite has taken place in cities.

If younger and older voters existed in equal numbers across the country, age-based polarisation wouldn't be causing political change. In the UK, however, the young and old are increasingly inhabiting two different countries. This was evident during the EU Referendum. Of the twenty local authorities with the youngest populations, sixteen voted to remain, while nineteen of the twenty local authorities with the oldest demographics backed Brexit.[18]

There are many potential reasons why the physical detachment of the young and old has occurred. One undoubtedly relates to the circumstances highlighted in Chapter 2, whereby work opportunities – particularly in the knowledge economy – are concentrated in urban hubs like London, Manchester, Bristol, Leeds and Liverpool. 'Many young people are finding themselves effectively forced out of rural areas to find economic opportunities, leaving behind ageing communities politically, economically and culturally adrift,' the Fabian Society notes.[19]

Another key factor in our current political settlement is education, which displays similar levels of physical and political polarisation. Close to 60 per cent of people educated to GCSE level or below voted Conservative in 2019. Meanwhile, 45 per cent of those educated to degree level or above voted Labour, and less than 30 per cent voted Tory.[20]

Again, this cleavage materialised as an electoral force during the EU Referendum. According to the Joseph Rowntree Foundation, fifteen of the twenty 'least educated' areas voted Leave, while all of the twenty 'most highly educated' areas voted Remain. At the more extreme ends of the spectrum, whereas 70 per cent of people with no qualifications voted for Brexit, more than 70 per cent of people with a postgraduate degree voted against the idea.[21]

Due to the rapid expansion of further and higher education in recent decades, there is a natural correlation between the age and educational composition of an area. Older populations are likely to be less well educated, and vice versa. These factors naturally intersect economics and work; younger, educated and mobile individuals seeking opportunities in areas with better job prospects, typically in university towns and cities.

The phrase 'left behind' has therefore been applied to areas that have been abandoned by the post-industrial, technological, university-educated economy. This is (another) disputed term, though it does seem to aptly embody the areas of the country populated by older, less well-educated people who have seen their local economies languish and their children leave home in search of opportunities elsewhere.

The question is: as a result of the conditions outlined above, what political values are nurtured in left-behind communities?

Primarily, older people with fewer qualifications tend to be more socially conservative. They came of age in an era governed by stricter social mores, in a monoethnic state, and are likely to hold more traditional attitudes to the family (and divorce), crime, immigration and social justice. They believe in effective, well-funded public services, because they rely on these institutions more than most, but they don't seek to rely on the state for their basic income. Their areas have a strong history of industrial employment, creating a strong aversion to welfare reliance. Their connection to Britain's past and to myths of imperial grandeur have nurtured an assertive strain of patriotism that is particularly sensitive to perceptions of national decline.

'Many of those who grew up in a more ethnically homogeneous, socially conservative Britain have a profoundly different view of what Britain is and ought to be than members of the youngest generations, who have grown up in a much more ethnically diverse and socially liberal country,' Maria Sobolewska and Rob Ford write in *Brexitland*.[22]

I have seen these beliefs in my life and in my work – and they are borne out by Michael Ashcroft's poll of more than 12,000 people, released the day after the EU Referendum. This huge survey revealed the disparities in social attitudes between the Remain and Leave camps. Some 80 per cent of people who said that 'social liberalism is a force for ill' voted in favour of Brexit; 68 per cent of people who said that 'social liberalism is a force for good' voted Remain. Around 80 per cent of those who said that multiculturalism is a force for ill voted Leave; 71 per cent of people who said it's a force for good voted Remain. Some 80 per cent of those who said that immigration is a force for ill voted for Brexit; 79 per cent who believe the opposite voted Remain.[23]

Cultural and social divides were far more significant than economic ones, Ashcroft found. Those who approve and disapprove of capitalism were evenly split among Remain and Leave voters – 51 per cent of Leavers seeing capitalism as a force for ill, 49 per cent holding the contrary opinion.[24]

In 2019, Labour's share of the vote increased in just thirteen seats – 2 per cent of all House of Commons constituencies.[25] This total is small, but it's still large enough to draw a pattern. These seats were characterised by a relatively large number of Black and minority ethnic voters, a significant number of professional workers, relatively high levels of deprivation, situated in or around large cities – especially London.

Compared to 2017, the party 'lost all types of voters everywhere', says the Labour Together report, 'except in London'.[26] The organs of the Labour movement have been barricaded in the capital. The leadership of the party, and its agenda, were extracted from this city – a place mirrored by other urban centres, but wholly disconnected from everywhere else in the country. In this context, it is entirely unsurprising that Labour gained votes in London, lost some votes in other cities, and haemorrhaged support in all other areas.

A common barb among populists and Brexiteers accuses Labour of belonging to the 'metropolitan elite'. This is rank hypocrisy, propounded by privately educated former city traders like Nigel Farage and assorted old Etonian aristotwats, led by Boris Johnson and Jacob Rees-Mogg. However, the hypocrisy of this accusation blinds the Labour movement to legitimate criticisms of its intellectual and physical concord with London. If Labour acted to solve this problem, it would be validating Farage – a fate seemingly worse than losing an election. And so it stumbles on in blissful ignorance.

There is a strategic reason why Farage, Johnson and the Vote Leave crew have deployed this 'metropolitan elite' gibe – and not just to distract from their own palpable privilege. The phrase unlocks the active resentment that many people in left-behind areas hold towards more affluent urban areas, particularly London. As Mattinson says in *Beyond the Red Wall*, 'the people all believe, to varying degrees, that they have been neglected and overlooked by power brokers in the South. London feels a long way away.'[27]

Therefore, Labour's occupation and adoration of London firstly fosters a general sense of disenfranchisement among Red Wall voters, who don't see their views and backgrounds reflected in the party. And given its intimate relationship with the capital, Labour is subject to the same resentment harboured by these voters towards London.

The fall of Red Wall seats is politically significant because it speaks to an identity crisis in the Labour Party. However, in charting this story, it's easy to erroneously imply that Brexit and the 2019 Tory landslide were solely products of a right-wing surge in former industrial seats. That is not the case. There are still powerful Conservative blocs in the home counties, the South, the East, and even parts of London. The UK electoral map shows a vast blue quilt in these parts of the country, punctuated by solitary red pinpricks. Lest we forget, Boris Johnson won two terms as London Mayor not long ago, while the South East delivered the largest proportion of Leave voters – 15 per cent of the national vote. There were

4.3 million Leave voters in the North, versus 4.1 million in London and the South East.[28] The Red Wall narrative is compelling, but it's an incomplete version of events.

In particular, the pro-Brexit coalition of 2016 and 2019 contains a number of contradictions that may unravel when slogans are converted into policies. Namely, almost half of the Leave-voting bloc could be assessed as relatively well-off, says the UK in a Changing Europe.[29] Many of these people, based in the home counties and the South, supported Brexit because they believe in small government and a free market. Less affluent Red Wall voters, by contrast, clamour for state-led regeneration of their areas and local services. Both groups cannot be fully satisfied.

People in former industrial communities were led to believe that Boris Johnson would 'bring the weaving sheds back into use in Accrington, reopen the mills, extend Darlington station, improve transport links across the whole of the North, create youth clubs and training opportunities, get us making things again. And growing things. And fishing things,' Mattinson says.[30]

The conscience-free promises of 2016 and 2019 were electorally popular in the Red Wall, but they set high expectations. 'People like working in industry, don't like working in shops and call centres, and want some pride back in their community and in their work,' says Buckley. Yet this regional revolution requires a high degree of planning and courage, neither of which are characteristics associated with Johnson. Modern British politics is febrile, and we could witness the rapid disintegration of the Vote Leave bloc, if the Conservative Party's pledges continue to inhabit a two-faced fantasy land.

And yet, there is no guarantee that Labour would be the beneficiary of Johnson's unmasking. Many Red Wall voters were disillusioned with politics before they were coaxed out of their apathy by the Vote Leave campaign. Politics has been a form of punishment for decades. The same groups of people have been battered by a seemingly never-ending cycle of deindustrialisation, globalisation and austerity. Any further betrayal is likely to shatter their faith in politics entirely – risking either mass disillusionment or extremism, rather than prompting their return to the Labour fold.

But it would be unfair to say that Labour is entirely ignorant to this state of affairs. 'The things that most mattered to people bled out of their communities for decades, and they wanted some control over what was happening to their lives,' Wigan MP Lisa Nandy tells me, explaining why people were so attracted to the slogans 'take back control' and 'levelling up'.

Nandy currently shadows Michael Gove, the Secretary of State for Levelling Up, Housing and Communities, and doubts the appetite and ability of the Conservative Party to deliver on its promises. 'Levelling up was also a con-trick,' she says, 'because it came from a government that not only had no intention of delivering it but had no idea what they were dealing with. A couple of clever people in Number 10 understood the scale of the anger and used it as a device to win an election. And as the scale of that con becomes clear, it doesn't just damage trust in Boris Johnson and the Conservatives – it undermines the legitimacy of the entire system.'

Greater Manchester Mayor Andy Burnham also acknowledges the scale of Labour's task – and the stakes for British democracy – having previously represented the Red Wall seat of Leigh. He tells me that local discontent palpably grew during his time as an MP, from 2001 to 2017. However, 'to counteract those forces is a massive thing,' he says, 'and when people are starting to feel neglected, it's a really big thing to turn around. The complaints were often about Wigan Council [historically run by the Labour Party] and the central government – they would often be interchangeable in people's minds. People would often see both as forces of darkness waged against Leigh.'

Indeed, another electoral disaster for Labour is not beyond the realms of possibility. There is no law of physics or politics that bestows Labour with the right to gain ground at the next election. There are fifty-eight seats across the country that could flip blue with just a small swing from Labour to the Conservatives, many of which will be vulnerable after the gutting of the Brexit Party.[31]

In comparison, the road to Downing Street for the Labour Party is steep – almost vertical. To win the number of seats needed to form a majority at the next election, Labour must increase its number of MPs by more than 60 per cent – a feat that has never been achieved by any major party. If Scotland doesn't provide some solace for Labour, it would need to win North East Somerset from Rees-Mogg in order to send the Tories scuttling back to the opposition benches. Even Clement Attlee would balk at the scale of this challenge.

But Labour will try, and so they must. It's therefore worth considering whether there is any way back for the party in the Red Wall, or among other socially conservative seats.

There is an ongoing debate in the movement about whether Labour should abandon the agenda that it has developed in recent years – premised on social liberalism, the green economy, ethical trade, wealth redistribution and a crackdown on exploitative labour. For many Labour campaigners, regaining the Red Wall would involve a journey towards Johnsonian nationalist-populism, violating the basic principles of left-wing thought.

Unfortunately for Labour, the movement contains a high concentration of rigid idealists; people who cry betrayal after even a modest dilution of the party's policies. Labour is the party of the self-righteous, populated by those who believe in educating voters before listening to them. In the wake of the 2019 election defeat, in February 2020, Corbyn devotee Richard Burgon – MP for Leeds East – proposed setting up a 'Tony Benn University of Political Education' to teach people about Labour's 'ideas, our history [and] internationalism'. Presumably such an institution would teach voters and members about the party's recent history of electoral annihilation.

However, for those who are principled yet not obstinate – who view politics as a series of electoral contests and not a meaningless ideological cock-waving competition – there is some hope.

The political chaos of the last few years, and the online rage associated with it, has nurtured the perception of a culture war between the liberal metropolitan class and small-town social conservatives; two clans with allegedly entirely opposing worldviews. Yet, the Culture War is a form of political posturing, primarily by the Conservative Party, rather than a manifestation of electoral reality – exaggerating divisions that don't really exist.

The contrived Culture War functions in two interrelated ways. For starters, it allows political parties and campaigners to signal their virtues to potential sympathisers in a world that is full of noise, with thousands of people competing for your attention. Thus, when Priti Patel signals that she would consider holding asylum seekers on an island in the South Atlantic, this may be an exaggeration of her views and a distortion of the strategy that she ends up implementing.[32] However, her prison island policy grabs headlines, in a way that a more rational and sensible policy never could. Culture War play-acting therefore allows her to reach far more voters than she would otherwise be able to.

The media is an agent of this crime, as it knows that extreme views provoke more intense reactions on social media, more clicks on its content and thus more revenue. Hence, there is an unspoken pact between politicians and the media to amplify the Culture War at every opportunity. For the Conservative politician, their ultimate ambition is to win over Labour's former heartlands, populated by large numbers of older voters who have traditional social attitudes. The Culture War is therefore more a reflection of Conservative electoral ambitions, and the media's broken business model, than of the state of the nation.

Consequently, and sadly, people in the Labour movement have been duped into thinking that the attitudes of non-urban Britain, particularly voters in Red Wall seats, are radically different to their own. As Ashcroft's polling demonstrated, the Brexit vote herded social conservatives towards the Leave campaign and liberals towards Remain – but the strength of feeling among and between these groups is overstated.

This perception of ideological warfare is amplified by the geographical separation of different viewpoints. Liberals and conservatives increasingly inhabit separate places, and so their impressions of one another are shaped by media carica-tures – as opposed to lived reality. 'White voters with low education levels move less often, and are becoming concen-trated in more ethnically homogeneous and less economically successful rural and small-town areas,' write Sobolewska and Ford in *Brexitland*. 'These trends magnify identity conflicts by increasing social segregation and reducing the level of contact and common experience between people on either side of the identity politics divide.'[33]

The late Jo Cox, former MP for Batley and Spen, used her maiden speech in the House of Commons to emphasise that 'we are far more united and have far more in common than that which divides us'. A range of polling data supports this view, indicating common ground between groups that are said to be belligerently opposed to one another, on territory that should be fertile for the Labour Party.

For all the post-Referendum rhetoric of tribes and traitors, Leave voters were actually relatively uncertain about the benefits of Brexit. Their choice was the consequence of despondency and disillusionment, rather than a burning conviction that Brexit would transform the nation. More than two-thirds of Leave voters thought that Brexit 'might make us a bit better or worse off as a country, but there probably isn't very much in it either way,' according to the Ashcroft polling.[34] Brexit was a vaguely defined idea used as a truncheon by millions of voters to express their fury at the current state of affairs.

This nebulous rage did not make for a coherent withdrawal plan, so extensive wrangling was required to crystallise the exact terms of Britain's departure. Ironically, the product of Vote Leave's consciously hazy manifesto – years of negotiations and parliamentary prevarications – hardened the views of Brexit voters in favour of a project they did not zealously support at the outset. Few Leave voters have switched to the Remain camp – polls still showing a 50:50 split in the electorate – despite their half-hearted enthusiasm for Brexit in 2016.

In fact, liberals and conservatives do overlap significantly. According to the 2020 British Social Attitudes survey, 55 per cent of people believe that migrants shouldn't have to earn more than £15,000 a year to be eligible for admission to the UK. Only 3 per cent of people agreed with the initial post-Brexit salary threshold set by the government, of £30,000 or more. Furthermore, 80 per cent of people think that migrant doctors should be given relative priority for entry, 60 per cent think that care workers should be given preferential treatment, while only 18 per cent say the same about bankers.[35]

Across the board, voters are in favour of a relatively relaxed immigration system that prioritises key workers over the masters of international casino finance. There exists a relatively progressive, liberal, moderate consensus on immigration – backing a system that is firm but fair – if it can be found by the Labour Party.

Indeed, Brexit merged two tectonic plates that now pull in opposite directions. One plate is occupied by libertarian luminaries – the likes of Daniel Hannan and Douglas Carswell – who seek to inflict another era of low-tax, low-spend Thatcherism on the UK. The other plate, however, houses the army of Brexit voters in former industrial areas who see leaving the EU as an opportunity for renewed state investment, and who deeply resent the inequalities created by Thatcher and perpetuated by Cameron.

'The public are not seeking a less strongly regulated economy,' the British Social Attitudes survey points out. People are generally supportive of individual EU regulations and are especially averse to less rigorous regulations for food production and sale – of the sort that could be expected after a free trade deal with the United States. 'There is little sign here at least of a public appetite for the less restrictive regulatory regime favoured by some of those who campaigned for Britain's exit from the EU,' the survey adds.[36]

Even on subjects more obviously related to Culture War conflicts, there is consensus. A YouGov poll from May 2021 found that 73 per cent of Red Wall voters and 78 per cent of Brits overall think that it's important to teach children about Britain's colonial history and its role in the slave trade.

Meanwhile, half of Red Wall voters and 54 per cent of all Brits think that a wide variety of different ethnic backgrounds and cultures is part of British culture – and only 33 per cent of Red Wall voters think that immigration has generally been a bad thing for the country, compared with 24 per cent of Brits overall.[37]

And while debates rage on social media about the efficacy of lockdowns and the merits of mask wearing, there has been enduring unity among the British public during the Pandemic. Some 93 per cent of people supported the first COVID lockdown in March 2020 – a consensus that persisted to January 2021, when 85 per cent of people backed a new lockdown amid rapidly spreading variants.[38]

It seems as though the commanders of the Culture War, the people who lounge on the dimly lit sofas of GB News and spew divisive delusions onto the pages of the *Daily Mail*, are in fact putting words into the mouths of the social conservatives they claim to represent. They have manufactured fictional Northerners; choosing to depict a fringe bigoted viewpoint rather than the humane consensus that actually exists.

The Culture War hyperbole also involves exaggerating the views of liberals and lefties – depicting the Labour Party as a cult of 'dead-eyed communist fanatics', in the words of author Frederick Forsyth, in a *Daily Express* column published three months before the 2019 general election.[39] Unfortunately, the Left has broadly fallen for this trick. Accused of treason and extremism, the Left has defended these positions. The vanguards of the movement have lined up to grab their 'I'm literally a communist' T-shirts, thus validating the caricatures created by the Right. The Left has danced along to a Tory tune, basking in self-righteousness while pointing a shotgun at their own foot.

In the real world, beyond the gates of Twitter, liberals are more conservative than the Culture War portrays, just as conservatives are more liberal. As the British Social Attitudes survey notes, there is widespread and consistent public support for ending freedom of movement, with three-fifths of voters backing an end to the policy. Even among Remain voters, half support a policy that is incompatible with freedom of movement. However, as stated, while EU immigration rules are broadly unpopular, most people do not want to pull up the drawbridge and turn Britain into a medieval, monoethnic state. More Leave voters than Remain voters believe that migrants should have to earn a minimum amount of money to be allowed into the country, but as many as three-quarters of Leave voters say that the minimum should be £20,000 or less.[40]

Contrary to the views espoused by pundits, newspapers, politicians and the assorted members of the Westminster cabal, on Brexit and the big social divides of our time, 'what is more remarkable is that the balance of opinion is often in a similar direction,' the Social Attitudes survey says.[41]

This harmony extends to economic affairs. When asked, 65 per cent of voters in England and 72 per cent of voters in Scotland believe that the income distribution in Britain is either 'unfair' or 'very unfair', while a clear majority in both countries believe that government efforts to reduce income inequalities have been unsuccessful. In fact, a majority of people in each income group – including the richest – believe that differences in wealth are unfairly large.[42]

Somewhat counter-intuitively, those with fewer educational qualifications are less critical of wealth inequalities in Britain than people with more qualifications – though a majority in both camps believe that wealth disparities are too great. Britons are equally pessimistic about the thorny issue of 'justice', with fewer than four in ten agreeing that justice prevails over injustice or that people generally get what they deserve. 'There is relatively little variation in these views within the British population,' the British Social Attitudes survey says.[43]

In theory, this should buoy the Labour Party, whose explicit mission is to rally against inequality and injustice. However, it would be naïve to assume that Labour's self-image corresponds with the perspective of voters.

There is a sophisticated, well-funded distortion apparatus in the UK dedicated to warping reality and the way that Labour is perceived. Attempting to conquer the country without a plan to reform this apparatus – and to reshape the narrative in a way that better reflects Labour's policies – is a fundamentally futile effort.

This is laid bare by the Labour Together post-mortem released after the 2019 election. When asked, most voters self-identify in the middle of a left–right scale (zero being the most left-wing option and ten being the most right-wing). Some 42 per cent of voters give an answer of between four and six. There is also an equal balance between left and right – 39 per cent of voters place themselves on the left and 39 per cent on the right, with the rest in the middle. Yet, on this same scale, more than 60 per cent of voters place Labour between zero and three, with almost 35 per cent of voters selecting zero.[44]

This is an uncanny reflection of the polling presented to senior Labour Party figures in 1985, as recalled by New Labour strategist Philip Gould in *The Unfinished Revolution*. 'The researchers produced a chart showing an "acceptable field" of politics where these voters thought debate was reasonable,' he wrote. 'Beyond this field were the unacceptable right and the unacceptable left. Nearly all Labour's policies were in the unacceptable left-field.'[45]

In the mid-1980s, voters believed that Labour advocated for disarmament, welfare dependency and mediocrity. Now, the public has swallowed the idea – brewed by the Right and served by the media – that Labour is a fanatical Marxist fringe plotting with Brussels to dethrone the Queen. This perception hasn't been aided by the voices in the Labour movement who've brought to life the Right's bogeymen, nor by recent Labour leaders who have located the party far away from the priorities of voters in the Red Wall and non-urban heartlands. Labour's recent agenda has been designed in and orientated around London, based on anachronistic class conflicts.

To win on a principled and popular programme, the party and the movement must broaden its geographical base – and it must refrain from throwing meat to its enemies. It must liberate itself from the one-dimensional distortions of the Culture War and manufacture an image of Labour that corresponds with the clear, communitarian, progressive consensus that exists in Britain.

The Conservative Party has not conquered the Red Wall. Its national coalition has brought together various groups of people who would almost certainly throw bottles at each other in a pub, yet who have been kept in nervous harmony by fanciful promises, belligerent media propaganda and the flagrant deception of charismatic leaders. This coalition will crack when expectation finally meets reality. The question is whether Labour can first overcome its instinctive propensity for self-sabotage.

The COVID pandemic has posed and will continue to pose a political dilemma for the Labour Party. The public's attitude towards the crisis and its aftershocks could still change, as the passing of time allows people to fully absorb the profusion of incompetence, death, corruption and sleaze that has been inflicted upon the nation. Generally speaking, however, the Conservative Party has avoided a political catastrophe.

The Pandemic has been marked by persistent public exasperation about the decisions of ministers, punctuated by two periods of revitalised support. The first was during the immediate onset of the crisis when a sense of national unity – our differences momentarily dissipating in the face of a common enemy – generated a sense of goodwill towards the government. The second was during the 'vaccine bounce' of spring/summer 2021, when the UK sprung ahead in its inoculation efforts.

This is shown in Boris Johnson's approval ratings, as tracked by YouGov, that went from zero in January 2020 (with equal numbers approving and disapproving of his performance) to +40 in mid-April, slumping to –25 in October before climbing again to neutrality by May 2021.[46]

Yet, while the standing of Johnson and his party has fluctuated, the scale of suffering inflicted on the country has not been accompanied by political reprisals. The Health Secretary Matt Hancock lost his Cabinet position over an affair with an aide, though not because he oversaw the deaths of more than 130,000 people from COVID. Dominic Cummings resigned as the prime minister's chief aide seemingly due to an ongoing spat with Johnson's then-fiancée Carrie Symonds, though not because he drove to Barnard Castle despite stay-at-home guidance during the height of the first wave. There has been a pact of solidarity among ministers – an understanding that, if they stand firm and deny the failures that occurred during the Pandemic, they all might get away with it. Ignorance is strength, after all.

This is a dangerous precedent. The first job of a government is to protect the health, wellbeing and security of its citizens. If it fails in this task and still wins elections, the public is effectively endorsing policies that shorten lives. This is a paradox rooted in the Red Wall, which has suffered disproportionately during the Pandemic.

During the first wave of COVID cases in the UK, from March to July 2020, seventeen of the twenty worst-hit areas were in the North and the Midlands – including relatively deprived Red Wall areas such as Bolton, Sunderland, Wigan, Hartlepool and Rotherham. The Royal College of Physicians found that mortality rates during the first wave were substantially higher in the North than in the rest of England. An additional 12.4 people per 100,000 died in the North from COVID during this period (98.4 compared to 86), researchers found, and 57.7 more people per 100,000 died in the North due to all causes.[47]

The COVID death rate in Greater Manchester was 25 per cent higher than in the rest of England during the first year of the Pandemic, from March 2020 to March 2021, according to the esteemed public health researcher Sir Michael Marmot. This resulted in 'jaw-dropping' falls in life expectancy, he said, and the widening of social and health inequalities – with life expectancy falling most sharply in poorer areas.[48] From June 2020 to July 2021, the North West experienced the highest annual COVID mortality rate, followed by London. The South East and the South West were the best-performing regions.[49]

The most disadvantaged have been chastened by COVID – an outcome that was anticipated as early as August 2020, when a Public Health England (PHE) report revealed that 'the mortality rates from COVID in the most deprived areas were more than double the least deprived areas, for both males and females'.[50] This evidence of unequal hardship has been buttressed by a report by the Northern Health Science Alliance (NHSA), calculating that 45 per cent of patients admitted to hospital with COVID in England have been from the most deprived 20 per cent of the population.[51]

Scientific studies and basic common sense have linked these deaths to the higher likelihood of pre-existing health conditions in deprived communities, more households with multiple occupants – thus encouraging the spread of the virus – as well as poorer working conditions, a lack of access to sick pay, and a greater volume of people working in human-facing professions. People 'working as security guards, taxi drivers and chauffeurs, bus and coach drivers, chefs, sales and retails assistants, lower skilled workers in construction and processing plants, and men and women working in social care had significantly high rates of death from COVID,' according to PHE, using figures from the Office for National Statistics.[52]

And while Chancellor Rishi Sunak has performed financial gymnastics to withhold regional support, there has evidently been a correlation between the prevalence of COVID and economic hardship in the North. During the first wave of the virus, for example, the North was hit with the worst economic outcomes, advertising the lowest number of job opportunities in the country by December 2020. At this time, the North was experiencing levels of unemployment not seen since 1994, according to IPPR North.[53]

London has since seen above-average increases in unemployment, an upsurge seemingly bred in poorer areas and among its younger population.[54] However, in the North, periods of unemployment are more likely to have profound consequences for those dumped out of their jobs. According to the NHSA, working people in the North are 39 per cent more likely to lose their job if they experience a spell of ill health compared to people in the rest of England. Moreover, if/when they return to work, their wages are 66 per cent lower on average than a person in a similar position in the rest of England.[55]

COVID has fatally exploited the health inequalities that have existed within and between regions for decades. These inequalities don't just depress the pound in your pocket or the standard of your education – they diminish your chances of being healthy, and of simply being alive. Yet, before and after the Pandemic, regional health inequalities have barely registered on the radar of either the Left or the Right.

The Royal College of Physicians sums it up as such: 'Over the past few decades the deep-rooted regional inequalities in health across England have continued to grow alarmingly. The COVID pandemic has made this alarm deafening.'[56]

Premature death rates in the North are 20 per cent higher across all age groups. This is equivalent to more than 1.5 million Northerners dying early, during the last fifty years, by virtue of their diminished health chances compared to the rest of England.[57] Indeed, Northerners experience worse health chances than Southerners across the board – among all social groups and genders.

It's not as though the situation has been improving, either. In fact, health inequalities have been worsening since 2010. This regression has been forensically unpicked by Marmot, a steely-faced academic with Einstein hair who could have been the head of security at Hogwarts. Having led a commission into the social determinants of health for the World Health Organisation a few years earlier, Marmot was commissioned in 2008 by Labour Health Secretary Alan Johnson to chair an independent review into health inequalities in the UK. Marmot completed the review in 2010, which he presented to the incoming coalition government. He has since tracked the growth of health inequalities in Britain, eviscerating the government in a 2020 report.

Marmot found that, in the intervening decade between his two reports, the poorest areas had seen a growth in sickness and premature death, while people in the richest places were living longer. 'Put simply, if health has stopped improving it is a sign that society has stopped improving,' Marmot wrote.[58]

In particular, life expectancy in London has increased more rapidly than elsewhere since 2010, Marmot says, now boasting the highest life expectancy in England – up from the fourth highest a decade ago. Three hundred miles away, the North East has seen the slowest growth in life expectancy, the figure for both men and women now standing at 2.8 years below London. The North East has also suffered the highest suicide rates for men in recent years, far exceeding London and the South East, which have the lowest male suicide rates.[59]

According to the NHSA, in the last five years of available data (2012–14 to 2016–18), almost half of local authorities in the North experienced a fall in life expectancy among men, women or both.[60] Blackpool has the lowest healthy life expectancy – the number of years you are expected to live in a good state of health – in England, at 53.7 years for men and 55.3 years for women.[61] This is considerably less than the national figure of 63.2 years. Men in Blackpool have an overall life expectancy of 74.4 years – matching the 1996 England-wide average.[62] A more recent Imperial College report found a 27-year gap in life expectancy for a man living in the healthiest parts of Kensington and Chelsea, compared with Blackpool.[63]

Across the capital as a whole, men have a life expectancy of 80.7 years and women 84.5 years, although this masks sharp differences between richer and poorer areas.[64] In Westminster, the life expectancy for women is 87.2 years, 84.9 years for men. On the opposite side of the city, both in terms of wealth and geography, the borough with the lowest life expectancy is Barking and Dagenham, at 82.3 years for women and 78.1 years for men – though these figures are still notably higher than life expectancy in Blackpool.[65]

The Royal College of Physicians and Michael Marmot ascribe these deteriorating health outcomes in the North, and in poorer areas, to one major source: public sector cuts carried out after 2010 by the two Conservative-led governments. 'We found austerity measures had disproportionately affected the North – particularly in its areas of high deprivation,' the former writes.[66]

Given its higher rates of deprivation, unemployment and ill health, the North was the primary victim of the Conservative government's decision to purge £27 billion from the welfare budget (a 25 per cent reduction). 'Austerity will cast a long shadow over the lives of the children born and growing up under its effects,' Marmot says.[67]

In fact, while the 2010 Marmot Review called on the government to address the social causes of poor health – including poverty, homelessness and insecure work – and to distribute resources equitably, Marmot found in 2020 that the exact opposite had occurred. Government spending on the key social determinants of health had fallen, and the funding was allocated in a less equitable way.[68] In other words: public money was in shorter supply and was less likely to be directed to deprived areas and those most in need. Absolute spending cuts were six times larger in the poorest places than in the richest, the IPPR notes, while working-age families in the lowest income groups were hit hardest by tax and welfare changes.[69]

'We're all in this together,' preached the Conservative Party slogan during the 2010 election campaign, promising that the cost of the financial crash would be borne by those with the broadest shoulders.[70] The data shreds this allegory. The country was pushed into recession, but the UK's total wealth increased by 13 per cent between 2014 and 2018 – subverting the rationale for austerity: that spending had to be deflated in line with scarcer national resources.[71]

In 2019, 96 per cent more people were sleeping on the streets than in 2011, according to Byline Times research. The number of emergency food parcels distributed by Trussell Trust food banks in 2020 was 402 per cent higher than it had been in 2010. Yet, the number of high-net-worth individuals living in Britain in 2020 was 26 per cent higher than it was in 2010, and from 2016 to 2018 the top three wealth deciles held 76 per cent of all wealth, while the bottom three held just 2 per cent.[72]

These wealth contours can be mapped on the physical geography of the nation. Average household wealth in the South East was 2.6 times that of the North East in 2017/18. And while London has become the richest region in Northern Europe since 2010, the UK boasts six of the ten poorest regions.[73] This has trickled down to health outcomes, creating a country in which people living in poorer areas suffer sickness and death at a younger age. 'Inequality in health services in the UK is profound, and health inequality in the UK is the most severe of any nation for which comparable data is available,' the IPPR says.[74]

In fact, healthy life expectancy fell in 80 per cent of Red Wall areas for either men or women from 2009–11 to 2017–19.[75] 'Forget ideological ideas about low tax and high tax, people are dying,' Marmot told me on the Byline Times Podcast, in a tone that barely concealed his rage, 'people are getting sicker and policies are not working. This is not just some arbitrary experiment and, in fact, we already know the outcome of the experiment: if you make poor people poorer, their health deteriorates.'

These facts should shame the nation, further unmasked by a pandemic that has festered among the disadvantaged. Yet, since 2010, the grim reaper has continued to win votes, gaining ground in the very areas that have fallen victim to his scythe. In a twisted irony of British politics, Labour-voting London has grown richer and healthier under Conservative rule, whereas the increasingly Tory-inclined North has become sicker and poorer.

6.

THE FOURTH ESTATE

The media is the playing field on which the proverbial political football is kicked around. Journalists are the referees – they set the rules and decide when someone has overstepped the mark. They are the gatekeepers of our national conversation. However, far from being representative of the nation, the UK media is a socially selective clique.

A disproportionate number of journalists – particularly in the Westminster lobby – are White, male and privately educated. An unhealthy number have also been the beneficiaries of overt nepotism. The Sutton Trust and the Social Mobility Commission came to this conclusion when they assessed the backgrounds of elite professions in 2019. According to their joint report, 'the media is an elite group that has among the highest proportions of independent and Oxbridge alumni among their number'. For example, 29 per cent of BBC executives attended private school and 31 per cent Oxford or Cambridge. And the commentator class is even more exclusive. Some 44 per cent of newspaper columnists attended independent school, while 33 per cent attended both independent school and Oxbridge, the report found.[1]

For context, fee-paying schools educate 7 per cent of students, while Oxbridge graduates make up less than 1 per cent of the overall population.[2]

Nor is this situation improving. 'Previous Sutton Trust research going back as far as 1986 has shown that the educational backgrounds of the country's media have, for a long time, looked very different to those of the population as a whole,' the report says, adding that the profession has grown 'more socially exclusive over time'. This applies to gender and race, alongside social class.[3] Women are 17 percentage points less likely than men to be hired as newspaper columnists, while around 94 per cent of journalists are White.[4]

These facts are well known, even if there isn't a great appetite for reform. Meanwhile, the question of regional inequality has once again been shunted to the sidelines. The media industry doesn't reflect the country, and so journalism acts as the medium through which regional divides are simultaneously downplayed and dismissed.

In this regard, the media is both the victim of self-inflicted wounds and structural processes beyond its control. To report on all the box-office events of national life, journalists must congregate in the throng of the action, in London. There's little use in watching the undercard when you're supposed to be reporting on the main bout. Politics, business, finance, arts, sport and law – they all have the same city on their address. London owns the nation's prized assets, and so opportunities to conduct national reporting outside the capital are naturally limited.

Yet, media outlets are still partly responsible for their collective evacuation to the fortress. An over-investment in advertising-based business models has prompted a recession in the industry since 2005, when the internet – and social media companies in particular – began to devour advertising revenues. In the twentieth century, advertising revenues made up roughly 75 per cent of the profits for most daily newspapers.[5] Between 1999 and 2014, newspaper advertising revenue fell in the United States by 65 per cent – a collapse that has occurred on both sides of the Atlantic.[6]

Publications have subsequently pared staff numbers and their horizons have narrowed. London is the base camp to which media outlets retreated after the cull. In 2010, the *New Statesman* reported that 40,000 mainstream journalism jobs had been lost in Britain over the previous decade – roughly a third of all jobs in the industry.[7] In the space of a few months during the early stages of the Pandemic, an additional 2,000 jobs were added to this redundancy list.[8] However, the public purse hasn't acted as a counterweight. The BBC has been instructed to carry out £800 million worth of cuts in recent years, shedding hundreds of roles in the process.[9]

And while opportunities in the industry have dried up, low-paid and insecure labour has become the norm. During my research for this book, I browsed Journo Resources – a helpful website for all aspiring reporters – that anonymously surveys journalists to provide advice on salary levels. The list reads like an epitaph to British journalism: broadcast journalist at the BBC (£25,000); broadcast journalist at Global Radio (£22,000); reporter at the *Daily Telegraph* (£24,000); senior features writer at Newsquest (£22,000); comment editor at the *i* Paper (£33,000). These are not amateur roles; they are reputable jobs at well-known outlets. The successful candidates will have been able to boast countless hours of academic study, internships and part-time work – for a job that pays barely more than the London Living Wage.

Unseen on jobs boards, however, is the bulging invisible economy, with work offered on an informal, freelance basis. Journalism is essentially a series of projects; reporters are engaged on tasks that have clearly defined boundaries and end-points. The nature of this work lends itself to time-limited employment for the duration of the project – a form of employment that is encouraged by a lack of money and a surplus of labour in the industry. Thus, many newsrooms now resemble a university library loaded with young people in various states of poverty, a decent proportion of whom will be replaced with another roster of low-wage workers within six months.

These are the perfect conditions for privilege to procreate. Not only are competitive recruitment rules abandoned – greasing the wheels of nepotism – but the financial risks associated with freelance and low-paid work inhibit people outside the capital.

On a salary of £25,000 a year, for example, a young journalist will be banking £1,700 a month. The average monthly cost of renting a one-bed flat in London is roughly £1,200 (not including bills), while you'll be looking at £750 a month if you share with a couple of mates.[10] Signing a lease usually involves a commitment to stay in the property for six months, or more typically a year – a commitment that may well extend beyond the length of your freelance role. Young journalists who migrate to the capital must therefore offer their financial security as collateral for work opportunities.

These financial risks are entirely nullified if your family lives in the capital, however, or if you can rely on another form of patronage. A rent of £1,000 a month is a heavy burden for someone in an unstable, low-wage profession, especially if you come from a poorer family. Being short of money during your childhood teaches you to be thrifty – an ethos that is violated by the idea of spending £12,000 a year on accommodation for a £25,000 a year job. The system is fundamentally rigged in favour of people who are able to luxuriate in early-career opportunities without having to pay rent.

In fact, as a young journalist migrating to London, it is almost entirely futile to have a plan for the future. The job and the capital erode your personal agency – your career and life choices determined by the financial demands of your landlord and the prudence of your employer.

Against my better judgement, this is the career path that I embarked on at a relatively young age. Under the unspoken threat that I would be forced to work for my dad if I didn't find something productive to occupy my time, I started blogging about politics in the long summer before university. It strikes me now that blogging was, among other things, a convenient distraction from thinking seriously about my future. And so, keen to sustain this blissful ignorance, I maintained the habit throughout university and into my early twenties.

What started as a distraction only became a career when, after graduating, I was nudged to apply for the annual BBC work experience scheme. I could have applied to work at any of the BBC's offices, but I picked London. The only reason I did this – opting for London instead of Salford, which was much closer to home – was because my girlfriend at the time lived in West London. Logically, I should have picked Salford. But the heart wants what the heart wants.

The unpaid two-week scheme cost £700 on accommodation, travel and food – funded out of my savings. Sure, many work experience programmes do now offer money to cover costs, particularly for individuals from disadvantaged backgrounds. However, geography typically isn't a prominent factor.

Spending nearly £1,000 on a short placement with no guarantee of future employment is irrational, and so aspiring journalists from outside the capital tend to search for opportunities closer to home. Work experience schemes and internships are some of the only pathways into a highly competitive media industry, yet these routes currently defy common sense for people in most regions.

Luckily, the BBC scheme did pay off in my case – though I still spent the next three years working in a number of low-paid freelance roles (my first 'job' paid just £100 a week). Under these financial strictures, I was forced to devise several creative strategies to avoid funnelling all my income to a landlord.

During one period, I commuted from the outskirts of Huddersfield to Salford every Monday and Tuesday, a journey that is more arduous than its 30-mile distance implies: typically, two hours in each direction. I would then leave home at 6 a.m. on Wednesday and catch a train down to London from Wakefield, staying for one night in a hostel and working two days in New Broadcasting House before scuttling back up North at 8 p.m. on Thursday – arriving through the door at 11 p.m. to spend Friday working from home.

A few months later, during the 2017 general election campaign, I was asked to work for six weeks in London – reporting for the World Service. Recruited at the last minute and struggling to find viable housing options, I spent each week living in a different Airbnb, ferrying a bag of clothes down from Yorkshire to London on Monday morning and returning to the North on Friday evening. I loved the work, though it was difficult not to feel a pang of resentment when London-based colleagues of a similar age sauntered into the office with fresh faces, a coffee cocked listlessly in their hand, while my suitcase was searched by security, compounding the pain of a three-hour journey before the working day had even started.

The capital made me work for its bounty. It gave me more than enough excuses to quit – signalling repeatedly that the opportunities provided by London belong to those who were bred in the city. Had my parents not supported my choices, had my willpower dwindled or had opportunities failed to materialise, I would have been forced into a very early retirement from the profession.

Yet, currently, few forces are engaged in the effort to achieve greater regional parity in the media. Recruitment processes rightly take into account the social background of candidates, as a means of achieving a more diverse workforce. However, geography is markedly absent from the media's diversity agenda.

A senior Scottish journalist accepted my application to the BBC's work experience scheme, I later learned, which stood to my advantage. However, aside from a helpful attitude from most of my bosses, I didn't receive any special dispensation based on where I lived.

I have no doubt that thousands of young journalists outside London have been through experiences more arduous than mine. I am also convinced that the ranks of Britain's most prestigious newspapers and broadcasters could be filled with talented people whose career ambitions disintegrated under the financial pressures imposed by London, the impenetrable capital.

For many people, this realisation dawns soon after completing their undergraduate degree. A master's qualification in journalism is virtually a prerequisite now, as legions of applicants crawl over one another for a limited number of jobs. Yet the most illustrious courses in the country are provided by City University in London, demanding £10,000 in fees and thousands more in accommodation costs. Even before you have the honour of winning a low-paid, precarious job in London, the education demanded by your future boss is virtually inaccessible.

The media digests and articulates the life of the nation, but the industry is not reflective of its people. Londoners – whose experiences are radically different to the rest of the country – dominate the airwaves. And even when outsiders puncture the fortress, there is an overwhelming pressure to conform to the London groupthink, surrounded as they are by the guardians of the capital. As psephologist and academic Rob Ford says: '90 per cent of political writers are London-based. So, the city's political mindset is the air they breathe.'[11]

This is even the case among outlets that have ostensibly pledged to better represent life outside London. GB News has hired extensively from the established network of Westminster swamp-dwellers, its chief political correspondent being a former private schoolboy from the South East, with its main studio firmly situated in central London.

This is the case throughout the media. All national newspapers – aside from those dedicated to affairs in Wales and Scotland – are headquartered in London, as are all the broadcasters aside from Channel 4, which has recently opened its new, nominal HQ in Leeds. *The Times* is based in London Bridge alongside the *Sun*; the *Telegraph* in Victoria; the *Financial Times* in the City; the *Mirror* and the *Express* in Canary Wharf; the *Guardian* in Kings Cross; the *Independent*, *Evening Standard* and *Daily Mail* in Kensington; the *New Statesman* in Blackfriars; the *Spectator* in Westminster.

New models of funding have been pioneered in recent years, reducing the media's reliance on ever-diminishing sources of advertising revenue. This has provided some hope that journalism can reverse its retreat. However, the relative success of a few titles has failed to compensate for an avalanche of job losses elsewhere. We are not on the brink of a media renaissance in the UK.

Until this changes, regional voices will continue to be squeezed out of the industry, along with their perspectives on life and politics. London is the centre of power, commerce and culture, trapping the media in the city. Bees can't make honey if they are separated from the hive. But a failure to adapt – editorially, ideologically and commercially – has further detached the media from the country outside its capital.

Despite recent government threats to defund the broadcaster, Culture War attacks on its reputation and periodic self-sabotage attempts, the BBC is still the most trusted news source in Britain, with the largest network of reporters. The BBC's total income in 2019/20 was £5 billion;[12] the *Guardian*'s annual revenue is some £250 million.[13]

Funded by the taxpayer, a higher standard is demanded of the BBC. It is a national institution, it holds a lofty place in our collective psyche, and we expect the style and substance of its coverage to reflect our lives. We don't just want the BBC to provide news about other places – we also want it to publicise our own experiences to the nation and the world.

With this in mind, the BBC has devoted considerable attention in recent years to recording workplace diversity – an effort to ensure that its staff, on and off air, are representative of the nation. In keeping with W1A tradition, there is a corporate maxim to accompany the BBC's plan – '50:20:12' – as stated in its 2020 creative diversity report: a workforce that is 50 per cent female, 20 per cent Black and minority ethnic, and 12 per cent disabled. The BBC's ambition is to better represent and engage with these groups, along with people 'from a range of socio-economic backgrounds'.[14]

How does this compare to the BBC's current performance? According to its 2018 equality report, women make up 43.3 per cent of senior leaders and 47.7 per cent of its total work-force, while 52 per cent of on-screen contributions are made by women. As for the representation of people from Black and minority ethnic backgrounds, 14.8 per cent of BBC staff and 10.4 per cent of leaders are non-White, and 27.3 per cent of on-screen contributions are made by people from non-White backgrounds. The equality report also reveals that 16.5 per cent of BBC public service staff were educated at fee-paying schools – a figure that rises to 24.4 per cent when the parameters are narrowed to those who work for network news.[15]

These figures indicate that the BBC substantially over-represents people from higher social classes – yet socio-economic diversity is not featured as one of its core targets. This exposes a flaw in the BBC's diversity process. Class boundaries are contested, and they are difficult to measure, but they are real and they manifest in pernicious ways. Rather than rushing headlong into the class quagmire, the BBC has instead swerved around the issue. This is a savvy PR decision but not one that will aid the cause of equality.

In fact, overall, the BBC's approach to diversity lacks nuance. There seems to be little understanding of intersec-tionality: the compounding co-existence of multiple forms of inequality. For example, someone will experience different strains of disadvantage if they are both Black and working class – as opposed to if they are Black and middle class. Ignoring the interactions between race and class, as tends to be the case in the BBC, acts to the detriment of those who lack the resources of their wealthier peers.

Regional inequality, meanwhile, has not featured on the BBC's diversity radar. The regional backgrounds of staff are not logged in the 2018 equality report, and no target is set for the better representation of regions in its 2020 diversity plan. The 2020/21 BBC annual report suggests that 52 per cent of staff are employed outside London – though we're unable to see how many of these people work on national and regional programming. Nor does the report record the regional backgrounds of its London-based workforce.[16]

The successful applicants to the BBC's annual journalism trainee scheme – much publicised by the corporation – belong to a range of social backgrounds, including different regions. However, with only a dozen journalists accepted, these hires represent a fraction of the BBC's annual intake of young staff members. Overwhelmingly, the BBC hires young people from the invisible economy – an informal market of freelancers who work on projects for short periods of time. Staying available in this economy is far easier if you live in London without a landlord.

And before I get cancelled, let me be clear: I believe it is imperative for the BBC to promote the equal representation of women, people from Black and minority ethnic backgrounds, and the disabled. I am not trying to play victim top trumps; I don't believe that regional inequality supersedes all other forms of discrimination. Rather, these forms of diversity can and should be promoted simultaneously. Regional inequality should be inserted – more than it is currently – into a multi-dimensional understanding of discrimination that takes into account all the above social conditions and their interactions.

To show you what I mean, take Bumpkin Files, an Instagram account that records the experiences of Black communities outside London. Karis Beaumont created the page after realising when she was younger that, 'there were little to no programmes on Black British history and whenever they were, these programmes were London-centric'.[17] A more developed understanding of life outside London does not exclude class, race or gender; quite the opposite.

These sentiments are echoed by Nazir Afzal, former Chief Crown Prosecutor for North West England, though not explicitly in relation to the media. 'In London, the Muslim community probably comes from more than fifty countries. In the North of England, it comes from a handful. The lack of recognition of a lack of diversity even among diverse communities troubles me. You cannot apply a policy to Muslim communities based on the Muslim community in London, because Muslims in the North of England are very different in terms of culture, background and heritage.'

Muslim communities further North are 'much more traditionalist', he says. 'The one-size-fits-all approach comes from living and working in London, as you have no sense of what it's like outside the capital – how people engage with issues and where people come from.'

The BBC has recently signalled its intention to take regional representation more seriously – though a nuance deficit still pervades its policies. The broadcaster is set to spend £700 million and move 1,000 jobs out of London by 2027/28, with BBC director general Tim Davie pledging that the exodus will allow the BBC to tell 'the stories that need to be heard from all corners of the UK' and that 'significant parts' of its news operation will be moved to different regions.[18]

Importantly, however, the BBC hasn't declared which of its programmes will be relocated. If past evidence sets an example for future action, the overwhelming majority of its flagship news programmes will be retained by London – serving to reinforce the psychological divide between the centre and the periphery.

This has been seen through the Salford experiment – the building of a BBC base in the Manchester docks, costing some

£200 million and opening in 2011. Only a fragment of the BBC's current affairs operation, primarily Breakfast and 5 Live, made the journey to Salford. The Centre for Cities concluded in 2017 that the BBC's relocation had made 'little positive impact' on jobs in Greater Manchester,[19] though the exact figures are disputed.[20]

When I worked in MediaCity, I was struck by its disloca-tion from Salford and Manchester – especially compared to New Broadcasting House, situated in the throng of Regent Street in central London. MediaCity is literally the end of the line, the final docking station for the tram before it winds back to Manchester. The site is not well connected to arterial train lines or to the local area. It's nestled awkwardly on the edge of two cities – an austere glass campus isolated from ordinary people.

'To create a media hub in an otherwise derelict piece of land next to the Manchester ship canal is a phenomenal achievement,' veteran broadcaster and Brummie Adrian Goldberg tells me. 'However, it is noticeably an island. You walk half a mile down the road to Salford proper, and it's a different world. The connection between the edifice of glass and steel in MediaCity and the local people of Salford is almost non-existent. It feels like a different world; it feels like something has been transplanted into this otherwise pretty run-down urban landscape. And something about that sits uneasily with me.'

The development of MediaCity has been followed in recent times by the creation of a new headquarters by Channel 4, located within spitting distance of Leeds train station, in a (stunning) converted 2,400-seat cinema. Dorothy Byrne, the former editor-at-large of the broadcaster, hopes that Channel 4 moves its entire news operation out of London. 'I think it would be very exciting if we could have a national news programme based in Leeds,' she tells me. 'Given that journalists don't generally live outside London, they believe the stereotypes about other areas, which is poor journalism.'

In her own career, Byrne has been forced to contend with these stereotypes. Her peers automatically assumed that Byrne came from a poorer background, for example, because she was born in Scotland. 'One of the things that I find very funny is the number of journalists who talk about Glasgow as a working-class city and Edinburgh as a middle-class city. And I say to them: in both those places they have middle-class people *and* working-class people. There are not whole cities outside of London with just one social class.'

However, while Channel 4 plans to base 300 of its 850 employees outside London by 2023, it has admitted that no national executives will work from its new command centre.[21] 'An organisation is always headquartered where its executives work, regardless of the address that's listed on its website,' says former Gordon Brown adviser Karl Milner, who now consults for the NHS and a number of public institutions in the North, 'and the executives have to be close to ministers.' As for the BBC, it hasn't disclosed whether any executives will be joining its 1,000-strong exodus from the capital.

Superficial devolution is the modus operandi of the BBC and other public bodies, partly because they have no other option. Displacing senior journalists and flagship programmes from the political, economic and cultural hub of the country would be an act of self-sabotage. So, under the watchful gaze of a government keen to signal the benefits of its 'levelling up' agenda, the BBC has pledged to invest some cash, disperse a few jobs and keep the prime minister happy for another day. The outcome of the move will be marginal, but the optics are good.

Ultimately, the media can't change the weather. The news will continue to remain firmly camped in Westminster, because that is where power lies in Britain. Westminster is the Jerusalem of British politics – a pilgrimage site for journalists reporting on the proclamations of those in power. Until this changes, the majority of jobs in media and politics will be based in London – and any attempts at redistribution will be substantially hollow.

However, the BBC does control some aspects of its own destiny, particularly in relation to recruitment and the nature of its content. In the latter regard, it is disappointing that regional affairs don't occupy a more prominent place in national BBC programming. For context, when I started free-lancing at one of the BBC's flagship domestic news programmes, I was soon summoned by an editor for a one-to-one meeting. They wanted to discuss the political and social issues of concern to the North – and while it was nice to be able to express my thoughts, it was also puzzling that none of the permanent members of staff were able to offer these insights.

Indeed, the media failed to anticipate Brexit – and has failed to properly explain its causes – due to its pervasive geographical ignorance. 'Brexit was the story that demonstrated just how damaging it has been for British television to be so London-centric,' says Byrne. 'London journalists called that vote wrong because they didn't know about people's lives elsewhere and what they were thinking. During the Brexit campaign, journalists kept going to Sunderland, and they treated the people of Sunderland as if they were Neanderthals – as though they were a different species who supported Brexit largely because they were irrational and misinformed.'

This failure to see beyond London, on the part of the BBC, is caused by its allergy to risk. Granted, the BBC employs some brilliant journalists working for innovative, world-class programmes. The World Service, for example, is the pinnacle of journalism – reporting from Beirut to Bogotá. But, generally speaking, the BBC is a cumbersome beast trying to navigate the narrow path that satisfies all of its stakeholders: the government, the public and its own internal bureaucracy. The BBC takes small, timid steps – it does not leap into the unknown.

The unknown, in this case, would be to call out or depart from a London-based worldview. This timidity was shown in the BBC's coverage of the riots that took place in Northern Ireland in April 2021. Violence had returned to the streets of Belfast – petrol bombs tinting the night sky – disturbances reportedly provoked by Brexit-related shortages, the funeral of Irish Republican Army member Bobby Storey, and the implementation of the Northern Ireland Protocol. Yet, the BBC relegated the topic down its news list, while the topic of Brexit was studiously avoided.

'It's wrong that what is happening in Northern Ireland is being rammed low down the news agenda because they don't want to call out Brexit,' former Downing Street director of communications Alastair Campbell told me at the time. 'There's a part of me that thinks you shouldn't reward the violent, by putting them on the top of every news bulletin. You've got to judge things according to the genuine news value. My point is: what's happening in Northern Ireland is dangerous and a consequence of the lies that were told on Brexit – and the government has to be held to account on that.'

If Molotov Cocktails were unleashed on the streets of London, or indeed any other mainland town or city, sleep-deprived reporters would be stationed on the BBC News channel for days. No such treatment was afforded to the riots in Northern Ireland – nervously studied by the BBC at a distance, as though in a foreign country.

The gaze of the media has settled on London, and the content of its reporting has been moulded in the capital's image. This is particularly true for economics and business reporting, both of which have changed markedly since the 1980s.

Alan Jones, originally from North-East Wales, joined the Press Association in the early 1980s as a news reporter. At that time, every newspaper had a 'labour' reporter, he says, covering strike actions, unions and industrial affairs. The *Financial Times* carried a page every day called 'the labour page', Jones recalls. Not long after joining the PA, Jones was given the title of labour correspondent, after covering a number of labour-related news stories, before taking up the rebranded title of 'industrial correspondent'. He has been doing this job ever since. However, despite Jones's longevity in the role, the industrial correspondent is now a near-extinct breed, and he is one of its few survivors – if not the last man standing.

'In the past, there were enough labour correspondents to mount a cricket team to play the union barons before the Trades Union Congress (TUC) started each year,' John Mair wrote for the BBC in 2011. 'Today, they could not umpire that match.'[22]

'There's hardly anyone who covers trade unions day-to-day,' Jones adds. 'I'm probably the only one, aside from maybe a few of the left-wing papers that periodically cover industrial affairs. Even the *Daily Mirror* doesn't have someone dedicated to covering unions. The BBC doesn't either.'

He guesses there were 'dozens' of industrial correspondents working for national and regional titles in the heyday of the job. 'I don't think it's justified,' he says, about the decision taken by most outlets to gut their industrial pages. 'Trade unions represent millions of people, and most days you would struggle to find even one quote from a union official.'

Jones says that his stories still gain some traction with regional titles, plus those in Scotland and Wales, but that attention has waned among national outlets. Indeed, industrial correspondents have been replaced at a national level by economics and business reporters, who report on finance, stock markets and venture capital. They cover high-level macroeconomic developments, and venerate 'entrepreneurs', rather than dwelling too heavily on the strife of workers.

This trend has several origins. Politically and economically, the financial and property sectors were unleashed by Margaret Thatcher's reforms of the 1980s, while the unions lost their struggle for supremacy, along with the industries they represented. This gave the impression that a new economy was being born – one that journalists could not ignore. Rather than telling the stories of those left behind, the media industry instead marched towards the new sources of economic power. Their journey ended in London.

Physically and intellectually dislocated from peripheral Britain and the graveyard of industry, newspapers and broadcasters extended their tentacles into the City and Canary Wharf, compounding the dominance of London and its all-consuming economy. This suited the government, and the right-wing press barons who were fans and beneficiaries of Thatcher's free market reforms. The turmoil created by Thatcherism – regional inequality, mass unemployment, the rise of the gig economy, property speculation and mass inflation – were portrayed as secondary issues by journalists occupying the new haven of high finance.

Meanwhile, as the economic centre of gravity shifted to London, so did the attention of political journalists. Thatcher's victory over the miners signalled the end of a domestic current affairs agenda previously dominated by regional labour conflicts. As the unions were crushed, the political trenches were once again burrowed in the corridors of Westminster, rather than on the picket lines of Yorkshire collieries.

'Over time, the job of the industrial correspondent became less important – politics began to take over. The top jobs are now political reporters. The lobby is all-powerful,' Jones says.

According to Peter Preston, former editor of the *Guardian*, the government actively encouraged this process – empowering the political lobby as a rival to the industrial press corps, the latter being more sympathetic to the cause of unions and workers. 'The group was undermined by past government decisions to brief the parliamentary lobby on industrial disputes (so cutting the labour followers out of the action),' Preston writes.[23]

Lobby journalists, as their name indicates, have special access to the parliamentary lobby where members of both Houses congregate. Not all political journalists have a lobby pass – only those from selected media outlets are afforded a spot at the top table. This relationship with power, the incestuous and secretive trading of gossip for coverage, is the basis of the lobby's strength – a cheque that is only payable in the Westminster Village, among London's political clique.

National political journalism in the UK is closed to places outside Westminster, and to journalists outside the lobby. In a palace that runs on the fumes of past glories, still performed in the present day through frilly garments and silly rituals, there is a strict social hierarchy. In this setting, the names of the big newspapers and broadcasters – like the public schools that educated their journalists – carry immense reputational weight. The protected status of these media institutions allows their journalists to hob-nob with politicians and advisers in a jumped-up drinking society – filling the latter with booze while draining their secrets.

There is a reason it is pejoratively labelled the 'Westminster bubble'. There is an extreme concentration of politicians, journalists and lobbyists in this one patch of London. Consequently, like over-aroused teenagers, its members ride on the rumour-mill – their awareness of national concerns subverted to the intoxicating, self-immersed tales of SW1.

Psychodramas thus become the currency of the lobby as they speculate on the political stock market, analysing which politicians have a higher share price. The structural issues affecting the nation, and the policies causing them, are eschewed in favour of Westminster horse trading.

This system rewards politicians who can manipulate the media circus – led by the prime minister himself. All the while, the fate of the lobby journalist is controlled by their level of access: by the number of MPs and ministers who are listed in their phonebook.

'Political editors whose greybeard predecessors treated Cabinet ministers like social inferiors now beg for scraps from minor officials,' says an anonymous lobby journalist writing for *The Critic*.[24]

This creates a system in which political reporters are psychologically trained not to expose the worst abuses of those in power. Their success relies on proximity to decision-makers – on their ability to exploit the patronage of politicians. Any latent radicalism within the lobby is therefore tempered by a fear of losing their contacts and being thrown out of the club.

This creates a herd mentality among lobby journalists, accentuated by their separation from other parts of the media ecosystem. The lobby functions as a distinct entity, detached from the outlets that employ its members. Westminster reporters attend the same events, work in the same parliamentary offices, but have different paymasters. As the experienced political reporter James Ball says: 'Lobby journalists can know each other better than they know journalists in their own newsroom, reinforcing the instinct to focus on politics – who's up, who's down – rather than policy itself.'[25]

This proximity encourages a form of collusion among lobby journalists, who often check with the herd before deciding whether a particular subject is newsworthy or not. The political agenda is therefore forged in a closed system, explaining why pundits have been so shocked by recent election results – during the few occasions when politics morphs from an elite hobby into a national democratic event.

Broadcasters are part of this system, paying avid attention to the opinion-setters in the written press before transmitting to the nation. Britain's newspapers skew to the right, which is consequently mirrored on our screens. The broadcast media, for example, has adopted the language of Thatcherite credit-card economics, falsely predicting doomsday scenarios if government spending exceeds tax revenues.[26]

The sycophancy of the Westminster press was particularly evident in its coverage of 'herd immunity' – the idea that COVID should be allowed to spread among the population, theoretically in order to build up a widespread natural resistance to the disease. The policy was adopted by the government at the outset of the Pandemic and privately briefed to ITV political editor Robert Peston, who hurriedly produced a range of content that echoed the government line. 'Back in early March 2020, a senior minister and senior scientific advisers used that precise term with me to describe the policy,'

Peston tweeted in May 2021, after the government denied that herd immunity was ever its ambition.

'Herd immunity will be vital to stopping coronavirus,' headlined one of Peston's articles when the policy was first adopted.[27] 'The strategy of the British government in minimising the impact of COVID is to allow the virus to pass through the entire population so that we acquire herd immunity,' he explained in another article for ITV, without commenting on the validity of the idea.[28]

Lobby journalists assumed that herd immunity was a valid concept – or their reports at least framed the idea as a valid one – while independent reporters who balked at its potential effects were either ignored or scorned. The concept only gained widespread infamy in early 2021, largely due to the testimony of former Downing Street chief aide Dominic Cummings, who told MPs that a continued belief in herd immunity would have caused a 'catastrophe'.[29]

The government did of course implement a series of lockdowns, eschewing the herd immunity approach. Given that the UK had lost 140,000 people from COVID, at the time of writing, it's difficult to imagine how many more lives would have been lost if herd immunity had continued to grip the government.

Based on briefings from insiders, another senior lobby journalist had some months earlier accused Cummings of spearheading the herd immunity policy. This story was entirely false, Cummings maintained, and the journalist in question had admitted that it was the worst mistake of his career, the former adviser told MPs.

So, the lobby failed to expose a potentially fatal government policy, while purportedly falsely accusing a senior adviser of wrongdoing. This is the product of a system that has lost its sense of context – isolated from the rest of London, and the rest of the country, in the Westminster 'madhouse', as described to me by Liverpool City Region Mayor and former MP Steve Rotheram. 'Most political hacks believe in the system,' Cummings said, when he attempted to explain why the media got it so wrong on herd immunity.

Of course, access to newsrooms was limited from March 2020 to the summer of 2021 – which may have prompted a shake-up in the regional balance of the media. Firstly, the Pandemic has normalised interviews conducted remotely, rather than in the studio, and viewers are now accustomed to the uninvited interventions of toddlers on Zoom. Given that the overwhelming majority of broadcast studios are based in the capital, the old process benefited pundits and experts living in London, while the new normal tips the scales towards regional parity.

Secondly, as in many other professions, the Pandemic has unchained journalists from the office, allowing them to work from home and to relocate out of the capital. It's likely that a much higher proportion of media jobs will now be offered on the basis of flexible or remote working – especially for early-career freelancers. If this happens, people outside the capital will be empowered to enter a profession that previously inhibited entry on the basis of geography.

However, given that Parliament will always operate in person, it seems unlikely that the lobby will be dispersed to the four corners of the country. 'Hybrid' working models require staff to live within commuting distance of the office – limiting the opportunities for outsiders to claim jobs in the capital.

And despite a widespread clamour for news during the Pandemic, COVID has delivered another kick in the ribs of the media industry. Data shows that, as retailers shut their doors, UK advertisers reduced their spending by £1.1 billion (or roughly half) year-on-year during the first COVID lock-down.[30] A few days after this story hit the headlines, the *Evening Standard* announced that it intended to cut 40 per cent of its newsroom staff.[31] With fewer people leaving the house to pick up a paper, newspaper sales and advertising revenues fell precipitously – inflicting a new wave of job losses on the industry.

This creates a precarious situation for regional titles. Reach, which owns the *Mirror*, the *Express* and dozens of regional titles, has told 75 per cent of staff that they will no longer have to travel into the office full-time – allowing the firm to reduce office space and costs. The plan is to maintain hub offices in cities, which may force some regional journalists to travel into London, or another city, if they want to use a desk.

This won't come as a shock to regional reporters, however, who are always the first to be sent wandering into no man's land as the generals of journalism hatch ill-conceived plans to ensure the industry's survival.

'I still believe that a journalist who has worked on a local paper has a more complete understanding of the trade than anyone – however brilliant – who has not. Because you learn, often painfully, the powerful effect your words can have on people, for good and ill. People you might well meet the next morning,' Matthew Engel wrote for the *New Statesman* in 2019.[32]

Yet the number of people passing through this apprentice-ship scheme has steadily declined in recent times, along with the status, circulation and revenue of regional titles. 'We've been selling our advertising space and not our journalism. It has lost us about £1 billion of ad revenue over the last decade,' says Tracy De Groose, former head of the news industry's marketing body, Newsworks.

The peak of newspaper profitability in the UK was reached in 2005, according to the Press Gazette. Since then 265 local titles have closed. In the eighteen months from the start of 2019 to August 2020, at least thirty-three local newspapers closed.[33] In September 2019, the *Guardian* estimated that 58 per cent of the country was served by no regional newspaper.[34]

The media industry worldwide, and especially in the UK, has to navigate an issue that other businesses do not. Namely, journalism is considered to be a public good. Everyone has the right to cheap, accurate information on the issues of the day, it is believed. This expectation is ingrained in Britain by the BBC, which is funded by the licence fee but is free at the point of access. Thus, while we expect to shell out monthly subscription fees for entertainment – via Netflix, Amazon Prime, Spotify, etc. – we are reluctant to pay for news, which is seen as a public right. It is also obviously easier to sell programmes about gorgeous, unhinged people flogging multi-million-pound houses in California than it is to sell a long-read about the geopolitical situation in the Balkans.

This state of crisis has been heightened by the explosion of information during the social media revolution. Indeed, it's no surprise that the newspaper industry peaked just a few years before the mass adoption of Facebook. Social media and the expansion of the internet drastically reduced the costs of creating information. Suddenly, everyone was writing a blog, free to access through an array of platforms. And as social media companies harvested billions of users – and their personal information – they became the go-to sites for advertisers, gazumping newspapers.

This is the scenario: a brand can place an advert in a newspaper (or on its website). This paper only has limited information about the demographics of its readership (age, wealth, location, etc.) – the people targeted by the advert. Moreover, there is no guarantee that everyone who buys a physical newspaper will see the advert. They may simply skip the page or leave the paper on a coffee table for weeks largely unread.

Alternatively, this same brand can place an advert on Facebook, which has detailed information on its 3 billion active users – their habits, interests and online actions. For example, Facebook can track whether someone has visited a particular brand's website, who can then be targeted with Facebook adverts by this brand. Facebook also allows the brand to track how many people have seen and engaged with the advert – making it easy to calculate whether the campaign was value for money.

In 2018, Facebook and Google hoovered up 60 per cent of revenues from the digital advertising sector in the United States, equating to roughly $65 billion, matched by 63 per cent of the UK market.[35] This is despite the fact that internet users spent 34 per cent of their time on Facebook and Google platforms.

The tech giants are dominant because they can offer 'targeted adverts, to reach specific individuals, with near-perfect accuracy,' says advertising executive David Moore. Facebook and Google's 'accuracy in identifying visitors stands in stark contrast with the identity knowledge of most publishers. How many publishers can claim to know the verified identities of 50 per cent or even 30 per cent of their visitors?'[36]

The mass information age has therefore been accompanied by a rapid decline in the circulation and profitability of newspapers. Sales of national and local printed newspapers fell by half between 2007 and 2017, according to a government report on the sustainability of journalism conducted by academic and journalist Dame Frances Cairncross. In a single decade, print advertising revenues fell by 69 per cent, Cairncross notes.[37]

'The decline in news publishers' advertising revenue results partly from the fact that the space for ads, once limited by the size of newspapers, is almost limitless online,' the review says. 'The power of the online platforms [i.e. Google and Facebook] results partly from their sheer scale, and partly from the wealth of personal data they harvest. Their superiority makes it hard for publishers to compete.'[38]

This presents an acute challenge for national newspapers, and an impossible situation for local and regional outlets with even smaller audiences. One solution may have been to abandon a business model that is delivering ever-diminishing returns. However, wedded to advertising, unwilling or unable to change, the owners of national and regional titles have continued to flog the dying horse.

For every 1,000 impressions that an advert receives on a website (i.e. when it is seen 1,000 times by readers), the publication typically earns a small fee. This fee is less than newspapers could expect to make on print adverts and fluctuates markedly between different publishers. Declining advertising revenues have prompted some publishers to simply increase the number of adverts on every page, while attempting to exponentially boost their website traffic through clickbait. Hence, your social media feed is saturated with articles promising that you WON'T BELIEVE Brad Pitt's latest tattoo; articles that assault your computer with half a dozen yoghurt adverts.

Unable to deliver the page-views needed to fund even a modest operation, most local newspapers have either scaled back dramatically or have already plunged into bankruptcy. Indeed, publications need millions or even billions of monthly hits to stay afloat. 'That scale will likely never be possible for local papers,' says the Cairncross review.[39]

Despite its detachment from commercial influences, this deterioration of local journalism has been matched by the BBC. Somewhat blunting its recent commitment to employ more staff outside London, the BBC has retrenched its regional and local output over the last decade. In July 2020, for example, the *Guardian* reported that the BBC was set to impose 450 redundancies on staff working for its regional programmes – constituting a sixth of BBC England staff.[40]

So, journalism is not standardised across the country. The national media occupies one city, fixated on its agenda, while peripheral areas receive either low-quality or non-existent coverage. For example, journalism researcher Rachel Howells found a 90 per cent decline in reports from Port Talbot council, public and political party meetings between 1970 and 2013, replaced instead by news that contained a high degree of rumour and speculation.[41] Meanwhile, a content analysis of almost 3,000 local newspaper articles in West Yorkshire found that 76 per cent cited only one source of information.[42]

However, the media industry is a complex mosaic, and there are notable variations and exceptions within and between regions. The *Yorkshire Post*, the *Manchester Evening News* and the *Liverpool Echo* are all examples of thriving regional papers that regularly deliver better journalism than their national rivals. Echoing economic trends that transcend journalism, the news desert seems to span across small towns, poorer cities and rural areas.

This shows that the commercial struggle endured by regional media outlets is an expression of the country's structural, regional imbalances. A report from the Reuters Institute in 2020 found that just 25 per cent of people in the UK would miss their local newspaper or news website 'a lot' if it went out of business, compared with 39 per cent in the US and 54 per cent in Germany. 'The value placed on local news seems to be partly related to the importance that countries place on their regions more generally – and the extent to which local politics matters,' the report says.[43]

Britain is highly centralised; London holds the unabridged rights to high politics, finance and culture. Decisions are generally made in the locus of national power and foisted upon subservient regions. Regional media titles are thus starved of fuel, given that local affairs are dictated by the capital. It's difficult to peep behind the curtain of power if you're not sitting in the front row, so journalists have flocked to London. This has depleted the quality, the content and the revenue of local outlets – causing a self-perpetuating cycle of commercial decline.

This is partly a symptom of Britain's weak devolution settlement, initiated over the last twenty years. Central government has reluctantly allowed regional figureheads to be appointed across the country; symbolic leaders whose political toolbox contains a large loudspeaker but few practical devices that can improve the wellbeing of their citizens. This form of devolution was pioneered in London, ironically, under the assumption that it would be effective everywhere else. Even in the field of devolution – whereby powers are dispersed to different areas of the country – a London-centric attitude has prevailed.

7.

DEVOLUTION

My flat isn't too far from City Hall, the office that has for thirteen years housed the Mayor of London and the London Assembly. Crouched on the southern bank of the River Thames, guarded by Tower Bridge, the bulbous, glass-clad structure resembles a flying beetle – or perhaps a shiny wart. Former London Mayor Ken Livingstone once called it a 'glass testicle'.[1]

The democratic levers of London are now set to move from City Hall to the Crystal Building in Newham, encased within an angular glass facade. If I were a supervillain looking for a new crib, both would be high on my list.

Buildings don't just keep officials dry and warm; they are the amphitheatres of democracy. They are supposed to embody the places they represent – and the spirit in which their affairs should be conducted. Many modern assemblies, for example, now use a horseshoe format in their debating chambers, to encourage more collegiate interactions between representatives and to dissuade the farmyard atmosphere seen in the House of Commons.

The design and placement of City Hall is therefore instructive. The building is glass, but its inner workings are shielded from view, at least from the outside, offering the pretence of transparency. City Hall was also never owned by the Greater London Authority (GLA). Ground-zero for local democracy in London is the property of the Kuwaiti sovereign wealth fund – formerly owned by a Bahamas-based company led by an Armenian businessman – and leased to the GLA for some £12 million a year.[2] In fact, the promenade surrounding City Hall is entirely owned by Kuwait, while the office blocks flanking the glass onion are occupied by the amorphous consultancy giants Ernst and Young, PricewaterhouseCoopers and KPMG. London is a city built on foreign capital and the rampaging excesses of the financial sector. And, for years, the capital's democratic instruments have occupied this polluted terrain.

The devolution of democratic power to the nations of the UK and the regions of England still seems like a relatively new event. However, we're now rapidly approaching twenty-five years since the process began. The 1997 Labour manifesto made an explicit commitment to devolution and, along with the Good Friday Agreement of 1998, Tony Blair's landslide victory triggered the distribution of powers to Scotland, Wales, Northern Ireland – and some parts of England.

London was the only area of England to gain devolved powers during the initial period of Labour's constitutional reforms – from 1997 to 2000 – holding its first mayoral election in the fifth month of the new millennium. Allegedly inspired by the mayoral system in America – there are some 1,400 city mayors in the United States – Blair sought to introduce executive figureheads who could neuter the factional squabbling of pre-existing local governments and provide clear, accountable leadership.[3]

Thus, a constitutional settlement has evolved in London over the last two decades. The mayor is responsible for city-wide planning – particularly with respect to transport, housing, police, and public investment – while the local boroughs and the City of London deliver the city's services: social care, education, street cleaning, waste removal and local planning.

Given the mayor's relative lack of power – he has the power to plan but not to introduce primary legislation – there have been doubts about whether Blair's ideal model was realised, or whether he ever wanted to dilute the authority of central government. 'The inspiration seemed to be less American Mayors of Chicago or [Los Angeles] and more the rubber-stamp parliament of the Russian Federation,' says left-wing writer Owen Hatherley.[4]

This perception seems to be confirmed by the slow pace of devolution in England. It was expected that other regions would follow London's lead, by electing city-region representatives. But, after voters in the North East rejected Labour's proposed devolution plan for the area, 78 per cent rebuffing the idea, further devolution in England was delayed by the government.

Local squabbles further complicated the process, with two regional deals collapsing following internal disagreements. Other areas of the country, including the ever-irreverent, habitually noncompliant Yorkshire, have been battling with the government to widen the scope of devolution – Whitehall repeatedly rejecting requests for one mayor to govern the whole county. So, there were no more mayors elected in English city-regions until 2017 – almost two decades after Livingstone stepped onto the throne in London.

In other words: the solution devised to fix England's democratic deficit was launched in the city with the most political and economic power – London – long before anywhere else. Meanwhile, the terms of devolution have been written by ministers in Westminster. 'The process has not been transparent to many of the wider stakeholders involved, such as councillors, civil society, trade unions and businesses – let alone the public, who have been almost entirely excluded from consideration,' says IPPR North.[5]

Not only has London enjoyed a devolved administration for longer than other regions, by a margin of two decades, the nature of devolution has also been conditioned to the needs of the capital. The disproportionate influence of London in national life imbues its mayor with a high degree of political importance. Regional mayors are symbolic leaders – local champions rather than policymakers – which acts to the advantage of the London Mayor, the figurehead of a super-power city that is comfortable flaunting its wealth, status and power.

'The legitimacy of the mayor's huge electoral mandate has been such that even ministers have found it hard to oppose elements of City Hall policy,' says local government academic Tony Travers.[6]

To illustrate: immediately after the EU Referendum, London Mayor Sadiq Khan launched a campaign called 'London is Open'. It was clearly intended to signal the divergence between the capital's support for Remain and the nationwide Brexit result. This was a symbolic act of defiance against the governing Conservative Party, that had orchestrated the Referendum, and a quiet middle finger to the rest of the country for forcing London out of the EU. London being 'open' suggested that other parts of the UK were closed.

I don't think that Brexit-voting regions particularly noticed or cared about this slogan or its significance – though many politically-inclined people in the capital have internalised the idea that London's politics is intellectually and morally superior to the rest of the country. Rather, the slogan exemplified

London's political confidence. The Mayor of London is more conspicuous than many Cabinet ministers, and he's happy to throw his weight around. He can change the political weather, even if his legislative capacity is limited.

On the other side of the spectrum, however, city mayors in more remote, less wealthy and seductive parts of England have been ostracised; unable to draft their own policies and otherwise languishing in the Westminster popularity contest.

The Mayor of London is a national political figure. All other regional leaders, aside from Greater Manchester Mayor Andy Burnham, are not.

This is likely to create a cycle in which prominent politicians avoid mayoral positions, reducing the status of these roles and perpetuating their lack of media clout. The regional inequalities that compelled the regional democratisation of power now underwrite the devolution settlement. The poor are weak, the rich are strong, and London is mighty.

Burnham has made an impact on politics since his election as mayor in 2017, partly due to his shrewd media tactics and indie-dad image, but also one suspects due to his former prominence in Westminster – having served in various government and shadow cabinet roles. Others, however, have barely made a ripple in the pond. Despite being the representative of nearly 3 million people, including those living in the country's second largest city, Birmingham, I struggle to picture West Midlands Mayor Andy Street. And I'm not alone – research conducted in March 2020 suggested that eight out of ten people in the West Midlands don't know the identity of the region's Mayor.[7]

'The whole media circus was really slow to pick up on devolution,' Liverpool City Region Mayor Steve Rotheram tells me. 'That's because we're the most politically centralised democracy in the OECD, and we have the most unbalanced economy in Europe. People aren't used to a federalist model because it simply hasn't existed before, in terms of England's regions.'

In contrast, London Mayor Sadiq Khan clearly feels as though his political power extends beyond the capital. The Mayor released a 'declaration of interdependence' in 2019, ostensibly to forge a consensus on devolution with the leaders of other English regions.[8] This campaign could be Khan's way of paving the ground for a future Labour leadership bid, although his charm offensive was more offensive than charming.

'It's time to change the narrative and stop pitting London and the rest of the UK against each other,' Khan says. Or, in other words: 'Stop giving London a hard time.' He claims that London doesn't deserve to be maligned by other regions, given its attraction to people who live outside the capital. 'Nine of the ten busiest rail stations in the country are in London,' he claims.

Khan deploys a number of poor arguments. 'Compared to economic output, public expenditure in London is the lowest among all UK regions,' he says. I have no reason to doubt the accuracy of this claim. Rather, I doubt its relevance. One of the functions of public spending should be to rebalance the economy. If state expenditure matched economic output, the poorest areas would receive the least money and the richest would receive the most, merely exacerbating inequalities.

Khan adds that 'rebalancing the economy cannot be achieved by making London poorer'. Literally no one is suggesting that London should be made poorer. Aside perhaps from restricting the income of predatory, offshore property developers who are extracting vast sums of wealth from ordinary Londoners. Overall, however, we want the rest of the country to grow at the same pace as the capital. We don't want to puncture London's tyres to win the race.

Meanwhile, Khan suggests that, 'No argument can be made from the macroeconomic data that London somehow benefits at the expense of the rest of the country, or vice versa.' There are a number of problems with the statement. Not least, if London exists in perfect harmony with the rest of the country, why does the capital accrue all the benefits from this arrangement?

As Khan acknowledges, the capital represents 25 per cent of the UK's total economic output. 'Compared to other European countries, London would be the eighth biggest economy in the continent – larger than Belgium, Sweden, Austria or Norway,' he adds. 'Between 2003 and 2015, London secured 39 per cent of all foreign direct investment (FDI) projects in the UK and 26 per cent of all FDI project-related jobs in the UK.'

Khan's declaration shows that London warps the politics of its advocates; a full-throated defence of the capital requires an adoption of conservative arguments. The Mayor's document argues against regional redistribution, on the basis that London is wealthier and more successful than everywhere else. Its underlying tone implies that the city is somehow inherently superior and is thus deserving of its riches.

In fact, Khan seems to call for the end of redistributive policies. 'London's role as a net contributor to the Exchequer means that for every pound contributed in recent years, around 30p is channelled to the rest of the UK in the form of net Exchequer contributions,' he says. Khan proposes a new agreement, in which regions keep their own share of tax revenues.

This is justified, seemingly, because London experiences acute problems of its own. 'In the last two decades the number of jobs in London has grown by 42 per cent and the number of people by 26 per cent, but the number of homes by only 16 per cent,' Khan says. This is undoubtedly true. However, he fails to acknowledge that regional redistribution may in fact ameliorate these issues. Indeed, if we create more jobs outside London, the demand for housing in the capital will reduce.

It appears as though the Mayor does not represent the consensus of thought, even among his fellow representatives in the capital. 'London is the economic hub of the UK – and we should appreciate and respect that. But that doesn't mean the rest of the country should suffer,' Dawn Butler, Labour MP for Brent Central, tells me. 'We've seen during the Pandemic that actually there is enough money to go around. There should be a mutual collaboration between areas – and a mutual benefit. It is not a case of investing in London or outside London. We are one country – and we need to work that way. We need to understand how we all intersect and how everyone can prosper.'

However, it speaks to the imbalances of devolution that the London Mayor can make these confident proclamations about national affairs, while other regional leaders have been marginalised from conversations about their own area. Of course, this is the way that democracy has functioned for centuries, even before the process of devolution. Dating back to 1571, a 'remembrancer' representing the City of London Corporation (essentially the capital's financial centre) has been allowed special access to the Houses of Parliament – to monitor any legislation that might act against the corporation's interests.

In terms of democracy – and much else – the UK is uniquely and perversely centralised. 'A nation of 55 million people living in diverse towns, cities and villages is still mostly governed from the capital in the corner,' says the IPPR.[9] And while the government's rhetorical fervour about devolution has blossomed in recent years, the project has been undermined by Westminster.

David Cameron's austerity campaign from 2010 onwards withdrew vast amounts of local government funding – cutting their budgets by more than half between 2009/10 and 2015/16.[10] This was a political ploy, cynics argue. At a national level, the Conservatives were credited with 'balancing the books', while councils – many of them run by the Labour Party – received the backlash when local services closed down. Austerity also shifted the balance of power in Britain back towards the centre, comparably weakening local spending powers. Since March 2010, local government employment has fallen by 30.7 per cent, whereas central government employment has in fact risen by 13.6 per cent, or 385,000, to 3.2 million.[11]

Thus, while Chancellor George Osborne proclaimed the virtues of the 'Northern Powerhouse', his policies were redirecting economic and political power back towards London. State and private sector investment is now heavily concentrated in London and the broader South East. Some 64 per cent of government research and development spending in England is directed towards London, the South East and the East, while London alone accounts for 52 per cent of venture capital investment.[12]

So, evidently, the country needs a devolution system that works. Not of the sort proposed by Sadiq Khan, whereby London gains more powers at the expense of the rest. Instead, disadvantaged areas must be given the necessary funding and powers to leap across the chasm. Local leaders have been trapped in recent years, unable to change the economic agenda of the central government yet simultaneously scapegoated for its failures.

'Regional devolution under the Tories has largely just led to the devolution of blame,' says Birmingham Yardley MP Jess Phillips. 'Devolution has been used by Westminster to create whipping boys for their failed policies.'

The exact form of this devolved settlement in England must be decided by the regions themselves, not dictated by Westminster. A lack of appetite for certain forms of regional democracy has been mistaken for a general opposition to the idea among England's regions. That is not the case. It is perfectly legitimate to hate lager and love ale, despite the fact that both are beers.

However, devolved powers must be extensive and they must be deployed effectively by regional leaders. People care about whether their services are delivered to a high standard. If devolved leaders aren't able to implement better policies than Westminster, support for devolution will understandably wane. 'People in my area don't really care who makes the decisions – how close their representatives are to them – they just want their bins collected,' says Phillips. 'They want decent services, good schools, their streets to be clean and their police officers to arrive when they call them. What matters, fundamentally, is whether their representatives are effective and responsive.'

The relative success of regional government is still being tested – limited by the constraints imposed by Westminster. Liverpool City Region Mayor Rotheram has been attempting to wriggle out of his straitjacket, however, stretching his regional powers. 'Unless the government tells us not to do something, we're going to venture into those areas,' he tells me. 'And unless we're doing something that they absolutely oppose, we're on safe ground.'

Rotheram cites the city's 'housing first' homelessness programme, which is outside the remit of Liverpool's original, formal devolution agreement. Liverpool, Greater Manchester and the West Midlands have collectively trialled the policy, first pioneered in Finland, which prioritises stable housing as the first response to assist those sleeping rough.[13]

'People in England see a democratic deficit in the way they are governed and are looking for a remedy in the form of self-government,' according to devolution expert Professor Charlie Jeffrey.[14] Statistics from IPPR North show that the further away from London you travel in every direction, the stronger local identity becomes. Twice the proportion of Northerners (61 per cent) identify strongly with an English county compared to Londoners (30 per cent), rising to 74 per cent in the North East.[15]

When the *Manchester Evening News* (*MEN*) surveyed local residents in April 2021, 85 per cent declared their support for greater devolution to Greater Manchester.[16] Such a resounding endorsement for greater regional powers was undoubtedly informed by local experiences during the Pandemic. Andy Burnham waded into the ring with Rishi Sunak and Boris Johnson – berating the government for imposing strict local restrictions on Manchester and much of the North while restricting economic support.

Burnham landed his punches, and in one memorable press conference in October 2020 he flayed Sunak and Johnson for offering insufficient relief funds to the region ahead of its move into 'tier three'. 'This is no way to run the country in a national crisis. This is not right. They should not be doing this. Grinding people down trying to accept the least they can get away with,' Burnham said, standing on the steps of Bridgewater Hall, surrounded by TV cameras.[17]

The *MEN* found that 57 per cent of people in the area approved of Burnham's handling of the Pandemic, compared to 48 per cent approval for central government. The affair did, however, signal the balance of power in British politics. Johnson and Sunak were the ones holding the money. Burnham's only option was to create a media storm.

I spoke to Burnham almost exactly a year after this row. It struck me that, for someone who came of age within the Westminster system, the Greater Manchester Mayor has now developed a deep frustration with how politics currently operates.

'It's an interesting thing to look back on,' Burnham muses, about his spat with Sunak and Johnson. 'I don't regret anything that we did. It was very much a Northern issue, the imposition of tier three. It was clear that they would never have put that paltry package of economic support on the table if they were dealing with London.'

Burnham has been a vocal critic of the special status afforded to London before and during the Pandemic – putting him at odds with much of the Labour movement. For this very reason, contrary to media speculation, I don't believe that Burnham is (currently) plotting a move back to Westminster, to take the Labour throne. His anger is raw, not politically calculated.

'When the Pandemic landed, we'd had all the talk at the general election of levelling up,' he tells me, 'but in 2020 the country went into default mode: they privatised the Pandemic response before they localised, and a London-centric attitude came to the fore once again. Everything was run from London, and the extent to which they listened to us was minimal.'

For all these grievances with Westminster, you suspect that Burnham enjoys being an outsider; the difficult Northerner who lacks patience for those who perpetuate the status quo, even within his own party.

'Whitehall doesn't like being answered back by the North,' he says, 'but that is the new reality, through the new, devolved entities they've created.

'Whitehall has to change, and to recognise that we don't want a system where everyone goes on bended knee to them; there has got to be a different relationship between national, regional and local government.'

He says that popular support for devolution has been building steadily since 2017, buttressed by these battles with Westminster. 'In 2017, it was common to hear people saying that I should go back to Westminster, that becoming mayor would be a non-job. It has changed through various events. The major one being the timetable chaos in May 2018 when the railways went into meltdown across the North. I think that event brought home to people that the voice of the North had got louder, thanks to devolution.

'And then you go into the Pandemic year and there was a real sense that we were not being treated properly. At that point, people could really see how it's helpful to have place-based advocacy, and how it's valuable to have a figure speaking for a much broader area than constituency-focused MPs.'

In many other countries, political structures add extra layers of regional representation – to ensure that dominant areas don't consume marginal ones when the national pie is being sliced. This isn't the case in Westminster.

Yes, the House of Commons is populated by 650 representatives, each from a different area of the country. However, the Westminster system encourages the concentration of power, among the governing party and within the executive. Therefore, if a particular region of the country votes consistently for the party of opposition, it is represented in Parliament but not in government. And if these seats are safe

– if there is no prospect of these constituencies switching from the party of opposition to the party of government – there is little political incentive for the government to invest in these areas. This incentive is reduced even further if ministers – the people who wield power – are not drawn from all nations and regions. For example, of the twenty-seven people who attend Cabinet at the time of writing, only three represent constituencies in the North of England.

This is partly a function of the first-past-the-post electoral system, tailored to produce a clear governing majority rather than to fairly represent all parties and regions. But neither is this state of affairs counteracted by the upper house, the House of Lords. In many federal states, the upper house bolsters regional representation – unlike the House of Lords, which is built on hereditary privilege and overt political bribery. The US Senate, while not without its own unique problems, welcomes two senators from each state regardless of size. In Australia, each state elects twelve senators (two small states elect two each) using a proportional voting system.

Isolated from the rest of the country, discounting the lessons provided by the rest of the world, Westminster has therefore hoarded power. This is evident in the current devolution settlement, with only relatively marginal responsibilities awarded to regional mayors and the local authorities that oversee them. As in London, regional mayors elsewhere largely wield the power to plan – to draft housing plans, transport plans and investment plans – and to allocate some resources within these policy areas, notably transport.

In general, however, mayors are hostages to events that are beyond their control. They polish the nuts and bolts of a machine operated by Westminster. For example, though regional mayors have authority over transport planning, investment in transport infrastructure is dictated by central government. Coincidentally or not, London has received disproportionate transport funds in recent years – more than twice the transport spending per person as the national average.[18] The fate of the country's flagship £100 billion rail project, HS2, likewise rests in Whitehall.

The public body responsible for co-ordinating transport services in Burnham's realm, Transport for Greater Manchester, has a core budget of some £300 million. Transport for London's budget is closer to £10 billion. This converts to the relative development of local transport systems. Burnham has promised an integrated bus, train and tram system in Greater Manchester by 2024.[19] This will involve bringing bus services under the mayor's control – abolishing the current system of multiple, competing private operators – and implementing simple, contactless payments across all modes of transport. This system has existed in London for two decades, with Oyster cards introduced in 2003.

In fact, despite virtually never visiting London as a child, I had a relatively good understanding of how its transport system functioned – thanks largely to the London Underground song, an Amateur Transplants parody of 'Going Underground'. 'Take your Oyster card and shove it up your arsehole,' is one of the many memorable lines that we belted across the playground.

Local government funding also comes with strings attached from Westminster. Long-term planning is hampered by the fact that budgets must be balanced within a year. Local administrations can't overspend one year and underspend the next, if they haven't built up reserves.[20] This limits the scale and the ambition of local reforms.

The bullying of local leaders by central government is not uncommon either, as a way of forcing them to accept

Westminster's agenda. The Mayor of London was effectively compelled to increase the cost and scope of the congestion charge – imposed on drivers in central London – in order to plug the city's income shortfall that had been caused by fewer people using public transport during the Pandemic.[21] Khan asked central government for a bailout, yet ministers were reluctant to deliver the full sum to the Labour mayor, especially during his re-election campaign. Similarly, central government priorities can often bulldoze local housing plans and targets – with leaders operating under the thumb of Westminster.

In turn, the subservient status of regional mayors may in fact weaken the case and the enthusiasm for devolution. Deprived of significant powers, yet still blamed for the blunders of Westminster, devolved leaders face an eternal struggle to stay relevant – something that has been achieved by Burnham but not by others. With only a slim trickle of powers flowing to the regions, voters may instead decide that it's best to turn off the tap entirely.

Westminster's superiority complex is difficult to break, despite its persistent inability to fix regional issues. The housing crisis in Cornwall is a prime example. Local property inflation is caused by unique circumstances – particularly the desirability of holiday housing and low wages. Solving this problem will require a nuanced appreciation of local circumstances, applying local rules – such as limiting second home purchases – that may not be relevant, or may even have adverse effects, if they were rolled out across the country.

Indeed, Cornwall is particularly ripe for further devolution, given its strong regional identity. In the 2011 Census, nearly 14 per cent of Cornwall's population stated their national identity as 'Cornish', with 9.9 per cent identifying as 'Cornish only'.[22] Withholding meaningful powers from the region, in this context, is an act of callousness rather than simple negligence. It's assumed that Westminster's incompetence is better for Cornwall than any form of significant regional democratisation.

Therefore, how can and should regional arrangements be enhanced? One proposal is to expand the boundaries of devolution, creating democratic structures that are larger than city-regions. One flaw in the city-regions algorithm is that economies and societies overflow their boundaries. The East–West train lines in the North of England – linking Liverpool, Manchester, Leeds, York and Newcastle – are a case in point. All roads lead to London, in the government's playbook, and so the improvement of these Northern lines has been long neglected. However, under the current devolution framework, planning for the improvement of East–West routes involves co-ordinating between multiple mayoral jurisdictions and navigating their different priorities. Seismic changes that could disrupt the balance of regional power in Britain are therefore shelved in favour of the pursuit of smaller, local victories.

Consequently, there are calls for the creation of a new tier of regional governance above city-regions. The IPPR, as a starting point, has proposed four regional jurisdictions in England.[23] The first would be 'the North', incorporating the North West, North East, Yorkshire and the Humber. A pretty formidable merger, this region would integrate 15 million people and an economy of £361 billion Gross Value Added (GVA) – larger than all the devolved nations. If this bloc was a standalone country it would be the tenth largest economy in Europe, and would have won thirty-two medals at the 2021 Olympics.

The second region would synthesise the East and West Midlands, representing £250 billion in GVA, twenty universities and more than 20 per cent of the UK's manufacturing output. The third region would be the South West, with 5.6 million people and a GVA of £139 billion, while the final region would be London and the South East. Emphasising Britain's warped economic geography, this region would far exceed the output of the rest, with a GVA of almost £900 billion – making it Europe's fifth-largest economy.

This idea is one of many proposals floating around the academic hive mind. It is a concept, not a detailed blueprint. But the idea of four regional power-blocs, sitting above city mayors, makes a lot more sense than the erratic patchwork of devolution implemented in recent years.

Ultimately, however, England's regions must be able to mould their own democratic settlement. Nothing will undermine the merits of regional government more rapidly than an ill-conceived plan thrust upon local people by deeply unpopular, distrusted Westminster politicians. As our current devolution model may yet prove.

So far in this chapter I have kept my focus on the English regions – but devolution is of course more widely applied outside the Tory kingdom.

Blair's post-1997 constitutional reforms triggered a new relationship between Scotland, Wales, Northern Ireland and the UK government in Westminster. The Northern Ireland Assembly was created in 1998, followed by the Welsh Assembly (now known as the Senedd or the Welsh Parliament) in 1999, along with the Scottish Parliament.

The Scottish Parliament can make laws on agriculture, fisheries, education and training, the environment, health and social services, housing, justice, policing, local government, and some aspects of tax and social security. The Welsh Parliament had no power to pass primary legislation when it was first created, only gaining the authority in 2011 to legislate on all devolved policy areas without first needing Westminster's approval. The Parliament gained some tax powers in 2018, followed by partial powers over income tax in 2019. Justice, the area on which the Scottish Parliament legislated most heavily between 1999 and 2018, is not devolved to Wales. Neither is policing, nor other aspects of home affairs.

I had the opportunity to visit the Senedd a few years ago, when I was helping to produce a current affairs programme in Wales. The external design, effectively a chopping board on stilts, is dwarfed by the internal beauty of the building. A plume of synchronised, narrow wooden beams explodes above the central chamber – like a static mushroom cloud – merging with a sweeping, curved ceiling with the same composition. The open-aspect first floor allows onlookers to peer through glass slats onto the floor of the debating arena below.

The Senedd shares many design features with the Scottish Parliament. Airy, modern and lavished with glass, they purposefully convey a political ethos: open, transparent, forward-thinking. The contrast with the Palace of Westminster – its aristocratic rituals, its intimidating architecture and its dark, stuffy corridors – is also entirely intentional. The main chambers in both Scotland and Wales adopt a circular format, with different parties positioned next to each other, rather than in head-to-head conflict. This collaborative approach flows through their voting systems, both adopting proportional electoral systems, thus requiring parties to work together in order to form governments and to pass legislation.

In a similar spirit, devolution has fostered a conviction that Scotland and Wales are laboratories of policy. In Wales, for example, the government has been a proponent of the foundational economy model – emphasising the importance of key services, both in the public and private sectors, that are the bedrock of the nation – including education, social care and basic infrastructure.

Therefore, the Welsh government has deployed a £4.5 million Foundational Economy Challenge Fund – to test how the state can best support the foundational economy – funding fifty-two projects.[24] Writing for the Institute of Welsh Affairs in 2020, former deputy minister for economy and transport Lee Waters captured the importance of the idea, investing in 'those basic services on which every citizen relies and which keep us safe, sound and civilised'.

'These aren't small parts of our economy. Estimates suggest they account for four in ten jobs, and £1 in every three that we spend – and in some parts of Wales represent the bulk of activity.

'They are also critical to our wellbeing because the interruption of their supply undermines safe and civilised life, but they are also more resilient to external economic shocks. Even if a change in the global economy tips the attitude of a large multinational company against investing in Wales, the foundational economy remains. And nurturing it is within our power.

'We don't simply want to grow these parts of the economy, we want to disrupt them – to change and improve the ways they work. Too often the foundational economy is dismissed as being characterised by low skill and poor productivity and therefore undeserving of attention.'[25]

Indeed, the Bevan Foundation has estimated that some 44 per cent of all low-paid jobs in Wales are located in the retail, hospitality and social care sectors.[26] During the Pandemic, a vast number of people working in these jobs will have been classified as key workers – their numbers bolstered by retail workers in the food industry – while others will have been furloughed for months amid repeated lockdowns. Yet, despite Westminster's cursory tributes to the sacrifices of key workers, their treatment has not improved. Instead, in the post-Pandemic economy, they merely face the prospect of more, gruelling, low-paid employment.

Waters also cites the success of Preston Council in North-West England, which has used its purchasing power to support local businesses – an approach that is being studied in Wales. Whereas 5 per cent of Preston Council's spending was channelled to local businesses in 2012/13, that figure rose to 18.2 per cent by 2016/17 – an increase of £75 million. More broadly, 79.2 per cent of the council's spending was directed to Lancashire-based firms by the end of this period, which constituted a £200 million increase compared to 2012/13 – a significant injection into the regional economy.[27]

The Welsh government has a solid record of economic innovation, within the boundaries of its devolution powers. After the 2008 financial crash, presaging the economic support packages offered during the Pandemic, it created a programme that encouraged firms to put their workers on state-subsidised training schemes rather than making them redundant – while also subsidising the hiring and training of workers who had recently been laid off.[28]

The Welsh government has also received plaudits for introducing a Future Generations Act, passed in 2015, which obliges government departments to consider the long-term implications of their policies.[29] More recently, the Welsh government has talked about plugging the 'missing middle' – drafting policies to increase the number of medium-sized, Welsh-owned firms that have healthy balance sheets, pay workers properly, and are rooted in the country – and will be trialling Universal Basic Income (UBI), whereby all adults are given a standard, unconditional, regular payment from the state.[30]

The details of the UBI trial are still hazy, and it's unclear whether a further rollout of the idea would ever be sanctioned by Westminster. Indeed, Scotland's study of UBI concluded that the devolved administrations did not have the power to run such a scheme. 'In the current landscape, any pilot would require considerable commitment from the UK government to make the necessary legislative, technical and procedural changes required,' the Scottish report said.[31]

And herein lies the problem for Wales in particular. The Senedd has 'economic development' powers but responsibility for industrial strategy and taxation largely rests in Westminster. Therefore, the Welsh economy – and the effort to revive the nation after a long period of deindustrialisation – risks slipping through the cracks. The Welsh government has instigated a number of well-intentioned economic policies, but it has largely only been allowed to tinker at the margins. All the nuclear buttons are stored in Boris Johnson's bunker. Neither Westminster nor Cardiff is fully responsible for the fate of the Welsh economy, so regional disparities are preserved by this marriage of inconvenience.

Ultimately, devolution is only as effective as the power it grants. The democratic gains of devolution are only substantiated if the institution has the authority to do more than fix potholes. This seems to be reflected in public sentiment, in both Scotland and Wales. As more powers are awarded to their respective parliaments, there seems to be a growing clamour for home rule – a trend that has been exacerbated by recent political developments in England.

England has imposed more than a decade of Conservative rule on Scotland and Wales, against their wishes. The two countries have repeatedly snubbed the Conservative Party, yet they have seen four consecutive elections in which a Tory prime minister has been placed in charge of their affairs. In the case of Scotland, further bruising has been caused by Brexit, when England (and Wales in this instance) overwhelmed Scotland's Remain vote and wrenched the UK out of the EU.

This sense of injustice was heightened during the withdrawal process. Article 50 – the official mechanism to leave the EU – was triggered without the agreement of the Scottish and Welsh governments. This was despite the prime minister pledging that the process would not be triggered without first agreeing 'a UK approach and objectives for negotiations'. The European Union (Withdrawal) Act 2018 – which instituted our departure into law – was also passed without Scottish consent. The Institute for Government called this an 'unprecedented assertion of parliamentary sovereignty to push through a bill that directly amended the terms of devolution'.[32]

'There was no engagement with the Scottish government, despite the fact it was simply representing the views of the Scottish people over Brexit,' Scottish National Parliament MP Owen Thompson tells me from his constituency office in Midlothian. 'We were ignored at every step, and I think that has contributed to people asking whether we have to put up with this any more.'

It's therefore unsurprising that faith towards Westminster has dissipated in Scotland and Wales. This is not the product of insidious secession campaigns; it's a manifestation of democratic reality. People in Scotland and Wales believe that their devolved governments better represent their interests – because they do. In 2017, 61 per cent of people in Scotland said they trusted the Scottish government to work in their best interests, matched by 66 per cent of people in Wales.

This compares to 27 per cent of Welsh voters who trust the UK government, and just 21 per cent of Scots.[33]

Thompson says that the relationship between Scotland and Westminster is equivalent to 'your wage every month going to your neighbour, who gives you back some of it, having decided what you're going to eat for your dinner every night. And just to top it off, your neighbour is Boris Johnson.'

Politics is local – ironically even more so in a globalised world. In a time of mass misinformation and distrust, voters sway towards parties and candidates that appeal to their regional interests; that are perceived to be standing up for them. In the May 2021 elections, Andy Burnham won another landslide victory in Greater Manchester; the SNP came close to a majority in the Scottish Parliament; the Labour Party likewise recorded a strong performance in the Senedd elections; while the Conservatives mopped up English councils. As politics and the world become more uncertain, voters increasingly seek strong, local, familiar candidates.

And though the SNP's record can and has been endlessly debated, the long-term trends in Scotland during the devolution era are positive. In 1999, prior to devolution, median weekly wages in Scotland for full-time employees were 5 per cent lower than for people in England – a gap that halved during the next two decades. Scotland has made gains while English regions, outside London and the South East, have lagged behind. Median full-time wages in the North-West mirrored Scotland in 1999, yet by 2019 Scottish wages were 5 per cent higher. In terms of productivity also, Scotland has surged. Prior to devolution, productivity in Scotland was 1.3 per cent lower than in the North West. By 2019, Scotland was ahead by 6.5 per cent.[34]

As in Wales, Holyrood has been a petri dish for progressive and innovative ideas. In 2006, Scotland banned smoking in public places, a policy adopted by Westminster a year later. Similarly, both countries have managed to repel some of England's more noxious policies – notably resisting the rapid inflation of tuition fees after the financial crash. In Scotland, for example, you can only be charged up to £1,820 a year for an undergraduate degree – compared to £9,250 in England. Interest rates on student debts in England are also criminal, meaning that graduates face ever-mounting levels of back-ground debt. In Scotland, 15.6 per cent of full-time university students came from the 20 per cent most deprived areas in 2017–18,[35] while a study in 2017 found that a 'fear of debt' was a significant deterrent for many English students wondering whether to go to university – a feeling that was pronounced among the most disadvantaged.[36]

The record of the Scottish government shows that 'if we were able to gain powers over all taxes and decision-making, we could become a much fairer and more equal society', Thompson claims. 'There's a real appetite for that in Scotland, especially after years of the Tories looking after their mates with contracts and tax cuts.'

In the realm of healthcare in particular, England and Northern Ireland have created an NHS marketplace in recent years – requiring the health service to contract work from other parts of the NHS, and from independent providers. This system was abolished in Scotland and Wales in 2004 and 2009 respectively, while Westminster has been accused of exposing the NHS to private sector exploitation. 'Since the abolition of the internal market and any further privatisation of clinical services NHS Scotland has been distinguished by organisational stability,' says the Centre for Health and the Public Interest.[37]

NHS Wales has not received the same plaudits, however – frequently used by Westminster Conservatives to bait their

Labour opponents. In January 2020, Wales recorded its worst ever (pre-Pandemic) accident and emergency (A&E) waiting times, although England's record is not exactly world class either.[38] In 2010/11, one in every twenty-five people attending major A&E facilities in England spent more than four hours in the department.[39] By 2014/15 this had risen to one in ten patients, and in 2018/19 it rose to almost one in five. According to Trevor Jones of the Bevan Commission, the delivery of healthcare in Wales is complicated by the splintering of the service into seven independent health boards. 'It's very difficult to have national implementation,' he says. There is an optimal level of devolution for services to operate efficiently, as NHS Wales demonstrates.[40]

Scotland, meanwhile, has suffered from a strong concentration of unemployment and deprivation at a local level – showing that, even within devolved administrations, regional inequalities can flourish. Scotland's approach has been to focus on community planning and neighbourhood-level interventions, to relieve these problems. However, with key components of social security still reserved to Westminster, there have been few signs of improvement in these deprived communities.[41]

This frustration with Westminster rule has peaked in Scotland over recent years and, despite the failure of the SNP's 2014 referendum campaign, the country may yet vote for independence. The Scottish government would thus acquire the full machinery of the state, allowing it to jettison Conservative programmes – and to apply for EU membership, if it wished.

But, from a purely practical perspective, there is considerable merit in Scotland's current devolution arrangement: steadily annexing powers from Westminster, while being able to rely on the financial safety-net of the Union. On Brexit in particular, Scotland will suffer from England's act of self-sabotage – like a spouse working to pay off their husband's gambling debt. The question is whether this justifies a divorce, or whether an amicable resolution can ever be found. This would seem to rely on the revival of the Labour Party, the success of which would bring Holyrood and Westminster in closer alignment. So long as the agents of Vote Leave continue to fly their flag over Downing Street, the people of Scotland will be keen to extract theirs from the Union Jack.

Undoubtedly, however, Scotland and Wales have provided a model for the democratisation of power across England's regions – even if, in both countries, there is an appetite and a need for greater sovereignty. Following this example, England's regions must acquire meaningful and growing powers, applied to large enough jurisdictions, allowing their agendas to significantly diverge from central government and reversing years of neglect and stagnation. Otherwise, global Britain's regional inequalities will continue to be an international aberration.

8.

RUST BELTS

There is an abrupt contrast between the tales of Britain's glorious past and the painful lived reality of many Brits. We once ruled the seas – so the stories say – conquered continents, perpetuated the rule of law, and beat the Germans, twice (not including 1966). Industry built the British Empire and enriched our towns and cities. Slavery, exploitation and barbarity also featured heavily, though that's not mentioned quite as much.

'Make us great again' is therefore a potent narrative – particularly in left-behind areas of the country. As in the United States, another superpower on the downward phase of its life-cycle, people have been taught to expect more. Grand nationalist myths have sustained these modern-day grievances, erasing the strife and poverty that also marked the era of empire.

As Sathnam Sanghera writes in *Empireland*: 'the idea that we are different to everyone else extends [deep] into our culture and psychology. There is a popular view that Shakespeare is the best writer any country has ever had, that we have the best pop music and the most beautiful countryside and that we alone defeated evil in the twentieth century.'[1]

These apparitions of past splendour and power accentuate the current, unhappy circumstances of small-town Britain. If anything, the political spasms of the last decade have been a protest against this slump from international supremacy to mediocrity. As Labour MP Clive Lewis tells me: 'Brexit was the last tantrum of empire.'

British perceptions of fallen glory are often toxic – manifesting through an ugly resentment towards other nations that have dared to rival our global prestige – as are their political ramifications. Foreign jealousy is easily mobilised by nationalists who link decline to diversity and liberalism. They both implicitly and explicitly suggest that the nation has been plagued by mass immigration, the emergence of liberal identity politics and a subsequent weakening of patriotism. Immigrants are of course some of the most patriotic people in Britain, often having fought to arrive here in the first place, and so a related fallacy has been constructed by the Right – of feckless hordes of asylum seekers and migrants sponging off the state.

National decline narratives are laced with reactionary attitudes, encouraging the vain, erroneous belief that past glory can be recaptured if we re-adopt the intolerant social attitudes of a bygone era.

However, while nationalists contort the past for their own political ends, stagnation is simply a fact of life for large parts of the country. In the modern era, one all-consuming city has surged ahead, imparting a sense of injustice on the rest of Britain.

The uneven fortunes of people living in metropolitan hubs versus those in former industrial heartlands is certainly not a phenomenon reserved to the UK. After the early 2000s, regional differences in GDP per capita have increased in most rich countries, as people and economic activity have concentrated in urban areas. According to the Organisation for Economic Co-operation and Development (OECD) – a grouping of thirty-six highly developed economies – only a third have experienced an increase in productivity among all their regions since 2008. Meanwhile, in two-thirds of the countries, their most productive region is twice as productive as their least.[2]

In most cases, capital cities lead the pack. They supply academic and work opportunities, culture and society – a potent cocktail that lures highly educated young people away from their home towns. People in capital cities are considerably better schooled than elsewhere; in twenty-six out of thirty OECD countries with comparable data, city regions have the highest proportion of people who have completed tertiary education.[3] Therefore, capital cities generally have mobile workers in mobile professions. They are employed in information-intensive sectors, motors of growth and innovation, while other regions are increasingly populated by older workers and older industries. In the OECD, capital cities consistently have the highest proportion of people who can potentially work from home.[4]

As in London, capital cities in most rich countries have swollen during the information age – acting as locus points for professional and financial services, high politics, culture and investment – attracting legions of graduates trained in spreadsheets and algorithms rather than bricks and mortar. The most developed metropolitan areas boast a GDP per capita that is 36 per cent higher than other cities of the same size – and 80 per cent higher than the rest of the country.[5]

However, despite the existence of regional disparities across the developed world, the UK suffers more than anywhere else. Regional inequality in the UK is worse than in the twenty-eight most advanced OECD countries, according to Philip McCann from the University of Sheffield.[6] And while more than 70 per cent of the UK lives in an urban region, based on the OECD's definition, one city reigns supreme.[7]

Across all indicators and among all large advanced industrial economies, the UK is the most regionally unequal, McCann concludes. 'It is likely that the enormous imbalances within the UK are heavily related to the over-centralised national governance system,' he says.[8] Indeed, local government spending accounts for 35 per cent of total public investment in the UK, compared to an OECD average of 57 per cent.[9] The UK, along with South Korea and the United States, display the largest differences in GDP per capita between their most and least prosperous metropolitan areas. In all these countries, the gap exceeds 70 per cent.[10]

The data is irrefutable. In terms of job prospects, London and the South East are in the top 20 per cent of all OECD regions, whereas the North East sits in the bottom 30 per cent. West Wales and County Durham have a GDP per capita that more resembles southern Italy, itself markedly poorer than the north of the country, or Romania in Eastern Europe.[11] The problem is also getting worse. London has the highest productivity of any UK region by some distance, as well as the largest productivity growth.[12]

The UK has a highly stratified geographical hierarchy, compared to other developed nations, with significant disparities existing between nations and regions even outside London. The West Midlands, for example, logged the highest youth unemployment rate in the country in 2017, 17.7 per cent, almost double the rate in Scotland.[13] Meanwhile, generational divides are exacerbating. The UK is one of the four nations in the OECD with the largest age disparities between regions – a symptom of older and younger people clustering in different parts of the country – alongside Canada, France and Australia.[14]

London's supremacy is celebrated in some quarters, particularly among those who revel in the capital's economic and political proceeds. A deeply unequal city, its landmarks flogged to offshore corporate interests and its housing owned by luxury development companies, London has somehow been cast in the role of the virtuous patron – allegedly spreading liberal politics and prosperity to less enlightened corners of the nation.

However, the Office for National Statistics (ONS) punctures this reverence. In a 2014 report, it points out that few other regions have benefited from London's excesses. 'London's productivity premium is outstanding, but more strikingly still is the weak performance of most other UK metropolitan areas. Few other cities appear to benefit from agglomeration economies or possible positive spill-overs from London,' the report says.[15] The ONS does not celebrate London's economic strength, nor imply that other regions should be grateful for the capital's outsized contribution to public finances.

In the same report, the ONS compares productivity levels in different areas of Europe. While London snatched the top prize, ranked as the most productive region on the continent, no other UK region reached the top sixteen. France, Spain and the Netherlands – by comparison – each logged two apiece, while Germany boasted five regions in the top sixteen. The UK was well represented in the relegation zone, however, delivering half of the least productive eighteen regions in Europe. France, meanwhile, had none in this bracket.[16]

It is a national hobby to compare Britain to Germany. This is rooted in a psychological national urge to reassert the proudest moment of our modern history: our gallant victory against the Nazis (like a football game, the war is fantasied as a contest between England and Germany, with few other actors involved). This must seem strange to Germans, not least since the 100-year anniversary of the war is fast approaching, and because our Bavarian rivals have been beating us ever since. In the realm of regional inequality, the story is no different.

Only thirty years ago, the German Democratic Republic (GDR) was a communist satellite of the Soviet Union – supervised by a vast state surveillance apparatus, the Stasi, which reportedly employed one informant for every 6.5 citizens in the country.[17] These 200,000 Stasi operatives wiretapped, bugged and tracked citizens – punishing them for the smallest acts of defiance, like refusing to wear a state-administered school uniform.[18]

At the time of reunification, during the early 1990s, GDP per capita in East Germany was 40 per cent less than in the capitalist West.[19] These were materially two different countries, with profoundly different recent histories and ways of life, tasked with engineering a stable, unified nation. In many ways, the former GDR still suffers from the baggage of its Soviet past. Unemployment is steadily higher in the East, while living standards are lower. In 2018, the average unemployment rate was 6.9 per cent in the six states of the former East Germany, compared with 4.8 per cent in the ten states of the West.[20] Workers also complain that big businesses locate low-skill, low-wage jobs in the East, expropriating the profits to the West.

Yet, the economic gap between East and West Germany is in many ways considerably less pronounced than the divergence between London and the rest of Britain.

In 2017, disposable income per head in East Germany was €19,909 per year; in West Germany it was €23,283, a 15 per cent surplus.[21] In England, disposable income per head was £21,609 in 2018; in London it was £29,362, a gap of 26 per cent.[22]

This latter comparison is of course distorted by the fact that London is included in the England-wide average, inflating the figure. Comparing the capital directly with other regions, a canyon appears. The difference between average disposable income in London and the North East is 42 per cent, and the gap between the capital and the North West is 37 per cent.[23]

East Germany has a much smaller population than the West (roughly 16 million versus 67 million), and its productivity is lower: its GDP per capita is 25 per cent below the West, €32,108 versus €42,971.[24]

London's GDP per capita, meanwhile, is 40 per cent higher than the England-wide average – £54,686 versus £32,857 – and a staggering 57 per cent ahead of the North East.[25]

This is an obscene state of affairs. The West of Germany is highly developed and prosperous; the East of Germany was its poor, ostracised brother. The West is the engine of Europe; the East periodically suffered from food shortages. Yet Britain is now more economically unequal than Germany, and the two countries are travelling in opposite directions. The Institute for Economic Research in Dresden has suggested that the East and West will converge economically by 2030.[26] London, as we know, continues to extend its lead over the rest of Britain.

So, while Germany has unified over the last thirty years, Britain has ruptured; not exactly embodying the collectivist, wartime spirit that is the source of such pride among those who still look fondly back to 1945.

*   *   *

The reunification of Germany after the fall of the Berlin Wall was a catalytic moment for the country. Two siblings that had been separated for decades were suddenly thrust into the same house and asked to make it work. Tearing down the Wall removed the physical barrier between East and West, but beyond it was an economic, social and cultural minefield. To prevent civil strife and potentially open conflict, the government rapidly embarked on a campaign to balance the wealth of the new, unified nation.

This campaign has even provoked jealousy from the richer West. Regions in the East now generally have better infrastructure than elsewhere in the country – despite decades of austere Soviet planning – by virtue of a $2 trillion reconstruction package invested by the federal government.[27] This is the same amount of money, roughly, that will be required to collapse regional inequalities in the UK and fulfil Boris Johnson's 'levelling up' pledge, according to the Centre for Cities – more than double the UK government's annual budget.[28]

As John Kampfner writes in *Why the Germans Do it Better*, describing the investment deployed by the unified German government: 'Railway lines and rolling stock have been modernised. A new network of Autobahnen has been built – all at a time when infrastructure in western regions has deteriorated due to a lack of spending. The amount that has been spent overall in the past thirty years has been staggering ... No country has seen such a long-term shift of funds and resources – a modern-day equivalent of the Marshall Plan.'[29]

And while previous generations of Germans may still be suffering from the legacy of the Soviet era, the lingering chill of the Cold War is now steadily thawing. An analysis in 2015 of sixteen German states showed that – apart from Bavaria –

East German regions have the best-performing schools in the country.[30]

This has been the outcome of generous state spending – a national mission that has endured for decades, rather than a catchword in a solitary, fleeting election cycle. Local and regional government economic spending in Germany exceeds the UK by a multiple of two-and-a-half, as a proportion of GDP – spearheaded by the solidarity surcharge, which marginally increases tax rates in the West of the country to pay for investment in the East.[31] In 2018, this policy raised €18.9 billion.[32] Regional and local government spending represents 48.1 per cent of total state expenditure in Germany, compared to an OECD average of 40.4 per cent.[33] In the UK, central government employs 61 per cent of public sector workers compared to just 10 per cent in Germany. The UK ranks near the bottom of OECD countries for local control of tax revenues (at less than 10 per cent of total tax).[34]

Social protection (welfare) and public services are the largest components of regional and local spending in Germany – equivalent to 49 per cent of the total outlay, compared to 28 per cent in the OECD area.[35] In short: state spending in Germany is uniquely devoted to welfare and public services, distributed by local and regional governments.

But far from acting as a drag on productivity and innovation – the accusation made by small-state libertarians in the UK – the German state has nurtured high productivity and growth. Productivity in Germany overall is now some 20 per cent higher than in the UK, while output in the East has overtaken many English regions.[36] These statistics may seem abstract, but they have a measurable impact on lives. While Germany is not a nirvana, and intense local problems do exist, since 1989 the country has guaranteed the health and prosperity of all regions. In Germany, the difference in average life expectancy between the bottom 20 per cent of regions and the top 20 per cent is one-and-a-half years. In the UK, this gap is a full three years.[37]

But the money invested by the German state did not just miraculously spawn into a healthier regional settlement. The cash was a fertiliser, but it also required an irrigation system, in the form of strong regional democracy. Notably, Germany has regional tiers of government that span larger areas than the UK's current city-region model. One of these German regions, North-Rhine Westphalia, is home to 18 million people and has 'used its devolved powers to modernise and diversify its industrial base', says IPPR North.[38] Such reforms are long overdue in the North of England and the Midlands.

Decisively, the German system allows a high degree of local fiscal autonomy. In other words, regions have the authority to decide how to spend money, allowing devolved administrations to tailor policies to their industrial and wider economic needs. The UK system, on the other hand, is akin to a Victorian patriarchy – the breadwinner hoarding the fruits of his labour while his children go to school with holes in their uniforms. And though austerity ransacked the budgets of local councils in the UK following the 2008 crash – particularly in the poorest areas – the German model is underpinned by an equalisation of resources between local, regional and federal government.[39]

In life, and certainly in politics, nothing is perfect. No system of thought or government boasts divine or practical supremacy. Germany does not break this rule. Indeed, regional disparities in the country are still above the OECD average, with Hamburg's GDP per capita diverging from Mecklenburg-Vorpommern by a margin of 60 per cent. Youth unemployment has fallen in practically all regions since 2007, but the figure in Berlin exceeded 11 per cent in 2018 – 7 per cent higher than in Bavaria and 5 per cent above the national average. Life satisfaction in the poorest regions is also lower in Germany than in the UK (6.3 out of ten versus 6.8), even if quality of life indicators are higher.[40]

Likewise, there is a deficit of East Germans in the country's elite. Only 1.7 per cent of top posts in politics, the courts, military and business are occupied by Ossis (the nickname given to former residents of the GDR), despite accounting for 17 per cent of the overall German population. And just 7 per cent of Germany's top 500 companies are headquartered in the East, according to Kampfner, with none of the top thirty residing in the former Soviet bloc.[41]

In some ways, this is an after-effect of the structural, commercial reforms implemented by the West before and during unification. In order to integrate the two economies, the West German government prescribed a shock treatment. The East German Ostmark was converted into Deutsche Marks at a rate of 1:1 – immediately inflating East German wages to 70 per cent of their western counterparts. However, the East German manufacturing sector collapsed – no longer buttressed by a weak currency and low export prices.[42] Simultaneously, the West German government initiated a fire-sale of East German enterprises, via a now-notorious federal agency called the Treuhandanstalt. Only 5 per cent of these firms were sold to Ossis.[43]

Consequently, there is a strange flow of money between the East and West: businesses owned by Western interests fund state spending, directed heavily towards the East, which then flows back to the West through profits and rents, 'recycled through eastern infrastructure projects and welfare recipients,' says international relations academic Gareth Dale.[44] There's an imbalance of regional power in Germany, even if the product of this system is a more equal country than Britain.

There is another aspect of Germany's economic geography that should be celebrated, however. The country boasts a handful of thriving metropolitan centres, rather than the crippling dominance of a superpower capital city.

Wolfsburg is a base for world-leading car manufacturing. Frankfurt is Germany's financial powerhouse. Schweinfurt is narrowly behind Frankfurt in terms of GDP per capita – a small manufacturing city populated by roughly the same number of people as Dewsbury in West Yorkshire. A site of mass production during the Second World War, the Bavarian city now specialises in ball bearings and bicycles.[45] Berlin, Germany's capital, lags behind other cities in terms of GDP per capita, but is the centre of federal government and is the country's cultural nucleus. The media is also decentralised, with *Der Spiegel* based in Hamburg, Reuters in Frankfurt and *Bild* in Berlin.

Take Hamburg. Located on the River Elbe between the North Sea and the Baltic, one of the final pit-stops before the Danish border, Hamburg is Germany's largest port and the third largest in Europe. The city specialises in aviation, health, international trade and transportation – and has a GDP per capita of some €60,000, the highest in Germany.[46] In terms of overall output, in 2017/18 Hamburg ranked tenth in Europe, though the Holy Roman city recorded just 20 per cent of London's total GDP.[47] Despite being the richest area of Germany, Hamburg doesn't have a debilitating housing crisis – perhaps one reason why it boasts the highest life satisfaction in the country. It's ironic that the UK considers itself to be a maritime nation, yet none of our ports rival Hamburg. Not that we would ever know, given that our interest in current affairs rarely extends beyond our own shores.

Felixstowe is the largest port in the UK yet only the eighth largest in Europe, Hamburg handling twice as much cargo every year.[48]

Even the relative population sizes of the largest German cities indicate a more balanced nation. Despite being the richest city, Hamburg is not the largest – housing a population roughly half the size of Berlin.[49] However, Berlin is only larger than fourth-placed Köln by a factor of three and a half. By contrast, London is larger than the UK's fourth-largest city, Sheffield, by a factor of seventeen. London's population is some 9 million; Sheffield's population is 600,000. London is even eight times larger than second-placed Birmingham, which houses 1.1 million people.

Frankfurt is Germany's fifth largest city, with a population of some 750,000. Its skyline punctuated by the vertical glass briefcases of Europe's banks, partitioned by the river Main, Frankfurt strikes a similar pose to central London. Yet, in what must surely be a source of confusion for the rulers of the English capital, Frankfurt is the financial epicentre of Germany – and mainland Europe – without hoarding all of the nation's cultural, political and economic assets. The big names of the German and international banking sector are represented in Frankfurt: scores of commercial banks, the European Central Bank, the German stock exchange (Deutsche Börse AG), the German central bank (Bundesbank) and branches of foreign central banks, and yet Frankfurt's financial might does not overwhelm the nation.[50]

For 150 years, Frankfurt and Berlin rivalled one another for financial supremacy, each courting domestic and foreign firms through their local stock exchanges. The dominance of Frankfurt's stock exchange was established in the post-war years, eventually becoming the site of the German stock exchange during the unification period of the 1990s.[51]

A financial divestment from London was never considered in Britain. Although Liverpool founded its stock exchange in 1836, followed by Manchester in the early twentieth century, neither was allowed to rival London.[52] In 1973, all stock exchanges in the British Isles amalgamated to form the Stock Exchange of Great Britain and Ireland – consolidating power in the capital. The Liverpool trading floor ceased to exist in May 1985, and the Manchester exchange is now a hotel owned by former Manchester United footballers Ryan Giggs and Gary Neville, having officially ceased trading in 2000. This signals the new Northern economy: Manchester is a powerhouse of football, not of high finance.

Britain's post-industrial heartlands are suffering from an identity crisis in the modern world, their sense of purpose clamped by libertarianism, globalisation and automation. However, Germany offers some hope, showing how former industrial regions are not inevitably plagued by dying high streets, bankrupt businesses and low-wage gig sector jobs.

Dortmund, the centre of commerce in the Ruhr area, situated in Germany's western bloc, provides an example of post-industrial regeneration. Practically wiped out during the bombing raids of the second world war, Dortmund rebuilt its prowess through the steel and coal industries throughout the latter half of the twentieth century. In 1980, roughly half of the city was employed in industrial production and the other half in services. Now, more than 80 per cent of people work in the service sector. This transformation hasn't been accompanied by poverty wages and instability, however. Instead, Dortmund offers routes into stable, professional jobs. The insurance sector has settled in the city, for example, with two-thirds of German insurance workers applying their trade in Dortmund. Meanwhile, a manufacturing base has been retained, acting as a 'power wheel' for the local economy and fuelling supplementary service-sector jobs.[53]

Germany still has profound regional inequalities, ranging from the stagnation of small, monoethnic towns in the East – recently harbingers of the far right – to the quandary of post-industrial development in the West. Many neighbouring areas in the Ruhr Valley and North Rhine-Westphalia have not been elevated by Dortmund's economic resurgence. Nearly half a million people once worked in the Ruhr coal and steel industries. Now, 'many towns have become nearly permanent social-welfare cases', says Deutsche Welle, as unemployment remains stubbornly high.[54] However, no nation will ever be entirely balanced, and Germany has shown the merits of endurance and persistence – addressing regional inequalities over a period of decades, using the full vigour and resources of the state, the pursuit of geographical parity embedded within the foundational principles of the nation.

After the war, the small city of Bonn, a western conurbation situated on the Ruhr, was selected ahead of Frankfurt as the seat of government. This was a purposeful decision, to encourage regional parity. 'By opting for this relatively small city, the new leadership sought to emphasise the provisional nature of the arrangements and the importance of decentralising power,' Kampfner says.[55] Ironically, British lawyers played a key role in drafting Germany's post-war constitutional settlement, yet these principles of decentralisation and regional equality weren't exported back to the United Kingdom.

The German decentralising spirit has persevered to the present day, even if its form has changed. In 2018, Berlin was the eighteenth wealthiest metropolitan area in Germany (in terms of GDP per capita), out of twenty-two.[56] Indeed, according to the Cologne Institute for Economic Research,

Germany is the only major European country that would see its GDP per capita increase without the input of its capital city. The UK's GDP per capita would fall by 11.2 per cent without London.[57]

The importance of decentralisation is recognised by regional leaders in the UK. 'In other parts of the world, where there is less centralisation, you see a greater spread of wealth,' Liverpool City Region Mayor Steve Rotheram tells me. 'We stuck everything in London. Over time, everything has been pulled back into the capital. Too many MPs spend too much time in London, departments are primarily based in London, so staff are inevitably Londoners or people from the South. Which means they've got a perverse incentive to ensure that London does well – because that's where they live.'

This state of affairs is not shared by Germany, though Berlin is certainly not a backwater. As well as being Germany's political and cultural capital, it hosts one of the highest densities of scientific research institutions in Europe.[58] Conde Nast Traveller has called Berlin 'one of the most achingly hip places on the planet',[59] and its economic growth rate is impressive – burgeoning on average by 4.4 per cent a year between 2008 and 2018, at a time when the nation as a whole averaged 3.5 per cent.[60]

To ensure the stability and prosperity of its newly unified nation, the German government applied an emergency dose of economic investment. The task wasn't left solely to the free market, under the baseless conviction that the invisible hand would elevate the poorer East. It was a collaboration, overseen by the government and embraced by business, guided by collectivist convictions that had rebuilt the German nation after the Second World War. Britain won the war; Germany won the peace. When we recognise this reality, perhaps we could learn some valuable lessons from our schnitzel-eating cousins across the North Sea.

However, Germany is the exception, not the rule. France, for example, has been wrestling with the issue of regional inequality for the best part of seventy years, with varying degrees of success. A national debate was first convened by Parisian geographer Jean-François Gravier, via his seminal 1947 book *Paris et le Désert Française* ('Paris and the French Desert').[61] Gravier described how Paris had suddenly and disproportionately inflamed at the expense of the nation-at-large. The capital city acted 'as a monopolist group devouring the national substance', he wrote.[62]

Gravier lamented how, since the mid-nineteenth-century, successive governments had concentrated national resources in the French capital – centralising economic, administrative and educational institutions – while spending extravagant sums on the capital's infrastructure and transport.[63]

The book was a symbol 'of the revolt against an unbalanced France', says *Le Monde*, 'between an overwhelming capital-region, where everything happens, and a beautiful sleepy province which arouses boredom and scares away talent towards the City of Light'.[64] Modern-day Britain seems to be suffering from exactly this complex.

The post-war era was marked by extremely uneven development, says Paris-based planning expert Matthew Wendeln.[65] Several traditional industries were gutted during this period; the farming, coal mining and the textile industries shedding jobs en masse. New service sectors emerged in their wake, triggering an imbalance between the sites of the old and new economies. Rural areas decayed while cities (Paris in particular) were overwhelmed by an influx of people seeking work. The situation was unsustainable for both.

'Can we base the future of a nation on internal bleeding? Can we base its rebirth on the congestive swelling of 4 per cent of its territory? And on the continuous impoverishment in men and in production of half of its provinces?'[66] Gravier posed these questions to the French establishment, aware that it already knew the answer – if only subconsciously.

Gravier's decimation of the status quo hence prompted government reforms. Eight years after the book was published, finance minister Pierre Pflimlin described regional economic development as 'the main goal of [the administration's] economic policy', ordering that a development plan should be drafted for every region, and insisting that industry should be exported out of Paris. Consequently, 600,000 manufacturing jobs were redistributed from the capital to the peripheries from the 1950s to the 1970s – although they didn't travel far. Most of the jobs remained within a 125-mile radius of Paris, Wendeln says.[67]

What's more, it was typically lower-status industries that moved out of Paris – reinforcing the economic and psychological pecking order between the modern commercial capital and the poorer hinterlands. Thus, a new strain of thought emerged in the 1960s, advocating for the development of urban regions each with a prosperous metropolitan core (bearing a strong resemblance to the city-regions supported by governments in the UK since the turn of the century). In the French blueprint, big cities would act as 'growth poles' – theoretically spreading prosperity throughout their respective regions.[68] However, as the prevailing force in the French economy, this emphasis on urban growth merely served to extend the supremacy of Paris.

Thus, regional economic inequalities in France have swelled in recent decades, hinged on the success of Île-de-France – the most prosperous area of France, encompassing the central arteries of Paris and its suburbs – akin to Greater London. Île-de-France has the highest productivity levels and the highest growth rates in the country, and even outguns London in some disciplines. The area represents 31 per cent of national GDP, despite covering just 2 per cent of French metropolitan territory,[69] while the UK capital contributes 23 per cent of national output.[70]

The service sector is ascendant in Île-de-France, representing 83.3 per cent of employment, while the region also leads the country in the automobile, clothing, pharmaceutical and IT sectors. Île-de-France has a 'very high concentration of resources', according to the French government, which enables the seamless transfer of workers, investment and knowledge in the area. In 2015, the region amassed 40 per cent of France's total research and development (R&D) spending, equivalent to €19.8 billion, thus attracting 38.2 per cent of the country's R&D workforce.[71] Île-de-France is a juggernaut, of the sort that would doubtless have prompted Gravier to unsheathe his pen for a second diatribe.

A new input in the modern era has been immigration, again emphasising the parallels between Paris and London. As of 2017, 19.5 per cent of Île-de-France had been born outside France – double the national average – while the region accommodated 40 per cent of all immigrants living in the country.[72]

In another reflection of London, there are sharp regional inequalities within Paris. The city has one of the highest rates of income inequality in the OECD relative to its population. The areas that flank the outer rim of Paris – the eighteenth, nineteenth and twentieth arrondissements – account for 38 per cent of welfare beneficiaries in the city but just 26 per cent of the total population. Almost 50 per cent of social housing in Paris is concentrated in just three of the twenty arrondissements (the thirteenth, nineteenth and twentieth).[73]

The severity of COVID in France varied along this income scale, with richer areas faring better than poorer ones. A *European Journal of Health Economics* study found that areas of France with higher levels of inequality tended to suffer more COVID deaths. 'When accounting for both the level of income and income inequality, we find that inequality kills,' its authors wrote.[74]

And while the richest parts of the city have the best access to jobs, public services and healthcare, they also suffer from spiralling housing prices – restricting the upward mobility of people from poorer families and districts, in what *Le Monde* labels the 'asphyxiation' of Paris.[75]

This isn't to say that regional inequalities are somehow inevitable – a natural, unavoidable facet of any developed nation. Rather, the French example exemplifies how common features of policy and leadership – the active choices of the state – have both ignored and nursed profound regional inequalities in multiple countries. Both France and Britain exhibit a dominant capital city enjoyed by the wealthy, an aversion to the devolution of government spending, and a perception among non-urban areas that they have been sacrificed on the altar of the post-industrial economy. Government recalcitrance has allowed regional imbalances to burst out of underlying economic, demographic and historical trends. This was not an act of divine fate.

Notably, there is now a common strain of resentment towards an urban-based elite on both sides of the Channel – nourishing the growth of reactionary, populist politicians. After the 2017 presidential election, Marine Le Pen, the figurehead of France's far right, said that she was fighting for the 'forgotten' peripheral France that had been suffering from unemployment and a lack of opportunities, neglected by the distant elite of diverse, metropolitan cities.[76] Le Pen was the runner-up in the election, winning more than 10 million votes, 34 per cent of the total, in a run-off against eventual winner Emmanuel Macron. A report from Angelique Chrisafis during the campaign described Le Pen's supporters as 'people living in modest towns and country villages far away from big cities, who have felt the sharp edge of France's decades of mass unemployment, who have seen factories close and local shops and services disappear'.[77]

It was the first time since 2002 that a National Front candidate had entered the final round of a presidential ballot, when Marine's father, Jean-Marie Le Pen, lost to Jacques Chirac with 18 per cent of the popular vote.

'If you go twenty kilometres North, South, East or West out of Paris you will find yourself in another France, which is far more immobile, hit by unemployment, worried about identity and marked by social and cultural divisions,' political scientist Pascal Perrineau commented during the 2017 campaign,[78] a description that could equally be applied to the coastal towns perched on the Kent coastline, or the fishing hubs of Lincolnshire, or the former mill towns of Yorkshire.

Indeed, the balance of state spending in France is also more akin to the UK than to Germany. Local and regional government spending accounts for just 19.8 per cent of total public expenditure in France, compared to a 40.4 per cent average across the OECD.[79]

In this shared cosmos, immigration has roused the left-behind. Older, White voters have been triggered into believing that city-based immigrants are plundering the nation's resources and enforcing their woke political agenda – all while peripheral regions stagnate, their political choices maligned as bigoted and misinformed. An August 2016

IPSOS survey indicated that 57 per cent of French people think there are too many immigrants in the country, and only 11 per cent think migration has a positive impact on the country.[80] As one Le Pen voter told Chrisafis: 'When there's no more bread at home, you don't invite in your neighbours.'[81]

This race-based hostility is pernicious and archaic. Politicians and the press have whipped up the tribal instincts of voters to buttress a populist, right-wing, authoritarian agenda. However, the immigrant bogeyman has been built on the separation of younger, diverse, liberal voters in thriving metropolitan hubs and older, conservative people in the stagnating peripheries. The latter are assumed to be dim-witted bigots, while the former are branded 'woke snowflakes'. Neither description is true, but the regional fissures in both France and Britain block the shared experiences – and the shared prosperity – that could explode these misconceptions.

A concurrent process has been seen in the United States: the evaporation of the American dream in former industrial regions, activating nativist political instincts. No American region has fared worse in the post-war period than the area known as the 'Rust Belt' – running through Pennsylvania, Ohio, West Virginia, Kentucky, Indiana, the Lower Peninsula of Michigan, northern Illinois and eastern Wisconsin.

These areas were previously renowned for their heavy industries, many of which have dwindled in recent decades. Detroit, the largest city in Michigan, was built on the success of the American motor industry, nicknamed 'Motor City'. In August 2021, the city recorded an unemployment rate of 25 per cent, exacerbated by the Pandemic.[82]

From the mid-1950s onwards, the big three automotive giants based in Detroit – Chrysler, Ford and General Motors – lost more than 40 per cent of their US market share. In just the period from 2000 to 2008, the US auto industry shed some 400,000 jobs, while 42 per cent of these losses occurred in Michigan alone.[83] This slump reached its nadir in 2008, when the financial crash caused a collapse in vehicle sales and pushed carmakers to near-extinction, only rescued by a last-ditch federal government bailout.

'By any number of metrics, the Rust Belt's share of aggregate economic activity has declined dramatically since the end of World War II,' says a macroeconomic analysis of the Rust Belt, published by Yale University.[84] Between 2000 and 2010, manufacturing employment in the United States fell by a third as nearly 6 million factory workers lost their jobs.[85] This was partly a symptom of the financial crash, partly the relocation of factories to cheaper labour markets overseas, and partly technology improvements reducing the demand for workers. From 1987 to 2016, US manufacturers increased their output by 80 per cent while reducing their workforce by 17 per cent.[86]

So, a Rust Belt revolt occurred in 2016 when key Midwestern states – Wisconsin, Michigan, Ohio and Pennsylvania – flipped to the Republicans. 'For the first time, the decades-long decline of the industrial Midwest could find an outlet in national partisan politics,' Michael McQuarrie writes in the *British Journal of Sociology*.[87] Megalomaniac billionaire Donald Trump spoke in brutal, unfiltered terms about the decline of the nation – his inauguration address peppered with references to 'American Carnage' – and offered straightforward solutions. Building a wall on the Mexico border; scrapping the North American Free Trade Agreement (NAFTA); challenging China. These were not ideas bred in an Ivy League policy lab. Trump's policies were simplistic, occasionally self-destructive and often downright offensive. But they resonated with the anger of disenfranchised voters in neglected, former industrial heartlands.

Crucially, Trump was an outsider. He was the beneficiary of a family fortune, but he wasn't part of the Washington 'swamp' that had betrayed the Midwest. In fact, Trump was mocked by both Democrats and Republicans prior to his election. This doubtless resonated with Rust Belt voters who felt scorned by the same elites.

The Rust Belt was cognizant of its relative disadvantage in modern America – a grievance that was enhanced by the height from which it had fallen. This place was literally the motor of American industrial capitalism during the twentieth century. It was the birthplace of Fordism; ground zero for the era of mass production, consumer spending and unionised labour. The age of affluence germinated in the Midwest – in areas that were gutted when the economy changed its allegiance and tied its fortunes to property, international capital and technology.

From 1973 to 2007, McQuarrie says, the Rust Belt suffered the 'systematic withdrawal of institutional, state and financial investment', redirected to the new economy – orientated around professional services and technology – and to cheaper manufacturing bases, domestic and international.[88] This process was partly encouraged by Democratic President Bill Clinton, who deregulated the finance sector and embraced free trade policies that encouraged the relocation of plants and factories overseas.

The era of American ascendancy, the post-war period, relied on the output of the Rust Belt. America's dwindling status as an unrivalled superpower in the late twentieth and early twenty-first centuries has therefore coincided with the economic decline of these industrial hubs. Perceptions of national and local failure are intertwined, forging the conviction that one cannot be revived without the other. 'Make America Great Again' was a national slogan that resonated strongly at a regional level. A national mission understood in a local context.

As in the UK, realising this promise would have taken billions (or trillions) of dollars and years of sustained investment in both political and economic redistribution. However, as a means of winning an election and converting low-income workers to right-wing politics, the promised revival of left-behind regions is fertile ground to plunder – particularly as progressives have abandoned the pitch entirely. Poor, older and less-educated White voters rowed behind Trump in 2016 – epitomised by a 16-point swing from the Democrats to Republicans among those earning less than $30,000 a year. The richer and better educated, meanwhile, swung decisively behind Hillary Clinton.[89]

The same flavour of grievances motivated pro-Brexit sentiments in the ostracised towns of Northern England, the Midlands and North Wales. Experiences of local and regional deterioration and neglect – dovetailing with perceptions of national decline – are reshaping the electoral map in Britain, America and across the West.

In America, this is a tricky knot to unpick. Federal, regional and local administrations overlap and regularly come into direct conflict. A coherent economic strategy, supported and implemented by all parties, is difficult to achieve.

However, France has a more developed architecture for addressing regional inequalities – that may provide some lessons to the UK. Indeed, overall, regional inequalities are more pronounced in the UK than in France. The OECD concluded in 2018 that France had the tenth largest regional disparities in GDP per capita among thirty OECD countries with comparable data.[90] The UK was sixth on this list, also recording the fourth largest increase in regional disparities between 2000 and 2016.[91]

In 2003, an amendment to the French constitution made the country a decentralised republic.[92] This might seem superficial and symbolic, but it fundamentally affects how France is governed. Notably, regions forge an agreement with the state every seven years, to decide on public policy priorities. This obligation both forces the state to pay attention to regional needs and allows policies to be constantly evaluated and refined.

Moreover, the campaign for regional equality is institutionalised by the French government. The prime minister chairs a National Conference of the Territories, involving ministers, local leaders and members of external bodies, to cohere a national strategy. The General Commission for Territorial Equality also operates at the centre of government as the long-term planning unit for fair geographical development. While the Northern Powerhouse Minister is only a recent phenomenon in the UK, a Minister for Territorial Development/Cohesion has been a part of the French government since the 1970s.[93]

There has been an ongoing debate in France since the late 1940s, periodically heeded by the government, the outcomes of which are worthy of study in Whitehall. Even so, France isn't a paragon of regional equality. Paris has engulfed the wealth of the nation while the peripheries wallow in past triumphs, conspiring with the far right to plot the takedown of the smug centre.

This serves as a warning to the UK. Firstly, to those in power: a few train stations and some more money on hospitals and police officers will not placate the Red Wall. People seek fundamental, structural change: the revival of their industrial prestige, the transformation of their high street and the modernisation of their transport networks. If this is possible – if London's monopolisation of wealth and opportunity can be broken – it will involve a wartime deployment of national resolve and resources. And if this effort is not successful, political extremism may harvest the dejected and disenfranchised.

Britain needs to embark on its own unification project – a national mission, not just a partisan election tool.

9.

UNIFICATION

If we are ever to rebalance Britain, London must join the effort. Reform won't be possible if the capital isn't an active participant.

The grey men who lurk in the corridors of power must recognise that fairer regional growth will benefit London. Houses will be more affordable, the morning mêlée on the Tube will be more bearable, poverty rates will fall, raising a family on a decent income will finally be possible, and the rest of the country will stop complaining about how much it hates the capital.

The status quo is not sustainable, for London or for the rest of the country. Overheating the city will eventually burn out its citizens. Westminster must also appreciate the national context: to create a prosperous, balanced and harmonious country, London can't stand alone in enlightened abundance.

However, for this to happen, attitudes must change. Currently, London's power brokers are invested in the exponential growth of the city. The capital's output exceeds the rest of the country to such an extent that even a modest abatement would jeopardise the GDP growth of the entire country. London therefore continues to swell, steadily consuming the South East. The underground will even extend to Reading, forty miles west of London, when the new Elizabeth line is opened.

This economic argument runs contrary to popular opinion. Voters are more willing than ever to vote for short-term economic pain in exchange for long-term returns. Indeed, people don't care about GDP growth if all the dividends are harvested by a small, property-owning cabal in London. They would be willing to support a temporary slow-down in total national output if the proceeds were more fairly distributed – among both social classes and regions – in five or ten years' time.

Those in favour of retaining London's supremacy typically highlight the benefits of clustering, known in official terms as 'agglomeration'. This is the source of London's profligacy: an economic hive that provides access to a vast pool of labour, financial markets, professional services, politicians and investors. It seems counterintuitive to demolish a system that delivers such extreme productivity benefits. But London's grip on national resources must be weakened for all to prosper. There is little point in London producing such extreme wealth when it is enjoyed by so few.

Unfortunately, stubborn attitudes to regional rebalancing continue to pervade in the capital. Currently, there is a perception within London that it is a self-made city, one that revels in its diversity and entrepreneurial spirit. This is ironically a conservative outlook, based on the conviction that London thrives due to its innate superiority, rather than the presence of a favourable dealer who keeps on supplying a favourable hand.

A similar attitude is held towards welfare in Britain. The poor are thought to be genetically stupid and feckless – a belief widely promoted by right-wing newspapers – and therefore undeserving of help. Conservative MP and Victorian broomstick Jacob Rees-Mogg, for example, was forced to apologise after he suggested that Grenfell victims who stayed in the burning tower, on the instruction of the fire brigade, lacked 'common sense'.[1] The rich, meanwhile, are thought to be inherently superior and thus deserving of their extreme wealth.

Likewise, there is a psychological certainty in the capital that London is naturally exceptional, justifying a tight-fisted approach to the rest of the country. After all, what have the peripheral regions done to deserve the capital's charity? This perspective has been entrenched by otherwise well-meaning progressive liberals, who have swallowed the cliché that people outside the capital are bigoted and racist because they voted for Brexit. So, while Brexit was a seismic event – an indication of the indignation felt by left-behind areas of the country – it may obstruct the cause of regional equality.

To its political cost, the Labour movement has been too busy salivating over its inflated intellect to realise that voters now have a much stronger attachment to place (local and national) than social class. Grounded in the capital, the Left has arbitrarily assumed that Brexit voters are stupid and prejudiced – an attitude that has shovelled votes to Boris Johnson – rather than reflecting on how progressives have bolstered regional injustice and abandoned the interests of their former heartlands. The terrain has been relinquished to the Conservatives, a party that fundamentally believes in (and is named after) the preservation of the status quo. Radical reform is not in the Conservative Party's DNA.

Unlike the fall of the Berlin Wall, it seems unlikely that the fall of the Red Wall will signify Britain's reunification moment. With politics, the media and the economy so deeply entrenched in the capital – a mutually sustaining relationship – it's improbable that we will see any substantial regional redistribution in the next decade. I don't want to sound defeatist, but I also don't want to trivialise the task ahead. There's a reason why regional inequalities are so deeply entrenched in Britain; I would be betraying the severity of the problem by suggesting that it can be miraculously fixed.

Equally, however, revolutions have never been triggered by people giving up and going to the pub. So, I'm going to itemise some of the ways that we can achieve greater parity between Britain's nations and regions. These are the solutions that I would implement if I was King of Britain, a shopping list that I would purchase with unlimited resources – without the inconvenient complications of electoral politics – after I had given up belting around Buckingham Palace on a quad bike.

The Palace of Westminster, a slowly disintegrating relic (a bit like Britain, some may say), is slipping into the Thames. Rats wander the corridors of power, at risk only from the high likelihood of fire.

All staff are due to move out of the building in 2025, for at least six years. The House of Commons is expected to move to Richmond House, a foreboding structure that looks like it was designed either by Darth Vader or Count Dracula. The House of Lords is set to move to a conference centre next to Westminster Abbey. The cost of renovating Parliament has been variously estimated at between £12 billion and £20 billion.[2] For context, as of August 2021, the total cost of the furlough scheme was £68.5 billion – and, in 2019/20, the UK spent £39.8 billion on national defence.[3]

Politicians, civil servants and journalists are sceptical about using this opportunity to relocate beyond Westminster, accustomed as they are to their favourite drinking holes down Whitehall. Even a temporary relocation of Parliament – an insufficient idea – exceeds the appetite of the Westminster bubble. Yet reforming the democratic relationship between our nations and regions means using the refurbishment of Parliament to move MPs and peers out of London permanently.

Indeed, the arguments in favour of a temporary relocation are not especially convincing. As Tim Wyatt wrote for CityMetric in February 2018: 'Pretty much anyone and any organisation which wants anything to do with government, policy or politics has set itself up in London – and they're certainly not going to relocate to Hull or wherever for six years just because MPs feel guilty about spending billions rebuilding the Palace they normally work in.'[4]

Tim is right – the political class wouldn't be keen on moving to 'Hull or wherever' for a few years (though they wouldn't have much choice), knowing they would soon be deported back to London. As a person who evidently cares deeply about regional equality, I'm sure Tim would agree that we can only truly encourage political heavyweights to leave London by relocating Parliament for good.

The benefits would be multifaceted. Primarily, it would bring democracy closer to the people. Westminster is an elite province of London, itself an outlier city that shares little with the rest of the UK. Moving the centre of power to somewhere else, anywhere else, would expose politicians to a more common existence.

The ostracism of politicians from ordinary life is palpable in the Palace of Westminster – a place in which one feels more likely to meet Dumbledore's ghost than a person on benefits. As Del Boy philosopher Russell Brand says: 'The whole joint is a deeply encoded temple of hegemonic power. The green, leather benches, the relentless oak panelling all look the same as the halls and chambers of Oxford University. Or

Cambridge. Or Eton. These great monuments to privilege and power all deploy a consistent design and symbology. A symbology which is alien to the majority but comfortably familiar to the privileged few. When most of us are in these rooms we feel daunted and belittled.'[5]

If Parliament sat in Hull, Manchester, Newcastle or Birmingham, politicians would be forced, through proximity, to see the lives of people outside the fortress. Also, more crucially, they would experience the same daily problems that have afflicted people outside London for the last forty years.

I can't imagine MPs being particularly pleased about commuting to work on a rusty, temperamental train that smells like a kitchen fire. Or seeing the local M&S disappear from their high street. Or suffering the incessant complaints of their children as they struggle to find job opportunities in the area. And they would probably start to do something about it.

'Power instinctively responds to location,' writes Simon Jenkins. 'Ministers and officials hire London banks, consultants and think-tanks because they know them, because they employ their children and friends. London gets a new railway because ministers experience the overcrowding. They subsidise its operas and museums because they use them.'[6]

These sentiments are echoed by Jonn Elledge, who notes that, 'In Brexit, the political class is already committed to one expensive project that will take decades to complete. At least this one might actually benefit the country – spreading jobs, rebalancing the housing market and ending the internal brain drain in which graduates of Northern universities head immediately for the South.'[7]

Politicians and civil servants would invariably be accompanied by an entourage of journalists who would soon discover that the rest of Britain is not a bigoted backwater populated by barely sentient lifeforms. Enlightened by their new horizons, reporters would cover issues of regional importance with enhanced gravity and nuance. The Westminster bubble will have burst.

Scottish National Party MP Owen Thompson agrees that the quality of democracy would improve if Parliament were shipped out of the capital. Currently, Thompson must travel 400 miles from his Midlothian constituency to attend Parliament, limiting the time that he can spend in his constituency.

'If you look at Members of Scottish Parliament, for example, a good number of them are able to travel back to their constituencies in an evening. So, if a community group is holding a meeting or a ceremony, they can attend,' he says, 'they can be a central part of their constituency and their community – whereas, for me, I can only do that normally on a Friday [when there are no votes or debates in Parliament].'

If Parliament moved to Leeds, for example, thousands of highly-skilled, educated, wealthy people would be encouraged to migrate northwards – spontaneously creating a new locus of power in Britain. The benefits would be far-reaching. It's likely that a renaissance of economic and social activity would mushroom around the gentrified masses of Londoners relocating to the North. New economic hubs would inevitably spawn in the area, gravitating towards the people who control the country's coffers. Meanwhile, kids from all parts of the country would be able to dream of entering these professions, without having to spend their savings on a mould-infested dungeon in Hounslow.

People who work in and around Parliament should not have to uproot their lives and move to a new city, say those who oppose the migration. This argument is made forcefully by people who are noticeably silent about the current situation, which compels people outside London to leave their home, their friends and family, to pursue job opportunities that are only available in London.

What's more, the shift to Leeds wouldn't be immediate. If the decision were made now, at the time of writing, the Westminster bubble would have three or four years to brace for the move. Civil servants, advisers and even MPs would have more than enough time to find a new job in London, if they would prefer to stay, or to formulate a plan for voyaging out of the capital.

Leeds is a fairly arbitrary choice, although Parliament's new home would need to fulfil two criteria. Firstly, it would need to be far enough away from London that commuting from the capital is discouraged. If the political elites were able to keep their cash, kids and culture locked down in the capital, the purpose of the move would have been undermined.

Secondly, the new base must be prosperous enough to endure the inevitable spike in house prices that would accompany the news. Housing and infrastructure plans would need to be drafted in alliance with the West Yorkshire Mayor, to ensure that London's housing crisis is not simply exported to Leeds, and that life in the city does not grind to a halt, its trains and roads overwhelmed by the influx of Parliament's foot soldiers.

Others, including Danny Dorling, have suggested that the new home of Parliament should be in the Midlands, located close to the proposed East–West split of HS2, so that power can be accessed easily from either side of the country. However, given that the government now seemingly plans to knobble HS2's right-hand flank, preventing a new East–West divide in the North of England may require redistributing Parliament to Leeds or another nearby city.

Moving the seat of power would be a costly operation. After all, Parliament would still need to be repaired. Letting it crumble into the Thames wouldn't exactly reflect the government's 'global Britain' mantra. However, as Dorling has suggested, the cost of the repairs and of procuring new offices elsewhere could easily be met by selling prime Whitehall real estate. As Dorling says, 'Downing Street would make a very nice boutique hotel.'[8]

Britain also wouldn't be making a great leap into the unknown. Throughout history, various countries have changed their capital cities in response to socio-economic conditions – an even more radical policy than I am proposing.

In recent times, Indonesia has been considering relieving Jakarta, on the island of Java, of its capital city status. Indonesia is currently suffering from an extreme concentration of national resources in Java, home to 60 per cent of the country's population and more than half of its economic activity. The government has been considering building an entirely new city in East Kalimantan, on Borneo, that is more central in Indonesia's archipelago of 17,000 islands.[9]

If Indonesia does pursue this route, it would be following Myanmar, which transferred capital city status from Yangon to Naypyidaw in 2005. Naypyidaw was likewise a planned city, as was Brasília when it replaced Rio de Janeiro as Brazil's capital in 1960, and Canberra when it became the capital of Australia in 1911.

I'm not suggesting that we build an entirely new capital city – or that we displace London's capital city status. I'm merely explaining that, across the world and throughout history, more ambitious reforms have been implemented to address the intense concentration of wealth and power in particular cities.

Boris Johnson speaks in noises rather than words or ideas, and so it has proven on the location of Parliament. Johnson has suggested that some parts of Whitehall should be scattered across the country: the Ministry of Housing, Communities and Local Government (MHCLG) announced in February 2021 that it would be creating a second base in Wolverhampton – allegedly the first central government department to be headquartered outside London. 'At least' 500 jobs will be based there.[10] The Cabinet Office is also set to move some staff to Glasgow, and three departments – including the Treasury – will relocate 750 officials from London to Darlington.[11]

Carefully placed rumours also suggested that Johnson was considering moving the House of Lords to York – although this was widely interpreted as a veiled threat to peers who were attempting to obstruct the prime minister's Brexit plans. The idea now appears to have been abandoned.

Indeed, Johnson's 'levelling up' agenda is designed to generate the most headlines with the least amount of money. After all, the prime minister is a functionary of London – its former Mayor – and one suspects that he would much prefer to be snorting caviar in Mayfair clubs than studying spreadsheets with Chris Whitty or learning how to improve the life chances of people in Chorley. In fact, the prime minister's former chief aide, Dominic Cummings, reportedly described the Conservative Party's route to political success as 'build shit in the North'. Not exactly a detailed manifesto.

In August 2020, the body in charge of Parliament's restoration said that moving the Lords out of Westminster was a matter for MPs and peers. However, after the decision was delegated to parliamentarians, the BBC reported that a temporary relocation had been 'effectively axed'.[12] In other words: the largest party in the House of Commons, the Conservatives, didn't want to put the threat into practice.

Thus, while some 450,000 civil servants are employed in the UK, only an additional 22,000 will be moved out of London by 2030, under current plans.[13] And while redistribution is welcome, no matter how small, these new homes appear to have been selected for political reasons. Darlington flipped from Labour to the Tories in 2019, while the local Tees Valley Mayor is a Conservative, as is the West Midlands Mayor (Wolverhampton being the region's second-largest city). Johnson is using bribery as a substitute for policy.

If we were starting from scratch – if the map of Britain was untouched – we would not choose one city as our political, economic and cultural capital. That's the plot of *The Hunger Games*, not the basis of a thriving, well-balanced nation.

London is a fortress. It is a superpower city guarded by its inhabitants, especially those whose pockets bulge with its power and wealth. Moving parliamentarians, civil servants and journalists out of the capital would have a profound, decentralising effect – dispersing money and influence to long-neglected areas of the country. Unfortunately, self-interest keeps getting in the way.

There is a pervasive belief in Britain that we don't have to play by the rules, either individually or collectively. We venerate the mischievous and practically worship those who have managed to succeed despite being generally drunk, hapless and unruly. Perhaps this is one of the many ways that the aristocracy has prevented a social coup – by perpetuating the belief that amassing wealth in the face of one's own vagrant behaviour is a sign of genius rather than privilege.

The Bullingdon Club, a University of Oxford society populated by its richest and most self-impressed students, has a long history of trashing restaurants and harassing locals.[14] If a bunch of working-class youths gave a similar performance, they would be hauled in front of the court of public opinion, labelled as 'chavs' and 'thugs' by the tabloids. The Bullingdon boys, by contrast, usually have a good chance of becoming prime minister.

This cult of the rascal has been evident over recent years, with catastrophic consequences. Throughout the Pandemic, the government has acted as though it can circumvent the laws of science, capable of formulating a novel response to COVID that would both suppress the virus and liberate the economy. Attempting to trick the virus, and ignoring mainstream scientific opinion, Britain locked down too late and opened up too early. More than 140,000 people have died at the time of writing – one of the worst death tolls in Europe.

Just a few years earlier, the UK collectively voted in favour of petulance by leaving the European Union – derived again from our collective insolence towards authority. 'I think it shows something about the state of our politics that a leader like Angela Merkel looks like a heroine,' public health expert Sir Michael Marmot told me on the Byline Times Podcast. 'She's sensible, she listens to science, she tells the truth. I think it's a dreadful statement about our politics that these things are considered exceptional.'

For once, just once, we need to show maturity. We need to stop trying to be the maverick or the class clown. For once, we need to implement proven and tested policies that actually work.

In the field of regional parity, Germany has set an example: investing in infrastructure, state services and welfare support over a period of decades, funnelled towards left-behind areas of the country under the jurisdiction of empowered regional and local leaders. Despite the chill of the Cold War spilling into the 1990s, Germany is now a more regionally equal country than Britain.

To catch up, we must dedicate billions (if not trillions) of pounds in the coming decades to improving train links, building new schools and hospitals, increasing pay for public-sector workers, investing in the research capacity of universities, and using the organs of the state to incubate pockets of economic heat outside the capital.

I don't think that a solidarity surcharge, of the sort that has been pioneered in Germany, would sit well among Brits. The solidarity surcharge is a crude levy that increases tax rates in the West to pay for government spending in the East. Ordinary Londoners, already punished by high housing costs, would justifiably balk at having to pay more tax than everyone else, and I doubt that people outside the capital would be too keen on being branded as charity cases.

However, regional redistribution could be carried out in more subtle ways, primarily through wealth taxes – a 1 per cent tax on individual wealth over a certain value, for example. This tax would be applied to people in all areas of the country. But, by virtue of their higher levels of wealth, it would be targeted at property owners in the capital and the South East. LSE academics recently considered the idea and found that a 1 per cent tax on wealth of more than £500,000 would raise £260 billion over five years.[15]

The government could even introduce a banded system. *The Times* calculated in May 2021 that a one-off wealth tax of 5 per cent on Britain's billionaires (applying just to their wealth above £1 billion) would raise £19 billion, even accounting for avoidance and the cost of setting up the scheme. A 5 per cent tax on all wealth over £100 million, a 10 per cent tax on wealth over £500 million and a 20 per cent tax on wealth over £1 billion could raise as much as £97 billion, the paper suggested.[16]

Alongside these measures, inheritance tax should be reformed. The current system applies a standard 40 per cent rate to estates worth more than £325,000, though there are exemptions for properties worth less than £1 million inherited by direct family members. To its credit, the Labour Party proposed a new, viable solution in its 2019 'Land for the Many' policy paper, whereby inheritance tax would be replaced by a lifetime gifts tax. 'Tax would be levied on the gifts received above a lifetime allowance of £125,000,' the paper says. 'When this lifetime limit is reached, any income from gifts would be taxed annually at the same rate as income derived from labour under the income tax schedule.'[17]

This would create a more progressive system, raising money from the proceeds of arbitrary property inflation, targeted at London and the South East. The Resolution Foundation has suggested that a lifetime gifts tax would have raised £15 billion in 2020/21, £9.2 billion more than the current inheritance tax system.[18]

And while the impetus for reform must flow from central government, Westminster has been too distracted by secondary agendas – not least party politics – to draft a substantial plan for regional rejuvenation. Therefore, while Whitehall must facilitate coherent, ambitious policies that transcend regional jurisdictions, central government must empower devolved administrations – trusting regional leaders to apply their local knowledge.

This should involve the creation of four overarching regional governments in England – the North, Midlands, South West and South East – as outlined by IPPR North. The democratic composition of these regions would be important, to ensure that power flows down to local areas. There would be no use in devolving power from Westminster to the North, if it's merely captured by an insular regional administration in Manchester, for example, that fails to accommodate the needs of Newcastle, Scarborough and Wakefield.

This should be accompanied by a renewed faith, among leaders of all stripes and dominions, in the importance of the foundational economy. The Pandemic has shown that in order to function – and to stay alive – we rely on bus drivers, doctors, nurses, lorry drivers, care workers, teachers, supermarket shelf stackers and the vast web of hidden heroes who grease the wheels of our collective existence. These people make up a substantial part of the economy, especially in left-behind regions, who have been starved of government support since the financial crisis. If we want to 'build back better', and to bring greater parity to a country ravaged by inequalities, key workers should finally be at the front of the queue when the government is injecting investment into the post-Pandemic economy.

Ultimately, Britain needs 'levelling up' on steroids; a fundamental reorganisation of democracy and state spending. Greater Manchester Mayor Andy Burnham describes this as 'hard-wiring' levelling up into the political system – ensuring that, as the party of government changes, the overall mission of regional equality perseveres.

'Our current system has got a London bias baked in,' he says. 'The government might invest a bit of money now and level up parts of the country, but a new government could take over and the impetus could disappear. What I think you actually need is to hard-wire levelling up into the way the country works.'

This would involve restructuring democratic institutions, Burnham says, to better reflect regional interests. 'All parts of the North need substantial regional devolution. The House of

Lords needs to be an elected senate of the nations and regions. And I would turn House of Commons elections into a proportional representation system. Every MP is fighting for their small constituency, and it prevents people from acting across a broad region. I would like to see MPs elected more on a regional basis than on a constituency basis.'

We need a 'complete rewiring of Britain', Burnham says, 'or else levelling up will be a fad that burns brightly but disappears quickly'. Levelling up is a 'slogan without any substance' currently, he notes, and 'to the extent that it changes anything it won't be permanent. And then we'll still be left with a very London-centric political system.'

And Burnham isn't alone in this view. 'Labour's instinct under the first past the post electoral system is to temporarily supplant the Tories and become a top-down centralising force,' says Labour MP Clive Lewis. 'The problem is that we lose three times as often as we win – so we don't get much opportunity to govern and often when we do, we tinker at the edges.'

Thus, Lewis says, Labour must support fundamental changes to the UK's democratic system – to create a vision of 'levelling up' that trumps the public spending commitments of the Conservative Party, with the ultimate aim of decentralising the British state. Leaving the EU – sold under the promise of people 'taking back control' – has merely 'replaced the EU with an increasingly authoritarian government at home', Lewis says. 'People can increasingly see that taking back control did not involve giving power to the British people, but instead simply awarding power to a handful of blokes down in London.'

Labour, he says, needs to claim the 'take back control' slogan and promise to fulfil the wishes of the British people by 'giving power to local communities, to regions. Labour has to frame its agenda through power, control, agency and democracy, rather than simply by promising more public spending than the Conservatives.'

The leadership of the Labour Party, however, remains hesitant about the merits of structural democratic reform. 'We have to close the gap between politics and people, and that involves bringing politics closer to people,' says Lisa Nandy, who is responsible for Labour's levelling-up policies.

Nandy suggests that the current devolution model is flawed – concentrating power in cities and hoping that their economic growth will trickle down to neighbouring towns. However, she also says that she is 'frustrated with the endless debate in Westminster – and actually some parts of local and regional government as well – about structures'.

Nandy believes that politicians in Westminster can and must represent the interests of neglected regions – and that the 'mindset' of leaders must change, rather than the democratic constraints under which they operate. The day after she took over as Labour's levelling-up chief, Nandy told her opposite number, Michael Gove, that she wants the rebalancing of the country to 'become as uncontentious as equal marriage by the time that David Cameron took office'.

'I want to build a political consensus around this,' she adds.

There undoubtedly needs to be a shift in attitude among the political establishment, recognising the ways in which certain areas of the country have benefited at the expense of others. But I'm unconvinced that levelling up will be achieved simply through the convictions of political pioneers, such as Nandy – persuasive and passionate though she is. Rather, I am more inclined to agree with Burnham and Lewis that structural reforms are needed in the operation of the Labour Party and the very nature of British democracy, in order to draft a new settlement between our nations and regions.

The current system is not simply flawed; it is entirely unsustainable – virtually undisturbed by the Pandemic. Average incomes rose by six times as much in London and the South East from December 2019, when the Conservatives swept up a raft of Red Wall seats, to December 2021, according to the New Economics Foundation.[19]

And despite Labour's decade-long journey through the political wilderness, the party will have a formative role in redressing Britain's regional imbalances. Indeed, the Conservative Party has presented little evidence to suggest that it will substantiate its slogans. Boris Johnson's tyranny of vacuity continues to predominate in a party that sees performative Brexit outrage as a substitute for serious policies. 'Take back control' and 'levelling up' described the process of disenfranchisement and disempowerment suffered by left-behind areas for generations but, beneath the rhetoric, there is a vacuum of genuine interest and ideas.

Education, for one, has been a neglected policy area in the levelling-up debate. 'Equality of opportunity' has been ingrained into the political dictionary since the Blair era – a pursuit of every administration, Labour and Conservative – yet, since 1997, marked inequalities have materialised between schools in London and the rest of the country.

This divergence was spurred by the London Challenge, led by Tim Brighouse, which transformed the capital's schools. The premise of the scheme was relatively simple: facilitate a dialogue between high-performing and travailing schools that share similar characteristics (primarily the social backgrounds of their students). This will encourage the lagging schools to learn from the best practice of the leading institutions; an informal mentorship scheme where teachers share notes on how to improve results. Meanwhile, government support programmes encouraged young, dynamic teachers to work in under-performing schools, further boosting attainment.

The London Challenge had a measurable impact on the capital's schooling system. In less than a decade, the capital soared up the regional league table, practically from last to first. London now boasts the best schools in the country, particularly in terms of secondary education performance and higher education entry rates.

However, the impetus for reform dissipated after New Labour's departure from office. The incoming Conservative government's austerity agenda hamstrung schools, while a succession of ministers were more occupied with altering the management structure of schools than exploiting past policies. Former Education Secretary Michael Gove is labelled as a radical reformer, even though he purged one of the most successful education policies of the twenty-first century.

Before the London Challenge disappears from memory entirely, its teachings must be applied to the rest of the country, working in partnership with devolved administrations. The policy should not be controversial in Conservative circles. Yes, it requires generous government funding, but its implementation doesn't rely on the heavy hand of the state. Schools are simply empowered to share their own solutions – an organic system of collaboration and improvement usurping top-down central government planning.

London is the media's home turf, in large part because all of our national institutions are based in the capital. The media has occasionally attempted to peer beyond the fortress, with increasing frequency since the Brexit vote, but its coverage is often clichéd and flimsy. There are few heavyweights of journalism devoted to unpicking the cultural, social and political convulsions that are afflicting peripheral Britain. The Westminster cabal is more concerned with the gossip that emanates from the hallowed corridors of power. Access is ranked above insight.

Ultimately, therefore, the media's ignorance towards places outside the capital won't significantly diminish until new hives of politics, economic, business and culture are created across Britain – dragging journalists out of the satellite state.

The Westminster lobby system could be abolished, for example, opening up the press gallery and Downing Street briefings to reporters from different beats, from a larger number of publications. This may collapse the current system, in which a coterie of political reporters skulk around the Palace of Westminster hoping to squeeze some hearsay out of unsuspecting advisers. But, although this would improve the quality of journalism in Britain, the political press corps still wouldn't evacuate beyond the boundaries of SW1. Until Parliament moves out of London, political journalism will continue to inhabit the Westminster village.

And yet, even in the current environment, the media can do more. Editors need to recognise that regional inequalities have saturated their newsrooms with staff from London and the South East. By better understanding the experiences of candidates outside the capital, the various ways in which they are prevented from accessing jobs in the media, editors can begin to bulldoze these obstacles to entry. This should involve taking into account the regional backgrounds of job applicants, thus mirroring other forms of social disadvantage, and setting targets for regional representation.

Relocation fees – a stipend paid to staff who are forced to move for a job – should also become more commonplace, and organisations should improve the overall support offered to people moving into the capital. People refrain from applying for jobs in London because they don't know where to live, how much they can expect to pay in rent, and how to navigate this strange, sprawling new universe. One solution would be to appoint a mentor to help each successful candidate with their move to the capital – a peer who can offer encouragement and advice.

Or staff should simply be encouraged to work from home. Many publications are now offering remote roles as standard, which is a welcome development. Editors should be explicit with staff about the future expectations of the job (i.e. whether it will ever be office based) and, if hybrid working is adopted, they should try to enable the participation of staff across the country. Rather than forcing their employees to move within the orbit of London simply to attend an occasional meeting, organisations should help their staff with ad hoc travel and accommodation so they can live wherever they like (within reason). This applies to all information-based industries, not just journalism.

Editors also need to understand how London warps their journalism, depicting a country that most people don't recognise. More energy and attention must be dedicated to commissioning writers and documentary makers who can articulate the UK's complex regional tapestry. This will involve a degree of humility from senior editors and reporters, appreciating their own limited horizons and delegating work to journalists who have local knowledge.

All of this will of course require some investment from organisations that are starved of cash. As the standard-bearer of British journalism, the best-resourced and most respected platform in the country, it is therefore incumbent on the BBC to dispel its instinctive timidity and lead the campaign for greater regional representation in the media. If the BBC sets an example, others will invariably follow.

This is not an exhaustive manifesto for the regional rebalancing of Britain, but rather a first draft. I hope that I have provided a rough sketch onto which policy makers and experts can forge a more vivid, detailed canvas – a new agenda that is desperately needed by the masses of people disenfranchised simply due to the random act of where they were born, and where they live.

According to the polling that I commissioned from Omnisis, some 55 per cent of people think that Boris Johnson will not be able to successfully level up the country, while only 22 per cent firmly think that he will fulfil his mission. Most people (58 per cent), meanwhile, don't think that the Conservative Party cares about fixing the inequalities between richer and poorer areas of the UK.[20]

Ultimately, the dominant Vote Leave faction of the Conservative Party only seems to understand the language of competition: the global horse race. In this allegory, Britain continues to run the same thoroughbred that it has overfed and overworked for decades. Germany breeds a full stable of specimen runners, while Britain shovels food towards its lone star, London, emaciating the rest of its fleet.

Until the country is saved from its capital, it will be impossible to avert our slide into international impotence and mediocrity. I don't care much for national glory myths, but I want Britain to be a fair and prosperous place to live, where freedom and opportunity prevail over privilege and exploitation – for everyone, regardless of region, race, gender, sexuality or religion. Right now, we are entirely failing to match that promise.

ACKNOWLEDGEMENTS

Fortress London has been years in the making – the book that I desperately wanted to write, though I could not have done so without the support, mentorship and occasional admonition of countless people.

First and foremost, I must acknowledge Mum and Dad, whose rants about 'that' London slowly seeped into my subconscious and eventually onto the pages of this book. I'm eternally fortunate to have parents who are brilliant drinking partners, therapists and friends. This book is for them, everything they have achieved and everything they have taught me.

The rest of my family have also shown incredible patience in journeying down my stream of consciousness about the book. Thanks in particular to my sister Ruth, brother-in-law Rob and nephew Harry, for making me laugh in moments of desperation – and to Nana Jean, Helen and Keith.

Among the patient masses have been the wider Byline Times family – including but not limited to Hardeep Matharu, Peter Jukes, Stephen Colegrave, Sian Norris, Adam Bienkov, Ella Baddeley, Iain Overton and all the Byline Intelligence Team – who have provided invaluable counsel and support.

Thanks also to John Sweeney, whose spag bol is not nearly as bad as it appears on Twitter.

I am not uncommon in saying that a great deal of my career can be attributed to Innes Bowen, my unmatched former colleague who decided to give this naïve, cocky Northerner numerous opportunities in the BBC big leagues. I continue to say to anyone who will listen that Innes was the BBC's best recruiter, which is a role she aptly transferred to the publishing world when she referred me to Jonathan de Peyer at HarperNorth.

Likewise, I'm massively grateful to Jon for taking a punt on *Fortress London*, and for being a calming influence as I navigated the obstacle course of writing my first book. Thanks also to Alice, Gen, Meg and everyone else at Harper North, whose enthusiasm for the book has spurred me on to meet their expectations.

In no particular order, I must also give thanks to Meesha – who suffered more than anyone else during the long months of research and writing – to Jenny Cater, Tom Duckham, Shafi Musaddique, Jack Sparling, Ben Stuart, Catrin Nye, Mukul Devichand and Clare Hudson. All have given me the opportunities of friendship, and of employment, without which my name would not be standing on bookshelves today.

I owe a debt of gratitude to all those who agreed to be interviewed for *Fortress London*, who humoured my ideas – even when they disagreed with them – and gave such thoughtful, knowledgeable responses. They maintained my otherwise dwindling faith that there is some hope left for this country.

I must also thank you, dear reader, for deciding to devote your time to my rants and ramblings. I hope this book will provide some ammunition for you to go forth and conquer the hypocrites and charlatans who currently rule our country, and to hopefully make Britain a better place for all, regardless of where we're all born.

Finally, a salute to Vin and Audrey Yearsley, who won't get to read this book, but who showed me unconditional love and pride that will motivate me no matter what obstacle comes next.

To you all – thank you.

ENDNOTES

PREFACE: THE FORTRESS

1. 'Regional ethnic diversity', Gov.uk (Aug. 2020), https://www.ethnicity-facts-figures.service.gov.uk/uk-population-by-ethnicity/national-and-regional-populations/regional-ethnic-diversity/latest
2. Jean-François Gravier, *Paris et le Désert Française* (Paris: 1947).
3. Geoff Tily, '17-year wage squeeze the worst in two hundred years', *Trades Union Congress* (May 2018).
4. Private rental market summary statistics in England: April 2019 to March 2020, *Office for National Statistics* (June 2020).
5. Maria Sobolewska and Robert Ford, *Brexitland: Identity, Diversity and the Reshaping of British Politics*, (Cambridge: Cambridge University Press, 2020).
6. Alex Nice, 'The ISC Russia report highlighted problems that cannot be solved by the intelligence services alone', Institute for Government (July 2020).
7. John Kenneth Galbraith, *The Affluent Society* (New York: Houghton Mifflin, 1958).
8. Robert Peston, *WTF?* (London: Hodder & Stoughton, 2017).
9. David Goodhart, *The Road to Somewhere: The Populist Revolt and the Future of Politics* (London: Hurst, 2017).
10. 'The English question: Young are less proud to be English', BBC News (June 2018), https://www.bbc.co.uk/news/uk-england-44142843
11. Andrew Gimson, Rachael Jolley, Sunder Katwala, Peter Kellner, Alex Massie, and Richard Miranda, 'This Sceptred Isle: Pride not prejudice across the nations of Britain', British Future (Apr. 2012), https://www.britishfuture.org/wp-content/uploads/2012/04/BritishFutureSceptredIsle.pdf
12. 'Regional ethnic diversity', Gov.uk.

13. 'London's Poverty Profile: The age distribution of the population', Trust for London (Apr. 2020), https://www.trustforlondon.org.uk/data/population-age-groups/#:~:text=The%20age%20distribution%20of%20the%20population&text=More%20than%20one%20in%202010,aged%20between%2030%20and%2034.&text=A%20relatively%20small%20proportion%20of,in%20the%20rest%20of%20England.
14. Michael Savage, 'Richest 1% have almost a quarter of UK wealth, study claims', Guardian (Jan. 2021), https://www.theguardian.com/inequality/2021/jan/03/richest-1-have-almost-a-quarter-of-uk-wealth-study-claims#:~:text=Almost%20a%20quarter%20of%20all,of%20inequality%20in%20the%20country
15. George Orwell, The Lion and the Unicorn (London: Secker & Warburg, 1941).
16. I have lightly edited some of these interviews to improve their comprehension and flow.
17. 'London's Poverty Profile', Trust for London, https://www.trustforlondon.org.uk/publications/lpp2020/#:~:text=28%25%20of%20people%20live%20in,ten%20(21%25)%20in%20Sutton.

1. EDUCATION, EDUCATION, EDUCATION

1. 'The Oxbridge files: which schools get the most offers?', The Spectator (March 2021), https://www.spectator.co.uk/article/the-oxbridge-files-which-schools-get-the-most-pupils-in
2. Children's Commissioner, 'Growing Up North: A generation of children await the powerhouse' (March 2018), https://www.childrenscommissioner.gov.uk/report/growing-up-north-a-generation-of-children-await-the-powerhouse-promise/
3. Tony McAleavy and Alex Elwick, 'School improvement in London: a global perspective', Education Development Trust (Jan. 2016), https://www.educationdevelopmenttrust.com/our-research-and-insights/research/school-improvement-in-london-a-global-perspective
4. Ibid.
5. Nida Broughton, 'Educational inequalities in England and Wales', Social Market Foundation (Jan. 2016), https://www.smf.co.uk/publications/educational-inequalities-in-england-and-wales/
6. Children's Commissioner, op cit.
7. Children's Commissioner, op cit.
8. Sally Weale, 'Northern secondary schools receive £1,300 less per pupil than London', Guardian (May 2016), https://www.theguardian.com/education/2016/may/23/northern-secondary-schools-less-funding-london-schools

9. Tom Barton, 'Parent school donations "exacerbating inequality"', BBC News (Dec. 2019), https://www.bbc.co.uk/news/education-50732685

10. Michael Young, *The Rise of the Meritocracy: 1870–2033* (London: Thames & Hudson, 1958).

11. 'Elitist Britain 2019: The educational backgrounds of Britain's leading people', The Sutton Trust and Social Mobility Commission (June 2016), https://www.suttontrust.com/our-research/elitist-britain-2019/

12. Alan Milburn, 'Letter of resignation in full', Sky News (Dec. 2017), https://news.sky.com/story/alan-milburns-letter-of-resignation-in-full-11154497

13. McAleavy and Elwick, op cit.

14. Merryn Hutchings, Charley Greenwood, Sumi Hollingworth, Ayo Mansaray, Anthea Rose, Sarah Minty and Katie Glass, 'Evaluation of the City Challenge programme', Institute for Policy Studies in Education, London Metropolitan University and Evaluation and Research Practice, Coffey International Development (June 2016), https://assets.publishing.service.gov.uk/government/uploads/system/uploads/attachment_data/file/184093/DFE-RR215.pdf

15. Marc Kidson and Emma Norris, 'Implementing the London Challenge', Institute for Government (Feb. 2014), https://www.instituteforgovernment.org.uk/sites/default/files/publications/Implementing%20the%20London%20Challenge%20-%20final_0.pdf

16. McAleavy and Elwick, op cit.

17. Hutchings et al., op cit.

18. McAleavy and Elwick, op cit.

19. 'Ethnicity and National Identity in England and Wales: 2011', Office for National Statistics (Dec. 2012), https://www.ons.gov.uk/peoplepopulationandcommunity/culturalidentity/ethnicity/articles/ethnicityandnationalidentityinenglandandwales/2012-12-11

20. 'Population of the UK by country of birth and nationality: July 2018 to June 2019', Office for National Statistics (Nov. 2019), https://www.ons.gov.uk/peoplepopulationandcommunity/populationandmigration/internationalmigration/bulletins/ukpopulationbycountryofbirthandnationality/july2018tojune2019

21. McAleavy and Elwick, op cit.

22. Hutchings et al., op cit.

23. Ibid.

24. Richard Adams, 'English schools funding has fallen faster than in Wales, says IFS', *The Guardian* (July 2018), https://www.theguardian.com/education/2018/jul/12/english-schools-funding-has-fallen-faster-than-in-wales-says-ifs

25. Michael Savage, 'Schools staff crisis looms as austerity hits teachers' pay', *Guardian* (Feb 2019), https://www.theguardian.com/education/2019/feb/09/teacher-pay-down-real-terms-since-2003

26. Diane Reay, 'British education: still selecting and rejecting in order to rear an elite', LSE British Politics and Policy (Aug. 2020), https://blogs.lse.ac.uk/politicsandpolicy/british-education-still-selecting-and-rejecting-in-order-to-rear-an-elite/

27. Lauren White, 'Things Posh People Have Said to Me', *NE Beep* (Sept. 2020), https://www.nebeep.com/things-posh-people-have-said-to-me/

28. Jack Rear, 'I know anti-Northern discrimination at British universities is real because I've experienced it', *Telegraph* (Oct. 2020), https://www.telegraph.co.uk/education-and-careers/2020/10/21/know-anti-northern-discrimination-british-universities-real/

29. Nazia Parveen, 'Students from northern England facing "toxic attitude" at Durham University', *Guardian* (Oct. 2020), https://www.theguardian.com/education/2020/oct/19/students-from-northern-england-facing-toxic-attitude-at-durham-university

30. Hannah Richardson, 'Oxbridge uncovered: More elitist than we thought', BBC News (Oct. 2017), https://www.bbc.co.uk/news/education-41664459

31. Maria Sobolewska and Robert Ford, *Brexitland* (Cambridge: Cambridge University Press, 2020), p. 25.

32. 'A plan for an adult skills and lifelong learning revolution', Education Committee (Dec. 2020), https://publications.parliament.uk/pa/cm5801/cmselect/cmeduc/1310/131002.htm

33. Children's Commissioner, op cit.

34. Nazia Parveen, op cit.

35. Phil McDuff, 'England lacks white working-class graduates. Quick fixes won't change that', *Guardian* (Feb. 2019), https://www.theguardian.com/commentisfree/2019/feb/18/england-white-working-class-graduates-universities-students

36. Richard Adams and Rachel Hall, 'Proportion of black school leavers going to university in England falls', *Guardian* (July 2020), https://www.theguardian.com/education/2020/jul/30/proportion-of-black-school-leavers-going-to-university-in-england-falls

37. 'Cambridge welcomes record number of black students', University of Cambridge (Oct. 2020), https://www.cam.ac.uk/news/cambridge-welcomes-record-number-of-black-students

38. 'Widening Participation in Higher Education, England, 2017/18 age cohort – Official Statistics', Department for Education (Dec. 2019), https://www.gov.uk/government/collections/widening-participation-in-higher-education

39. Nerys Roberts and Paul Bolton, 'Educational outcomes of Black pupils and students', House of Commons Library (Oct. 2020), https://commonslibrary.parliament.uk/research-briefings/cbp-9023/

40. Sally Weale, 'Oxford Union condemns itself as racist over cocktail poster', *Guardian* (June 2015), https://www.theguardian.com/education/2015/jun/01/oxford-union-racist-colonial-cocktail-poster

41. 'Plymouth University Tory group suspended over T-shirts', BBC News (October 2018), https://www.bbc.co.uk/news/uk-england-cornwall-45735591

42. Luke O'Reilly, 'Student "wore racist slogan at Leicester University event"', *Evening Standard* (Oct. 2019), https://www.standard.co.uk/news/uk/student-wore-racist-slogan-at-leicester-university-event-a4266921.html

43. Mikey Smith, 'Tory students face race probe over "disgusting" Black Lives Matter messages', *Mirror* (June 2020), https://www.mirror.co.uk/news/politics/tory-students-face-race-probe-22158034

44. David Batty, 'Universities failing to address thousands of racist incidents', *Guardian* (Oct. 2019), https://www.theguardian.com/world/2019/oct/23/universities-failing-to-address-thousands-of-racist-incidents

2. CRADLE TO GRAVE

1. John Burn-Murdoch, 'Small towns left behind as exodus of youth to cities accelerates', *Financial Times* (Nov. 2017), https://www.ft.com/content/2312924c-ce02-11e7-b781-794ce08b24dc

2. Michael Savage, 'Brain drain of graduates to London leaves cities facing skills shortage', *Guardian* (Mar. 2018), theguardian.com/money/2018/mar/18/regions-london-brain-drain-graduates-metro-mayors

3. Ibid.

4. Richard Berry, 'London and the South East feature disproportionately in parliamentary CVs', *LSE Democratic Audit* (Aug. 2013), https://blogs.lse.ac.uk/democraticaudit/2013/08/08/london-and-the-south-east-feature-disproportionately-in-parliamentary-cvs/

5. David Goodhart, *Head, Hand, Heart: The Struggle for Dignity and Status in the 21st Century* (London: Penguin, 2021).

6. David Edgerton, *The Rise and Fall of the British Nation: A Twentieth-Century History* (London: Penguin, 2018).

7. Ibid.

8. 'TV Interview for London Weekend Television *Weekend World*', *Margaret Thatcher Foundation* (Jan. 1983).

9. James Ball, 'The Thatcher effect: what changed and what stayed the same', *Guardian* (Apr. 2013), https://www.theguardian.com/politics/2013/apr/12/thatcher-britain

10. Ibid.

11. Edgerton, op cit.

12. Ball, op cit.

13. Roch Dunin-Wasowicz, 'De-industrialisation rather than globalisation is the key part of the Brexit story', LSE Brexit (Apr. 2017), https://blogs.lse.ac.uk/brexit/2017/04/28/de-industrialisation-rather-than-globalisation-is-the-key-part-of-the-brexit-story/

14. Alan R. Townsend, 'The Urban-Rural Cycle in the Thatcher Growth Years', Royal Geographical Society (1993).

15. 'Historic economic data for regions of the UK (1966 to 1996)', Office for National Statistics (Oct. 2016), https://www.ons.gov.uk/economy/regionalaccounts/grossdisposablehouseholdincome/adhocs/006226historiceconomicdataforregionsoftheuk1966to1996

16. Ball, op cit.

17. Ibid.

18. 'Did Labour decimate manufacturing?', Full Fact (Mar. 2013), https://fullfact.org/economy/did-labour-decimate-manufacturing/

19. Gordon Brown, 'How to fix regional inequality', *Prospect* (Nov. 2016), https://www.prospectmagazine.co.uk/politics/regional-inequality-regions-nations-constitution

20. Phil Carradice, 'The birth of Barry Docks', BBC News (Nov. 2011), https://www.bbc.co.uk/blogs/wales/entries/e2ab2169-5cbd-3fae-a049-d7bd37ba501a

21. Travers Merrill and Lucy Kitson, 'The End of Coal Mining in South Wales: Lessons learned from industrial transformation', International Institute for Sustainable Development (May 2017), https://www.iisd.org/system/files/publications/end-of-coal-mining-south-wales-lessons-learned.pdf

22. Swansea Council, 'Swansea Economic Profile' (Apr. 2021), https://www.swansea.gov.uk/economicprofile

23. Welsh Government, 'Gross Disposable Household Income by area and measure', StatsWales (June 2020), https://statswales.gov.wales/Catalogue/Business-Economy-and-Labour-Market/Regional-Accounts/Household-Income

24. 'Income estimates for small areas, England and Wales: financial year ending 2018', Office for National Statistics (Mar. 2020), https://www.ons.gov.uk/employmentandlabourmarket/peopleinwork/earningsandworkinghours/datasets/smallareaincomeestimatesformiddlelayersuperoutputareasenglandandwales

25. Local Development Plan Team, 'Key data Port Talbot' (2009), https://www.npt.gov.uk/ldpexamination/LDP20%20Port%20 Talbot%20Key%20Data%20Paper%20(February%202009).pdf

26. Simon Usborne, 'The thinking outside the box: The Amazing world of online retail giant Amazon', *Independent* (Oct. 2013), https://www.independent.co.uk/news/uk/home-news/the-thinking-outside-the-box-the-amazing-world-of-online-retail-giant-amazon-8869562.html

27. 'Port Talbot Man Takes Charge at Amazon in Swansea', BusinessNewsWales (May 2019), https://businessnewswales.com/port-talbot-man-takes-charge-at-amazon-in-swansea/#:~: text=Amazon%20has%20announced%20a%20new,opened%20 its%20doors%20in%202008

28. 'Amazon set to hire 10,000 UK workers', BBC News (May 2021), https://www.bbc.co.uk/news/business-57109282#:~:text= Amazon%20is%20to%20hire%2010%2C000,confidence%20 in%20the%20British%20economy%22

29. James Bloodworth, *Hired: Undercover in Low-Wage Britain* (London: Atlantic Books, 2018).

30. George Orwell, *The Road to Wigan Pier* (London: Victor Gollancz, 1937), p.19.

31. Edgerton, Op. cit.

32. 'High streets in Great Britain: March, 2020', Office for National Statistics (Aug. 2020), https://www.ons.gov.uk/ peoplepopulationandcommunity/populationandmigration/ populationestimates/articles/highstreetsingreatbritain/march2020

33. Hilary Osborne and Sarah Butler, 'Death of the high street: how it feels to lose your job when a big chain closes', *Guardian* (Mar. 2019), https://www.theguardian.com/business/2019/mar/06/death-of-the-high-street-how-it-feels-to-lose-your-job-when-a-big-chain-closes

34. Elise Uberoi, Georgina Hutton, Matthew Ward, Elena Ares, 'UK Fisheries Statistics', House of Commons Library (Nov. 2020), https://commonslibrary.parliament.uk/research-briefings/sn02788/

35. Nick Statt, 'Amazon says fully automated shipping warehouses are at least a decade away', The Verge (May 2019), https://www. theverge.com/2019/5/1/18526092/amazon-warehouse-robotics-automation-ai-10-years-away

36. Rupert Neate, 'Amazon had sales income of €44bn in Europe in 2020 but paid no corporation tax', *Guardian* (May 2021), https:// www.theguardian.com/technology/2021/may/04/amazon-sales-income-europe-corporation-tax-luxembourg

37. Joseph Rowntree Foundation and UK in a Changing Europe, 'What do people want from Brexit?', UK in a Changing Europe (July 2019), https://ukandeu.ac.uk/wp-content/uploads/2019/07/

What-do-people-want-from-Brexit-full-report-JRF-and-UK-in-a-Changing-Europe.pdf

38. 'Annual region labour productivity', Office for National Statistics (July 2021), https://www.ons.gov.uk/economy/economicoutputandproductivity/productivitymeasures/datasets/annualregionallabourproductivity

39. Robert Zymek and Ben Jones, 'UK Regional Productivity Differences: An Evidence Review', Industrial Strategy Council (Feb. 2020), https://industrialstrategycouncil.org/sites/default/files/attachments/UK%20Regional%20Productivity%20Differences%20-%20An%20Evidence%20Review_0.pdf

40. 'Gross weekly earnings of full-time employees by region', Office for National Statistics (May 2021), https://www.ons.gov.uk/employmentandlabourmarket/peopleinwork/earningsandworkinghours/datasets/grossweeklyearningsoffulltimeemployeesbyregionearn05/current

41. Feargal McGuiness, 'Household incomes by region', House of Commons Library (Apr. 2018), https://commonslibrary.parliament.uk/authors/feargal-mcguinness/

42. Zymek and Jones, op cit.

43. Andy Pike, Danny MacKinnon, Mike Coombes, Tony Champion, David Bradley, Andrew Cumbers, Liz Robson and Colin Wymer, 'Uneven growth: Tackling city decline', Joseph Rowntree Foundation (Feb 2016), https://www.jrf.org.uk/report/uneven-growth-tackling-city-decline

44. Angela Monaghan, 'Seven things you need to know about the UK economy', *Guardian* (Apr. 2014), https://www.theguardian.com/business/economics-blog/2014/apr/24/uk-economy-seven-things-need-to-know-ons-g7

45. Scott Lavery, 'Public and private sector employment across the UK since the financial crisis', Sheffield Political Economy Research Institute (Feb. 2015), http://speri.dept.shef.ac.uk/wp-content/uploads/2018/11/Brief10-public-sector-employment-across-UK-since-financial-crisis.pdf

46. Ali Shalchi, Chris Rhodes and Georgina Hutton, 'Financial services: contribution to the UK economy', House of Commons Library (Feb. 2021).

47. 'Legal services' £60bn economic contribution must be heeded in Brexit talks', The Law Society (Jan. 2020)

48. 'UK legal sector shows strong growth driven by record exports, regions, nations and LawTech', TheCityUK (Jan. 2019), https://www.thecityuk.com/news/uk-legal-sector-shows-strong-growth-driven-by-record-exports-regions-nations-and-lawtech/

49. 'Top 200 UK Law Firms', Conscious, conscious.co.uk/site/our-clients/top-200-law-firms/

50. 'Unparalleled expertise in management consultancy', The Global City, https://www.theglobalcity.uk/management-consultancy

51. 'Brexit anxiety helps UK consulting market hit £11 billion', Consultancy.uk (Jan. 2020), https://www.consultancy.uk/news/23499/brexit-anxiety-helps-uk-consulting-market-hit-11-billion

52. Philip McCann, 'Perceptions of regional inequality and the geography of discontent: insights from the UK', *Regional Studies* liv (Jun 2019), https://www.tandfonline.com/doi/full/10.1080/00343404.2019.1619928

53. Phillip Inman, 'Number of Europe's poorest regions in UK "more than doubles"', *Guardian* (Dec. 2019), https://www.theguardian.com/business/2019/dec/10/number-of-europes-poorest-regions-in-uk-more-than-doubles

54. 'Joint Strategic Needs Assessment Blackpool' (Mar. 2020), https://www.blackpooljsna.org.uk/Home.aspx

55. Zymek and Jones, op cit.

56. The Foundational Economy Collective, *Foundational Economy: The Infrastructure of Everyday Life* (Manchester: Manchester University Press, 2018).

57. Niamh Foley, 'Public sector employment by parliamentary constituency', House of Commons Library (Dec. 2020), https://researchbriefings.files.parliament.uk/documents/SN05635/SN05635.pdf

58. Professor John Tomaney, 'Book Review: Foundational Economy: The Infrastructure of Everyday Life', *LSE Review of Books* (Sept. 2018), https://blogs.lse.ac.uk/lsereviewofbooks/2018/09/11/book-review-foundational-economy-the-infrastructure-of-everyday-life-by-the-foundational-economy-collective/

59. Colin Crouch, 'Foreword', in The Foundational Economy Collective, *Foundational Economy: The Infrastructure of Everyday Life* (Manchester: Manchester University Press, 2018).

60. Ali Shalchi, Chris Rhodes and Georgina Hutton, House of Commons Library.

61. Centre for Cities, 'Cities Outlook' (Jan. 2009), https://www.centreforcities.org/publication/cities-outlook-2009/

62. Ibid.

63. Ibid.

64. David Brindle, 'Public sector job cuts: is the tide finally turning?', *Guardian* (Sep. 2018), https://www.theguardian.com/society/2018/sep/03/years-austerity-tide-starting-turn-public-sector-job-cuts

65. Sarah Longlands, Carys Roberts, Jack Hunter and Rosie Lockwood, '1 in 4 North East Public Sector Jobs Lost Since

Austerity Began', IPPR North (June 2019), https://www.ippr.org/news-and-media/press-releases/ippr-north-1-in-4-north-east-public-sector-jobs-lost-since-austerity-began

66. 'Child poverty continues to rise as pandemic response falls short for families', Child Poverty Action Group (Mar. 2020), https://cpag.org.uk/news-blogs/news-listings/child-poverty-continues-rise-pandemic-response-falls-short-families

67. George Bangham, 'In this coronavirus crisis, do families have enough savings to make ends meet?', Resolution Foundation (April 2020), https://www.resolutionfoundation.org/comment/in-this-coronavirus-crisis-do-families-have-enough-savings-to-make-ends-meet/

68. Martin Williams, 'Finance industry wages rise faster than any other sector', *Guardian* (Feb. 2013), https://www.theguardian.com/careers/finance-industry-wages-earnings

69. 'Average weekly earnings by sector', Office for National Statistics (July 2021), https://www.ons.gov.uk/employmentandlabourmarket/peopleinwork/employmentandemployeetypes/bulletins/averageweeklyearningsingreatbritain/july2021

70. 'As it happened: Cameron's austerity speech', *The Times* (June 2010), https://www.thetimes.co.uk/article/as-it-happened-cameron-austerity-speech-wxjkcfttz2s

71. Juliette Jowit, 'Strivers v shirkers: the language of the welfare debate', *Guardian* (Jan. 2013), https://www.theguardian.com/politics/2013/jan/08/strivers-shirkers-language-welfare

72. Adam Bychawski, 'UK faces insecure job "crisis" as government plans to pull pandemic safety net away', openDemocracy (July 2021), https://www.opendemocracy.net/en/opendemocracyuk/uk-faces-insecure-job-crisis-as-government-plans-to-pull-pandemic-safety-net-away/

73. David Bol, 'Rishi Sunak defends Universal Credit cut on Scotland visit', *Herald* (July 2021), https://www.heraldscotland.com/politics/19478975.rishi-sunak-defends-universal-credit-cut-scotland-visit/

74. Dan Bloom, 'George Osborne defends his brutal Tory welfare cuts that are still driving families to food banks', *Mirror* (Oct. 2018), https://www.mirror.co.uk/news/politics/george-osborne-defends-brutal-tory-13510616

75. John Lubbock, 'UK's Outsourcing of COVID Response Has Cost More Than the GDP of 140 Countries', Byline Times (July 2021), https://bylinetimes.com/2021/07/12/uk-outsourcing-covid-response-has-cost-more-than-the-gdp-of-140-countries/

76. Sam Bright, Hardeep Matharu, Katie Tarrant, Max Colbert, Daisy Bata and Iain Overton, 'Mapping the Pandemic: £2 Billion in Contracts Awarded to Conservative Associates', Byline Times

(Mar. 2021), https://bylinetimes.com/2021/03/31/mapping-the-pandemic-contracts-to-conservative-associates/

77. Billy Kenber, 'Britain accused of blowing £400m in space race with Elon Musk', *The Times* (Dec. 2020), https://www.thetimes.co.uk/article/britain-accused-of-blowing-400m-in-space-race-with-elon-musk-0fzjcg52k

78. Colin Crouch, op cit.

79. Joanna Wardill, 'Campaigners welcome news that Northern's final Pacer train has been removed from service', *Yorkshire Post* (Nov. 2020), https://www.yorkshirepost.co.uk/news/people/campaigners-welcome-news-that-northerns-final-pacer-train-has-been-removed-from-service-3051541

80. Owen Hatherley, *Red Metropolis: Socialism and the Government of London* (London: Repeater Books, 2020).

81. 'New transport figures reveal North to receive "indefensible" £2,555 less per person than London', IPPR North (Jan. 2018).

82. Professor Sir Michael Marmot, 'Health Equity in England: The Marmot Review 10 Years On', The Health Foundation (Feb. 2020), https://www.health.org.uk/publications/reports/the-marmot-review-10-years-on

83. Deborah Mattinson, *Beyond the Red Wall: Why Labour Lost, How the Conservatives Won and What Will Happen Next?* (London: Biteback, 2020).

84. Sam Bright, 'The Runaway Train: Whistleblowers Accuse HS2 of "Concealing the Truth" Over Controversial Project's Costs', Byline Times (July 2021), https://bylinetimes.com/2021/07/22/the-runaway-train-whistleblowers-accuse-hs2-of-concealing-the-truth-over-controversial-projects-costs/

85. 'The Prime Minister's Levelling Up speech: 15 July 2021', Gov.uk (July 2021), https://www.gov.uk/government/speeches/the-prime-ministers-levelling-up-speech-15-july-2021

86. Andy Bounds, 'Pledge to level-up UK questioned after northern transport budget cuts', *Financial Times* (Jan. 2021), https://www.ft.com/content/2c22f6b7-a73a-411b-8b27-2b21db4006bc

87. Rachel Hall, 'The jobs aren't there: why graduates are leaving northern towns', *Guardian* (May 2019), https://www.theguardian.com/education/2019/may/16/the-jobs-arent-there-why-graduates-are-leaving-northern-towns

88. Peter Walker and Aubrey Allegretti, 'Sunak's £1bn of "town deals" will nearly all go to Tory constituencies', *Guardian* (Mar. 2021), https://www.theguardian.com/uk-news/2021/mar/03/sunaks-1bn-of-town-deals-will-nearly-all-go-to-tory-constituencies

89. Luke Raikes and Marcus Johns, 'The Northern Powerhouse: 5 years in', IPPR North (June 2019), https://www.ippr.org/blog/the-northern-powerhouse-5-years-in

90. Sam Bright, '"Levelling Up Fund" Gives £1.25 Billion to Areas that Have Lost £25.5 Billion', Byline Times (Oct. 2021), https://bylinetimes.com/2021/10/29/levelling-up-fund-gives-1-25-billion-to-areas-that-have-lost-25-5-billion/

91. Sam Bright, 'How the Red Wall Has Been Levelled Down Since 2010', Byline Times (Oct. 2021), https://bylinetimes.com/2021/10/27/how-the-red-wall-has-been-levelled-down-since-2010/

92. 'Brexit: Official forecasts suggest economies throughout UK will be hit', BBC News (Feb. 2018), https://www.bbc.co.uk/news/uk-politics-42977967

3. CAPITAL IN THE CAPITAL

1. Joel Golby, 'London Rental Opportunity of the Week', VICE, https://www.vice.com/en/topic/london-rental-opportunity-of-the-week

2. Joel Golby, 'It Costs $800 a Month to Live in a Box Inside a London Apartment', VICE (Sep. 2015), https://www.vice.com/en/article/3bjvpv/london-rental-opportunity-of-the-week-a-fucking-shed-a-shed-in-someones-front-room-987

3. Joel Golby, 'It's Finally Happened, a Space Literally Described as a "Harry Potter Room"', VICE (May 2016), https://www.vice.com/en/article/nnkmdg/london-rental-opportunity-of-the-week-its-finally-happened-finally-a-space-literally-described-as-a-harry-potter-room

4. Joel Golby, 'It is Never Going to Get Worse Than This, Truly, in Surrey Quays', VICE (Aug. 2017), https://www.vice.com/en/article/j55xep/london-rental-opportunity-of-the-week-it-is-never-going-to-get-worse-than-this-truly-in-surrey-quays

5. Joel Golby, 'A £750 Camp Bed in Penge!', VICE (Aug. 2018), https://www.vice.com/en/article/43pqkm/london-rental-opportunity-of-the-week-a-pound750-camp-bed-in-penge

6. Danny Dorling, Inequality and the 1% (London: Verso, 2014), 83–84.

7. Matt Padley, 'A Minimum Income Standard for London 2019', Centre for Research in Social Policy, Loughborough University (Feb. 2020), https://repository.lboro.ac.uk/articles/report/A_minimum_income_standard_for_London_2019/12199613

8. Julia Stuart, 'UK house prices', Trussle, https://trussle.com/mortgages/house-prices

9. Statista Research Department, 'Average house prices in London 2019–2020, by borough', Statista (Jun 2020).

10. 'House prices in Manchester', Zoopla, https://www.zoopla.co.uk/house-prices/manchester/

11. 'House Prices in Leeds', Rightmove, https://www.rightmove.co.uk/house-prices/leeds.html
12. 'House prices in Durham', Zoopla, https://www.zoopla.co.uk/house-prices/durham/
13. Industry Insight, 'London Property in 2030: The "Unaffordable Capital"', Arthur (May 2016), https://www.arthuronline.co.uk/blog/property-news/london-property-prices-2030/
14. Stuart, op cit.
15. Grace Gausden, 'How did house price inflation in the last decade compare to the 1980s, 1990s and 2000s?', This is Money (Jan. 2020), https://www.thisismoney.co.uk/money/mortgageshome/article-7864489/How-did-house-price-inflation-2010s-compare.html
16. Anna Minton, *Big Capital: Who is London For?* (London: Penguin Books, 2017).
17. 'Homes without residents', Action on Empty Homes (June 2019).
18. Brigid Francis-Devine, 'Poverty in the UK: statistics', House of Commons Library (Mar. 2021), https://commonslibrary.parliament.uk/research-briefings/sn07096/
19. 'English Private Landlord Survey 2018', Ministry of Housing, Communities and Local Government (Jan. 2019), https://www.gov.uk/government/publications/english-private-landlord-survey-2018-main-report
20. 'Homes without residents', Action on Empty Homes.
21. Marc Da Silva, 'The proportion of income spent on rent drops despite increases in rental level', Landlord Today (Jan. 2020), https://www.landlordtoday.co.uk/breaking-news/2020/1/the-proportion-of-income-spent-on-rent-drops-despite-increases-in-rental-level
22. 'Homes without residents', op cit.
23. Ibid.
24. Anna Minton, op cit.
25. Margaret Thatcher, 'Leader's speech, Blackpool 1975', BritishPoliticalSpeech, http://www.britishpoliticalspeech.org/speech-archive.htm?speech=121
26. Martin Williams, 'A quarter of Tory MPs are private landlords', openDemocracy (July 2021), https://www.opendemocracy.net/en/dark-money-investigations/quarter-tory-mps-are-private-landlords/
27. Dorling, op cit.
28. Carl Cullinane and Rebecca Montacute, 'Pay as you go? Internship pay, quality and access in the graduate jobs market', Sutton Trust (Nov. 2018), https://www.suttontrust.com/wp-content/uploads/2019/12/Pay-As-You-Go-1.pdf
29. Ibid.

30. Sarah Butler, 'Initiative to crack down on unpaid internships launched in the UK', *Guardian* (Feb. 2018), https://www.theguardian.com/society/2018/feb/08/initiative-to-crack-down-on-unpaid-internships-launched-in-the-uk

31. Paul Johnson, 'A bad time to graduate', Institute for Fiscal Studies (Apr. 2020), https://ifs.org.uk/publications/14816

32. Anna Bawden, 'Almost two-thirds of people who lost jobs in UK pandemic are under 25', *Guardian* (Mar. 2021), https://www.theguardian.com/society/2021/mar/23/almost-two-thirds-of-people-who-lost-jobs-in-uk-pandemic-are-under-25

33. Johnson, op cit.

34. Jack Peat, 'Graduate jobs drop by 60.3% since last year', London Economic (Aug. 2020).

35. 'English higher education 2020: The Office for Students annual review', Office for Students (Dec. 2020), https://www.officeforstudents.org.uk/annual-review-2020/

36. Helen Crane, 'Here's where you should buy a home for access to the best London schools', City AM (Aug. 2019), https://www.cityam.com/heres-where-you-should-buy-a-home-for-access-to-the-best-london-schools/

37. Kate Hughes, 'Quarter of UK parents move house for the school catchment area', *Independent* (Aug. 2017), https://www.independent.co.uk/money/spend-save/uk-parents-move-house-school-catchment-area-quarter-best-education-a7908046.html

38. Crane, op cit.

39. Ibid.

40. Steve Gibbons, 'The link between schools and house prices is now an established fact', LSE British Politics and Policy (Sep. 2012), https://blogs.lse.ac.uk/politicsandpolicy/school-house-prices-gibbons/

41. Hughes, op cit.

42. 'How to run the bank of mum and dad … The definitive guide', Family Building Society, https://www.familybuildingsociety.co.uk/tips-and-guides/bank-of-mum-and-dad-research-and-guides

43. Kath Scanlon, Fanny Blanc, Annie Edge and Christine Whitehead, 'The Bank of Mum and Dad: How it *really* works', Family Building Society and LSE (Jan. 2019), https://www.lse.ac.uk/business/consulting/reports/the-bank-of-mum-and-dad-how-it-really-works

44. Ibid.

45. Chihiro Udagawa and Dr Paul Sanderson, 'The impacts of family support on access to homeownership for young people in the UK', Social Mobility Commission (Mar. 2017), https://assets.publishing.service.gov.uk/government/uploads/system/uploads/attachment_data/file/602541/Impact_of_family_support_on_homeownership.pdf

46. 'The Politics of Housing', Social Market Foundation (Nov. 2013), https://www.smf.co.uk/publications/the-politics-of-housing/

47. Udagawa and Sanderson, op cit.

48. 'Over 50s hold 75% of housing wealth, a total of £2.8 trillion', Savills (Apr. 2018), https://www.savills.co.uk/insight-and-opinion/savills-news/239639-0/over-50s-hold-75--of-housing-wealth--a-total-of-%C2%A32.8-trillion-(%C2%A32-800-000-000-000)

49. 'The Fund', Norges Bank Investment Management, https://www.nbim.no/

50. Rupert Neate, 'Covid led to huge London property exodus, says Hamptons', *Guardian* (Dec. 2020), https://www.theguardian.com/business/2020/dec/26/covid-led-to-huge-london-property-exodus-says-hamptons

51. Callum Jones and Louisa Clarence-Smith, 'Capita plans to shut offices as staff work for home', *The Times* (Aug. 2020), https://www.thetimes.co.uk/article/capita-plans-to-shut-offices-as-staff-work-from-home-9xvfttmh5

52. Louise Eccles, 'Home-working during Olympics is "skiver's paradise" says Boris as he ignores Government's message to avoid traffic chaos', *Daily Mail* (July 2012), https://www.dailymail.co.uk/news/article-2168493/Boris-Johnson-Home-working-London-2012-Olympics-skivers-paradise.html

53. Jones and Clarence-Smith, op cit.

54. 'Average UK house price surges by 8.5% to hit record high in December', *Sky News* (Feb. 2021), https://news.sky.com/story/average-uk-house-price-surges-by-8-5-to-hit-record-high-in-december-12220686

55. 'Towns with the biggest house price rises in 2020 revealed', Sky News (Dec. 2020), https://news.sky.com/story/towns-with-the-biggest-house-price-rises-in-2020-revealed-12174576

56. Rupert Jones, 'Private rents fall in UK's biggest cities by up to 12% amid Covid crisis', *Guardian* (Jan. 2021), https://www.theguardian.com/money/2021/jan/27/private-rents-fall-in-uks-biggest-cities-by-up-to-12-amid-covid-crisis

57. Monica Costa Dias, Christine Farquharson, Rachel Griffith, Robert Joyce, and Peter Levell, 'Getting people back into work', Institute for Fiscal Studies (May 2020), https://ifs.org.uk/publications/14851

58. 'New lease of life: young renters lured back to the heart of London', *Financial Times* (Apr. 2021), https://www.ft.com/content/84b5183e-53fd-4326-8797-6274ece49f06

59. Rachael Kennedy, 'COVID-19: Is work from home here to stay? What UK businesses are planning post-lockdown', Sky News (Feb 2021), https://news.sky.com/story/covid-19-is-work-from-home-

here-to-stay-what-uk-businesses-are-planning-post-lockdown-12226622

60. Rupert Neate, 'Covid led to huge London property exodus, says Hamptons', *Guardian* (Dec. 2020), https://www.theguardian.com/business/2020/dec/26/covid-led-to-huge-london-property-exodus-says-hamptons

61. 'House Price Affordability Index 2019/20', Open Property Group, https://www.openpropertygroup.com/guides/house-price-affordability-index-2019-2020/

62. Neate, op cit.

63. Mark Magill, Claire Miller and Jeff Raines, 'Cornwall housing crisis: Figures confirm everyone is moving to Cornwall – and where from', CornwallLive (July 2021).

64. Gavin Knight, 'English out: Cornwall's fightback against second homes', *Guardian* (May 2016), https://www.theguardian.com/uk-news/2016/may/31/cornwall-fightback-second-homes-house-prices-ban

65. Tom Wall, 'Tensions rise in Bath as influx of Londoners prices out local families', *Guardian* (Sep. 2018). https://www.theguardian.com/society/2018/sep/02/tensions-rise-in-bath-exodus-of-londoners-prices-out-local-families

66. 'How St Ives' crackdown on rich Londoners buying second homes has removed demand and sent house prices plunging', iNews (July 2019), https://inews.co.uk/news/uk/st-ives-cornwall-londoners-second-homes-demand-house-prices-the-economist-316397

67. 'Sun, surf, flat whites and Rolls-Royces – Cornwall's frenzied housing market', *Financial Times* (May 2021), https://www.ft.com/content/b08b377f-5d77-4bc3-8116-be58b8e1090e

68. 'Owners of holiday lets in Cornwall claim £80m of government coronavirus grants', ITV (Apr. 2020), https://www.itv.com/news/westcountry/2020-04-27/owners-of-holiday-lets-in-cornwall-have-claimed-50m-of-government-coronavirus-grants

69. 'New lease of life', *Financial Times*, op cit.

70. Mayor of London, 'Housing in London: 2019: The evidence base for the Mayor's Housing Strategy', Greater London Authority (Sep. 2019), https://data.london.gov.uk/dataset/housing-london

71. 'Home ownership', Gov.uk (Feb. 2020), https://www.ethnicity-facts-figures.service.gov.uk/housing/owning-and-renting/home-ownership/latest

72. Mayor of London, op cit.

73. 'Malaysian investors complete acquisition of Battersea Power Station's commercial assets', Propertyfundsworld (Mar. 2019), https://www.propertyfundsworld.com/2019/03/15/274023/malaysian-investors-complete-acquisition-battersea-power-stations-commercial

74. Simon Jenkins, 'London is the wild west of the global property market – and it needs a sheriff', *Guardian* (Oct. 2020), https://www.theguardian.com/commentisfree/2020/oct/23/london-global-property-market-overseas-tycoons-apartments-empty
75. Minton, op cit.
76. Jack Peat, 'Almost £11 billion-worth of London housing is sitting empty', London Economic (Oct. 2019), https://www.thelondoneconomic.com/property/almost-11-billion-worth-of-london-housing-is-sitting-empty-165592/
77. 'About Homelessness', Streets of London, http://www.streetsoflondon.org.uk/about-homelessness#:~:text=More%20than%2011%2C000%20people%20sleep,from%20the%20rest%20of%20us
78. Martine Berg Olsen, 'There's been a 165% increase in homelessness since the Tories took power', *Metro* (Jan. 2019), https://metro.co.uk/2019/01/31/165-increase-homelessness-since-tories-took-power-8419274/
79. 'Homes without residents', Action on Empty Homes.
80. Owen Hatherley, *Red Metropolis: Socialism and the Government of London* (London: Repeater Books, 2020).
81. Caroline Davies, 'Baby girl was found dead in mother's arms in Grenfell Tower stairwell', *Guardian* (June 2017), https://www.theguardian.com/uk-news/2017/jun/28/baby-found-dead-mothers-arms-grenfell-tower
82. Roisin O'Connor, 'Akala on the Grenfell Tower fire: "These people died because they were poor"', *Independent* (June 2017).
83. 'Kensington and Chelsea', Public Health England (Sep. 2016).
84. Rajeez Syal and Harrison Jones, 'Kensington and Chelsea council has £274m in reserves', *Guardian* (June 2017), https://www.theguardian.com/uk-news/2017/jun/19/kensington-chelsea-council-has-274m-in-reserves-grenfell-tower-budget-surplus
85. 'London's Poverty Profile 2020', *Trust for London* and *WPI Economics* (Apr. 2020).
86. Ibid.
87. Ibid.
88. Ibid.
89. Sarthak Agrawal and David Phillips, 'Catching up or falling behind? Geographical inequalities in the UK and how they have changed in recent years', Institute for Fiscal Studies (Aug. 2020), https://ifs.org.uk/publications/14969
90. Akala, *Natives: Race and Class in the Ruins of Empire* (London: Two Roads, 2018).
91. Aamna Mohdin, 'Nearly a million more young adults now live with parents – study', *Guardian* (Feb. 2019), https://www.

theguardian.com/society/2019/feb/08/million-more-young-adults-live-parents-uk-housing

92. Ryan Bassil, 'The Grim Reality of Renting in London With No Safety Net', VICE (June 2020), https://www.vice.com/en/article/889gxa/the-grim-reality-of-renting-in-london-with-no-safety-net

4. LEFT BEHIND?

1. Owen Hatherley, *Red Metropolis: Socialism and the Government of London* (London: Repeater Books, 2020).

2. 'How Labour's most rebellious member went from being an outsider to its newest leader', Business Insider (July 2021), https://www.businessinsider.in/politics/how-labours-most-rebellious-member-went-from-being-an-outsider-to-its-newest-leader/slidelist/48963467.cms#slideid=48963468

3. 'Jeremy Corbyn's speech to Annual Conference 2016', Labour Policy Forum (Sep. 2016), https://www.policyforum.labour.org.uk/news/jeremy-corbyn-s-speech-to-annual-conference-2016

4. 'It's time for real change: The Labour Party Manifesto 2019', Labour Party (Nov. 2019), https://labour.org.uk/wp-content/uploads/2019/11/Real-Change-Labour-Manifesto-2019.pdf

5. 'Mission Statement', Peace and Justice Project, https://thecorbynproject.com/

6. Owen Jones, 'The north-south divide is a myth – and a distraction', *Guardian* (May 2014), https://www.theguardian.com/commentisfree/2014/may/04/north-south-divide-myth-distraction

7. 'Ethnicity facts and figures: Unemployment', Gov.uk (Jan. 2021), https://www.ethnicity-facts-figures.service.gov.uk/work-pay-and-benefits/unemployment-and-economic-inactivity/unemployment/latest

8. Jane Coaston, 'The intersectionality wars', Vox (May 2019), https://www.vox.com/the-highlight/2019/5/20/18542843/intersectionality-conservatism-law-race-gender-discrimination

9. Aditya Chakrabortty and Jessica Elgot, 'Leak reveals Labour plan to focus on flag and patriotism to win back voters', *Guardian* (Feb. 2021), https://www.theguardian.com/politics/2021/feb/02/labour-urged-to-focus-on-flag-and-patriotism-to-win-voters-trust-leak-reveals

10. Sam Bright, 'Brexit to Blame for Driver Shortages, Voters Say', Byline Times (Oct. 2021), https://bylinetimes.com/2021/10/06/brexit-is-to-blame-for-lorry-driver-shortages-voters-say/

11. Dani Rodrik, 'The great globalisation lie', *Prospect* (Dec. 2017), https://www.prospectmagazine.co.uk/magazine/the-great-globalisation-lie-economics-finance-trump-brexit

12. Deborah Mattinson, *Beyond the Red Wall: Why Labour Lost, How the Conservatives Won and What Will Happen Next?* (London: Biteback, 2020), 28.
13. Claire Ainsley, *The New Working Class: How to Win Hearts, Minds and Votes* (Cambridge: Polity Press, 2018), 88.
14. Ibid.
15. Tobias Phibbs, 'Labour Country: How to rebuild the connection with rural voters', Fabian Society (Mar. 2018), https://fabians.org.uk/wp-content/uploads/2018/03/FABJ6015-Rural-Labour-Report-180320-WEB.pdf
16. Adrian Pabst, 'Introduction: Blue Labour and the Politics of the Common Good', in Ian Geary and Adrian Pabst (eds), *Blue Labour: Forging a New Politics* (London: IB Tauris, 2015), 1–13.
17. Paul Embery, *Despised: Why the Modern Left Loathes the Working Class* (Cambridge: Polity Press, 2021).
18. Jon Bloomfield, 'Progressive Politics in a Changing World: Challenging the Fallacies of Blue Labour', *Political Quarterly*, 91:1 (2019), 89–97.
19. 'Andy Burnham: "End the London-centric Labour Party"', BBC News (May 2021), https://www.bbc.co.uk/news/av/uk-politics-57041672
20. 'MPs and Lords: London', UK Parliament, https://members.parliament.uk/
21. 'Election Review 2019', Labour Together (Jun. 2020), https://www.labourtogether.uk/review
22. Maria Sobolewska and Robert Ford, *Brexitland: Identity, Diversity and the Reshaping of British Politics* (Cambridge: Cambridge University Press, 2020), 200.
23. Ibid.
24. Phibbs, op cit.
25. Tim Bale, Paul Webb and Monica Poletti, 'Grassroots: Britain's party members: who they are, what they think, and what they do', Mile End Institute, Queen Mary University of London (Jan. 2018), https://esrcpartymembersprojectorg.files.wordpress.com/2018/01/grassroots-pmp_final.pdf
26. Ibid.
27. Ibid.
28. Bobby Duffy, Kirstie Hewlett, Rachel Hesketh, Rebecca Benson, and Alan Wager, 'Unequal Britain: Attitudes to inequalities after Covid-19', King's College London (Feb. 2021), https://www.kcl.ac.uk/policy-institute/assets/unequal-britain.pdf
29. Ibid.
30. Ibid.
31. Carole Cadwalladr, 'The great British Brexit robbery: how our democracy was hijacked', *Guardian* (May 2017), https://www.

theguardian.com/technology/2017/may/07/the-great-british-brexit-robbery-hijacked-democracy

32. Owen Polley, 'Let's drop our obsession with America and stop importing its problems', The Article (Nov. 2017), https://www.thearticle.com/lets-drop-our-obsession-with-america-and-stop-importing-its-problems

33. William H. Frey, 'The US will become "minority white" in 2045, Census projects', Brookings (Mar. 2018), https://www.brookings.edu/blog/the-avenue/2018/03/14/the-us-will-become-minority-white-in-2045-census-projects/#:~:text=The%20new%20statistics%20project%20that,populations%20(see%20Figure%201)

34. 'Ethnicity and National Identity in England and Wales: 2011', Office for National Statistics (Dec. 2012), https://www.ons.gov.uk/peoplepopulationandcommunity/culturalidentity/ethnicity/articles/ethnicityandnationalidentityinenglandandwales/2012-12-11

35. 'Population of the UK by country of birth and nationality: July 2018 to June 2019', Office for National Statistics (Nov. 2019), https://www.ons.gov.uk/peoplepopulationandcommunity/populationandmigration/internationalmigration/bulletins/ukpopulationbycountryofbirthandnationality/july2018tojune2019

36. 'Ethnicity facts and figures: Regional ethnic diversity', Gov.uk (Aug. 2018), https://www.ethnicity-facts-figures.service.gov.uk/uk-population-by-ethnicity/national-and-regional-populations/regional-ethnic-diversity/latest

37. 'Racially and religiously-motivated hate crime hits a new high in 2020, Home Office statistics reveal', Sky News (July 2021), https://news.sky.com/story/racially-and-religiously-motivated-hate-crime-hit-a-new-high-in-2020-home-office-statistics-reveal-12356632

38. Statista Research Department, 'People shot to death by US police, by race 2017-2021', Statista (Aug. 2021).

5. RED WALL

1. James Kanagasooriam, 'How the Labour party's "red wall" turned blue', Financial Times (Dec. 2019), https://www.ft.com/content/3b80b2de-1dc2-11ea-81f0-0c253907d3e0

2. Deborah Mattinson, Beyond the Red Wall: Why Labour Lost, How the Conservatives Won and What Will Happen Next? (London: Biteback, 2020).

3. Full methodological details and tables are available on the Omnisis website.

4. George Orwell, *The Lion and the Unicorn* (London: Secker & Warburg, 1941).
5. 'City factsheet: Leeds', Centre for Cities, https://www. centreforcities.org/city/leeds/
6. 'Wakefield State of the District: Population', Wakefield Observatory (2015)
7. 'City factsheet: Wakefield', Centre for Cities, https://www. centreforcities.org/city/wakefield/
8. 'UK votes to leave the EU', BBC News, https://www.bbc.co.uk/ news/politics/eu_referendum/results
9. 'Election Review 2019', Labour Together (Jun. 2020), https:// www.labourtogether.uk/review
10. Ibid.
11. 'Jeremy Corbyn approval rating', YouGov, https://yougov.co.uk/ topics/politics/trackers/jeremy-corbyn-approval-rating
12. 'Election Review 2019', Labour Together.
13. Ibid.
14. Ibid.
15. Ibid.
16. Lord Ashcroft, 'A reminder of how Britain in the EU referendum – and why', Lord Ashcroft Polls (Mar. 2019), https:// lordashcroftpolls. com/2019/03/a-reminder-of-how-britain-voted-in-the-eu-referendum-and-why/
17. Centre for Towns, Twitter (Apr. 2021).
18. Matthew Goodwin and Oliver Heath, 'Brexit vote explained: poverty, low skills and lack of opportunities', Joseph Rowntree Foundation, https://www.jrf.org.uk/report/brexit-vote-explained-poverty-low-skills-and-lack-opportunities
19. Tobias Phibbs, 'Labour Country: How to rebuild the connection with rural voters', Fabian Society (Mar. 2018), https://fabians.org. uk/wp-content/uploads/2018/03/FABJ6015-Rural-Labour-Report-180320-WEB.pdf
20. 'Election Review 2019', Labour Together.
21. Goodwin and Heath, op cit.
22. Maria Sobolewska and Robert Ford, *Brexitland: Identity, Diversity and the Reshaping of British Politics* (Cambridge: Cambridge University Press, 2020).
23. Ashcroft, Lord Ashcroft Polls, op cit.
24. Ibid.
25. 'Election Review 2019', Labour Together.
26. Ibid.
27. Mattison, op cit.
28. Ros Taylor, 'Brexit: how both sides of the political divide have co-opted the "left-behind" North to fuel their agendas', The

Conversation (June 2019), https://www.createstreetsfoundation.org.uk/wp-content/uploads/2021/09/8560_PS_Create_No_Place_Left_Behind_FINAL.pdf

29. 'Comfortable Leavers: The expectations and hopes of the overlooked Brexit voters', UK in a Changing Europe (Apr. 2021), https://ukandeu.ac.uk/research-papers/comfortable-leavers-the-expectations-and-hopes-of-the-overlooked-brexit-voters/

30. Mattinson, op cit.

31. 'Election Review 2019', Labour Together.

32. Peter Walker and Jessica Walker, 'Priti Patel looked at idea of sending asylum seekers to South Atlantic', *Guardian* (Sept. 2020), https://www.theguardian.com/politics/2020/sep/30/priti-patel-looked-at-idea-of-sending-asylum-seekers-to-south-atlantic

33. Sobolewska and Ford, op cit.

34. Ashcroft, Lord Ashcroft Polls, op cit.

35. 'British Social Attitudes survey: 37th Edition', NatCen Social Research (2020), https://www.bsa.natcen.ac.uk/latest-report/british-social-attitudes-37/fairness-and-justice-in-britain.aspx

36. Ibid.

37. Patrick English, 'Is the stereotypical image of "Red Wall" residents actually accurate?', YouGov (May 2021), https://yougov.co.uk/topics/politics/articles-reports/2021/05/17/stereotypical-image-red-wall-residents-accurate

38. Connor Ibbetson, 'Brits support new national lockdown', YouGov (Jan. 2021), https://yougov.co.uk/topics/politics/articles-reports/2021/01/05/brits-support-national-lockdown-jan-2021

39. Frederick Forsyth, 'How Labour Party has been overrun by dead-eyed communist fanatics', *Daily Express* (Sep. 2019), https://www.express.co.uk/comment/columnists/frederick-forsyth/1183172/Labour-party-communism-far-left-jeremy-corbyn

40. 'British Social Attitudes survey', op cit.

41. Ibid.

42. Ibid.

43. Ibid.

44. 'Election Review 2019', Labour Together, op cit.

45. Philip Gould, *The Unfinished Revolution: How New Labour changed British politics for ever* (London: Abacus, 1998), 48.

46. 'Boris Johnson's approval rating', YouGov, https://yougov.co.uk/topics/politics/trackers/boris-johnson-approval-rating

47. Clare Bambra, Hannah Davies and Luke Munford, 'COVID-19 and the north-south health divide', Royal College of Physicians (Apr. 2021), https://www.rcplondon.ac.uk/news/covid-19-and-north-south-health-divide

48. Patrick Butler, 'Jaw-dropping fall in life expectancy in poor areas of England, report finds', *Guardian* (June 2021), https://www.

theguardian.com/uk-news/2021/jun/30/life-expectancy-key-to-success-of-levelling-up-in-uks-poorer-areas-covid-pandemic

49. Public Health England, 'COVID-19 confirmed deaths in England (to 30 June 2021): report', Gov.uk (Aug. 2021), https://www.gov.uk/government/publications/covid-19-reported-sars-cov-2-deaths-in-england/covid-19-confirmed-deaths-in-england-to-30-june-2021-report

50. 'Disparities in the risk and outcomes of COVID-19', Public Health England (Aug. 2020), https://assets.publishing.service.gov.uk/government/uploads/system/uploads/attachment_data/file/908434/Disparities_in_the_risk_and_outcomes_of_COVID_August_2020_update.pdf

51. Like Munford, Clare Bambra et al, 'COVID-19 and the Northern Powerhouse: Tackling inequalities for UK health and productivity', Northern Health Science Alliance (Nov. 2020), https://www.thenhsa.co.uk/app/uploads/2020/11/NP-COVID-REPORT-101120-.pdf

52. 'Disparities in the risk and outcomes of COVID-19', Public Health England, op cit.

53. Helen Pidd, 'Covid deepens south and north of England inequalities, study finds', *Guardian* (Dec. 2020), https://www.theguardian.com/inequality/2020/dec/07/covid-deepens-south-and-north-of-england-inequalities-study-finds

54. Lucy Harley-McKeown and Oscar Williams-Grut, 'London now unemployment capital of UK as jobless rate hits 7.2%', Yahoo News (Apr. 2021), https://consent.yahoo.com/v2/collectConsent?sessionId=3_cc-session_45a9e4b1-457b-4890-a9e3-9466746dedc8

55. Munford, Bambra et al, op cit.

56. Ibid.

57. Ibid.

58. Sir Michael Marmot, 'Health Equity in England: The Marmot Review 10 Years On', The Health Foundation (Feb. 2020), https://www.instituteofhealthequity.org/about-us/the-institute-of-health-equity/our-current-work/collaborating-with-the-health-foundation-#:~:text=UK%20life%20expectancy%20stalled%20at,health%20inequalities%20(health%20inequities)

59. Ibid.

60. Munford, Bambra et al, op cit.

61. 'Healthy life expectancy', Lancashire County Council, https://www.lancashire.gov.uk/lancashire-insight/health-and-care/health/health-inequalities/healthy-life-expectancy/#:~:text=Healthy%20life%20expectancy%20(HLE)%20at,also%20one%20of%20the%20lowest.

62. 'Life Expectancy', Blackpool Joint Strategic Needs Assessment (June 2021), https://www.blackpooljsna.org.uk/Home.aspx

63. 'Health state life expectancies, UK: 2016 to 2018', Office for National Statistics (Dec. 2019), https://www.ons.gov.uk/releases/healthstatelifeexpectanciesuk2016to2018

64. 'Life expectancy by London borough', Trust for London, https://www.trustforlondon.org.uk/data/life-expectancy-borough/#:~:text=Healthy%20life%20expectancy%20for%20women,to%20the%20COVID%2D19%20pandemic

65. 'Life expectancy falling in parts of England before pandemic – study', BBC News (Oct. 2021), https://www.bbc.co.uk/news/uk-58893328

66. Bambra, Davies and Munford, op cit.

67. Marmot, op cit.

68. Ibid.

69. Ibid.

70. 'Full text of David Cameron's speech', *Guardian* (Oct. 2009), https://www.theguardian.com/politics/2009/oct/08/david-cameron-speech-in-full

71. Marmot, op cit.

72. Jake Tacchi, 'An Unequal Kingdom: 12 Graphs that Show We Were Never "In This Together"', Byline Times (July 2021), https://bylinetimes.com/2021/07/21/an-unequal-kingdom-12-graphs-that-show-how-we-were-never-in-this-together/

73. Marmot, op cit.

74. Luke Raikes, 'The Devolution Parliament: Devolving power to England's regions, towns and cities', IPPR (Feb. 2020), https://www.ippr.org/research/publications/the-devolution-parliament

75. Sam Bright, 'Healthy Life Expectancy has Fallen in 80% of Red Wall Areas Since Conservatives Took Power', Byline Times (Oct. 2021), https://bylinetimes.com/2021/10/15/healthy-life-expectancy-has-fallen-in-80-of-red-wall-areas-since-conservatives-took-power/

6. THE FOURTH ESTATE

1. 'Elitist Britain 2019: The educational backgrounds of Britain's leading people', The Sutton Trust and Social Mobility Commission (June 2019), https://www.suttontrust.com/our-research/elitist-britain-2019/

2. Caitlin Saunders, 'There's nothing normal about the Oxbridge 1%', The Cambridge Student (Aug. 2014), https://www.tcs.cam.ac.uk/there-s-nothing-normal-about-the-oxbridge-1/

3. 'Elitist Britain 2019', op cit.

4. Mark Spilsbury, 'Diversity in Journalism', National Council for the Training of Journalists (Nov. 2017), https://www.nctj.com/downloadlibrary/DIVERSITY%20JOURNALISM%204WEB.pdf

5. Albert Scardino, 'After Years of Swimming, Newspapers Tread Water', *New York Times* (Nov. 1988).

6. Matthew Yglesias, 'Newspaper print ad revenue has declined 73% in 15 years', Vox (Apr. 2014), https://www.vox.com/2014/4/28/5661250/newspaper-print-ad-revenue-has-declined-73-in-15-years

7. 'UK journalism jobs decline steeply over last decade', *New Statesman* (Sep. 2010).

8. Freddy Mayhew and William Turvill, 'More than 2,000 newspaper jobs hit as hundreds of publications across UK face Covid-19 cuts', PressGazette (Apr. 2020), https://pressgazette.co.uk/more-than-2000-newspaper-jobs-hit-as-hundreds-of-publications-across-uk-face-covid-19-cuts/

9. 'BBC announces latest job cuts and 400 roles to leave London', National Union of Journalists (Mar. 2021), https://www.nuj.org.uk/resource/bbc-announces-further-job-cuts-and-500-roles-to-leave-london.html

10. Jess Commons, 'Here's What You Can Rent Around The UK For £1,250', Refinery29 (Nov. 2017), https://www.refinery29.com/en-gb/rent-around-the-uk

11. Andy Beckett, 'How London became a Labour city – and what it means for British politics', *Guardian* (May 2016), https://www.theguardian.com/politics/2016/may/11/how-london-became-a-labour-city-and-what-it-means-for-british-politics

12. John Woodhouse and Yago Zayed, 'TV license fee statistics', House of Commons Library (Jan. 2021), https://commonslibrary.parliament.uk/research-briefings/cbp-8101/

13. Jim Waterson, 'Guardian broke even last year, parent company confirms', *Guardian* (Aug. 2019), https://www.theguardian.com/media/2019/aug/07/guardian-broke-even-last-year-parent-company-confirms#:~:text=The%20Guardian's%20parent%20company%20has,and%20increased%20contributions%20from%20readers

14. June Sarpong, 'BBC Creative Diversity Report', BBC (2020), http://downloads.bbc.co.uk/aboutthebbc/reports/reports/creative-diversity-report-2020.pdf

15. 'BBC Equality Information Report 2017/18', BBC (2018), https://www.bbc.co.uk/diversity/strategy-and-reports/equality-information-report-2018

16. 'BBC Group Annual Report and Accounts 2020/21', BBC (2021), https://downloads.bbc.co.uk/aboutthebbc/reports/annualreport/2020-21.pdf

17. Bashirat Oladele, 'Capturing The Beauty Of Black British Life Outside London', Refinery29 (Aug. 2021), https://www.refinery29.com/en-gb/instagram-photos-capturing-black-british-life

18. 'BBC publishes blueprint for the biggest transformation in decades', BBC (March 2021), https://www.bbc.co.uk/mediacentre/2021/across-the-uk

19. Dean Kirby, 'BBC move from London to Salford had "little positive impact" on jobs', iNews (Aug. 2017), https://inews.co.uk/news/bbc-move-london-salford-little-positive-impact-jobs-83990

20. Stephen Chapman, 'BBC and councils reject "flawed" report into MediaCityUK's impact', Prolific North (Aug. 2017), https://www.prolificnorth.co.uk/broadcasting/digital/2017/08/bbc-and-councils-reject-%E2%80%9Cflawed%E2%80%9D-report-mediacityuk%E2%80%99s-impact

21. Jim Waterson, 'No top Channel 4 bosses will move to Leeds HQ', *Guardian* (June 2019), https://www.theguardian.com/media/2019/jun/11/no-top-channel-4-bosses-will-move-to-leeds-hq#:~:text=No%20senior%20Channel%204%20executives,quit%20rather%20than%20leave%20London

22. John Mair, 'Have we heard the last of labour correspondents?', BBC (Jan. 2011), https://www.bbc.co.uk/blogs/collegeofjournalism/entries/747059e4-22e4-3488-ab92-377a6f7639a6

23. Peter Preston, 'The gates have closed for good on the industrial correspondent', *Guardian* (Mar. 2011), https://www.theguardian.com/media/2011/mar/27/gates-close-industrial-correspondent?CMP=gu_com

24. Anonymous hack, 'From feral beasts to pussycats', *The Critic* (Feb. 2020), https://thecritic.co.uk/issues/february-2020/from-feral-beasts-to-pussycats/

25. James Ball, 'A modest proposal for 2019: scrap the parliamentary lobby', *Guardian* (Dec. 2018), https://www.theguardian.com/commentisfree/2018/dec/26/scrap-parliamentary-lobby-westminster-journalists

26. Stephen Bush, 'No, the UK has not "maxed out its credit card"', *New Statesman* (Nov. 2020), https://www.newstatesman.com/politics/the-staggers/2020/11/no-uk-has-not-maxed-out-its-credit-card

27. Robert Peston, 'Herd immunity will be vital to stopping coronavirus', *Spectator* (Mar. 2020), https://www.spectator.co.uk/article/Herd-immunity--will-be-vital-to-stopping-coronavirus

28. Robert Peston, 'British government wants UK to acquire coronavirus "herd immunity"', ITV (Mar. 2020), https://www.itv.com/news/2020-03-12/british-government-wants-uk-to-acquire-coronavirus-herd-immunity-writes-robert-peston

29. Toby Helm, 'Dominic Cummings claims ministers backed herd immunity against Covid', *Guardian* (May 2021), https://www.theguardian.com/politics/2021/may/22/dominic-cummings-claims-ministers-backed-herd-immunity-against-covid

30. Mark Sweney, 'UK advertisers pulled more than £1.1bn spend during Covid lockdown', *Guardian* (Aug. 2020), https://www. theguardian.com/media/2020/aug/04/uk-advertisers-spend-covid-lockdown-coronavirus

31. Mark Sweney and Jim Waterson, 'Evening Standard to cut one-third of staff as Covid-19 hits advertising', *Guardian* (Aug. 2020), https://www.theguardian.com/media/2020/aug/07/evening-standard-to-cut-115-jobs-as-covid-19-hits-advertising

32. Matthew Engel, 'The rise and fall of local newspapers', *New Statesman* (Dec. 2019), https://www.newstatesman.com/politics/2019/12/the-rise-and-fall-of-local-newspapers

33. Charlotte Tobitt, 'UK local newspaper closures: At least 265 titles gone since 2005, but pace of decline has slowed', PressGazette (Aug. 2020), https://pressgazette.co.uk/uk-local-newspaper-closures-at-least-265-local-newspaper-titles-gone-since-2005-but-pace-of-decline-has-slowed/

34. Tim Adams, 'Final editions: why no local news is bad news', *Guardian* (Sep. 2019), https://www.theguardian.com/media/2019/sep/29/local-newspapers-closing-down-communities-withering

35. Kurt Wagner, 'Digital advertising in the US is finally bigger than print and television', Vox (Feb. 2019), https://www.vox.com/2019/2/20/18232433/digital-advertising-facebook-google-growth-tv-print-emarketer-2019

36. David J. Moore, 'Identity crisis: Why Google and Facebook dominate digital advertising', Digital Content Next (May 2020), https://digitalcontentnext.org/blog/2020/05/19/identity-crisis-why-google-and-facebook-dominate-digital-advertising/

37. Dame Frances Cairncross, 'The Cairncross Review: A sustainable future for journalism', Gov.uk (Feb. 2019), https://www.gov.uk/government/publications/the-cairncross-review-a-sustainable-future-for-journalism

38. Ibid.

39. Ibid.

40. Ibid.

41. Jim Waterson, 'One in six jobs to go as BBC cuts 450 staff from regional programmes', *Guardian* (July 2020), https://www.theguardian.com/media/2020/jul/02/local-tv-stars-to-go-as-bbc-cuts-450-staff-from-regional-programmes

42. Caincross, op cit.

43. Freddy Mayhew, 'Covid-19 has prompted boom for TV news, dip in media trust worldwide and surge in misinformation – 2020 Digital News Report', PressGazette (June 2020), https://pressgazette.co.uk/covid-19-has-prompted-boom-for-tv-news-dip-in-media-trust-worldwide-and-surge-in-misinformation-2020-digital-news-report/

7. DEVOLUTION

1. 'Inside London's new "glass egg"', BBC (July 2002), http://news.bbc.co.uk/1/hi/uk/2129199.stm
2. Express KCS, 'Mayor's office sold in £1.7bn Kuwaiti deal', City A.M. (Dec. 2013).
3. T.G, 'Why Britain is copying America's "metro mayors"', Economist (Dec. 2015), https://www.economist.com/the-economist-explains/2015/12/18/why-britain-is-copying-americas-metro-mayors
4. Owen Hatherley, 'Mayors Are Blairite Nonsense and We Don't Need Them', Novara Media (Apr. 2021), https://novaramedia.com/2021/04/16/mayors-are-blairite-nonsense-and-we-dont-need-them/
5. Luke Raikes, 'The Devolution Parliament: Devolving powers to England's regions, towns and cities', IPPR North (Feb. 2020), https://www.ippr.org/research/publications/the-devolution-parliament
6. Tony Travers, 'Has devolution to City Hall benefited London and Londoners?', in Akash Paun and Sam Macrory (eds), Has Devolution Worked? The first 20 years, 71–81.
7. Peter Madeley, 'Andy who? Eight in 10 people don't know the identity of the West Midlands Mayor', Express and Star (Mar. 2020), https://www.expressandstar.com/news/politics/2020/03/13/andy-who-eight-in-10-people-dont-know-the-identity-of-the-west-midlands-mayor/
8. Mayor of London, 'London and the UK: A declaration of interdependence', Greater London Authority (Aug. 2019), https://www.london.gov.uk/business-and-economy-publications/london-and-uk-declaration-interdependence
9. Luke Raikes and Arianna Giovannini, 'The Devolution Parliament', IPPR (Nov. 2019), https://www.ippr.org/blog/the-devolution-parliament
10. Centre for Cities, 'Cities Outlook' (Jan. 2009), https://www.centreforcities.org/publication/cities-outlook-2009/
11. Raikes, IPPR North, op cit.
12. Ibid.
13. Nick Tyrrell, 'Calls to extend homelessness prevention pilot', Liverpool Echo (July 2021), https://www.liverpoolecho.co.uk/news/liverpool-news/calls-extend-homelessness-prevention-pilot-21159602
14. Charlie Jeffrey, Richard Wyn Jones, Ailsa Henderson, Roger Scully, and Guy Lodge, 'Taking England Seriously: The New English Politics', Centre on Constitutional Change (2014), https://

www.centreonconstitutionalchange.ac.uk/sites/default/files/
migrated/papers/taking_england_seriously.pdf

15. Raikes, IPPR North, op cit.

16. Niall Griffiths, 'The vast majority of Greater Manchester residents
want more powers for the mayor, according to new poll',
Manchester Evening News (Apr. 2021), https://www.
manchestereveningnews.co.uk/news/greater-manchester-news/vast-
majority-greater-manchester-residents-20343128

17. Andrew Bardsley, '"It's brutal to be honest" – Extraordinary
moment Andy Burnham learns of new coronavirus guidelines live
on TV', *Manchester Evening News* (Oct. 2020), https://www.
manchestereveningnews.co.uk/news/greater-manchester-news/andy-
burnham-coronavirus-tier-three-19137922

18. Raikes, IPPR North, op cit.

19. Jennifer Williams, 'Black-and-yellow buses, bike hire and a tram to
Middleton – Andy Burnham unveils his second term public
transport vision', *Manchester Evening News* (May 2021), https://
www.manchestereveningnews.co.uk/news/greater-manchester-
news/black-yellow-buses-bike-hire-20563149

20. Paul Swinney and Simon Jeffrey, 'Levelling up local government in
England', Centre for Cities (Sep. 2020), https://www.
centreforcities.org/publication/levelling-up-local-government-in-
england/

21. Ross Lydall, 'Sadiq Khan forced to hike congestion charge after
Government's Transport for London bail-out', *Evening Standard*
(May 2020), https://www.standard.co.uk/news/london/sadiq-khan-
congestion-charge-tfl-bailout-government-a4441361.html

22. Sarah Longlands and Anna Round, 'Why Devolution Matters: The
case of Cornwall', IPPR North (Mar. 2021), https://www.ippr.org/
publication/why-devolution-matters-the-case-of-cornwall

23. Raikes, IPPR North, op cit.

24. 'Foundational Economy', Business Wales, https://businesswales.
gov.wales/foundational-economy

25. Lee Waters, 'It's time to focus on the everyday economy', Institute
of Welsh Affairs (Jan. 2020), https://www.iwa.wales/
agenda/2020/01/its-time-to-focus-on-the-everyday-economy/

26. 'Why the foundational economy must be fair', Bevan Foundation
(May 2021), https://www.bevanfoundation.org/views/
foundational-economy-fair-work/

27. 'The Preston Model', Centre for Local Economic Strategies, https://
cles.org.uk/the-preston-model/

28. Gerald Holtham, 'Has devolution led to more effective government
in Wales? The case of the economy', in Akash Paun and Sam
Macrory (eds), *Has Devolution Worked? The first 20 years*, 57–70.

29. Ibid.

30. 'Foundational Economy', *Business Wales*, op cit.
31. Martin Shipton, 'Universal Basic Income pilot: Scotland concluded that the devolved administrations did not have the power to run a scheme', WalesOnline (May 2021), https://www.walesonline.co.uk/news/politics/universal-basic-income-pilot-scotland-20619622
32. Akash Paun and Bronwen Maddox, 'Overview: Has devolution worked', in Akash Paun and Sam Macrory (eds), *Has Devolution Worked? The first 20 years*, 7–18.
33. Emily Gray and Ben Page, 'Has devolution enhanced public trust in the political system?', in Akash Paun and Sam Macrory (eds), *Has Devolution Worked? The first 20 years*, 109–121.
34. Alex de Ruyter and David Hearne, 'Scottish devolution a "disaster"? Let's look at the data', The Conversation (Nov. 2020), https://theconversation.com/scottish-devolution-a-disaster-lets-look-at-the-data-150339
35. Liam Kirkaldy, 'How devolution changed Scotland', Holyrood (Feb. 2019), https://www.holyrood.com/inside-politics/view,how-devolution-changed-scotland_9936.htm
36. Clair Callender, 'Poorer students aren't applying to university because of fears of high debts', The Conversation (June 2017), https://theconversation.com/poorer-students-arent-applying-to-university-because-of-fears-of-high-debts-78694
37. Matthew Dunnigan, 'What has devolution meant for the NHS in Scotland and England?' Centre for Health and the Public Interest (Sep. 2014), https://chpi.org.uk/blog/devolution-meant-nhs-scotland-england/
38. 'Welsh NHS records worst ever A&E waiting times', ITV (Jan. 2020), https://www.itv.com/news/wales/2020-01-23/welsh-nhs-records-worst-ever-a-e-waiting-times
39. Carl Baker, 'NHS pressures in England: Waiting times, demand, and capacity', House of Commons Library (Dec. 2019).
40. Andy Bounds, 'Welsh government struggles to improve weak and fragmented NHS', *Financial Times* (Apr. 2021), https://www.ft.com/content/5a2e98bc-2b17-4460-812c-7348e1f2720c
41. Linda Christie, Ken Gibb, Alan McGregor, and Alex McTier, 'Economic Regeneration in Scotland: Past Lessons; Current Practice; Future Challenges', What Works Scotland (Aug. 2017), http://whatworksscotland.ac.uk/wp-content/uploads/2017/08/WWSEconomicRegenerationinScotlandLessonsPractice Challenges.pdf

8. RUST BELTS

1. Sathnam Sanghera, *Empireland: How Imperialism Has Shaped Modern Britain* (London: Viking, 2021), 182–3.
2. 'OECD Regions and Cities at a Glance', OECD iLibrary (Nov. 2020), https://www.oecd-ilibrary.org/urban-rural-and-regional-development/oecd-regions-and-cities-at-a-glance_26173212#:~:text=OECD%20Regions%20and%20Cities%20at%20a%20Glance%202020,more%20resilient%20economies%20and%20societies
3. Ibid.
4. Ibid.
5. Ibid.
6. Philip McCann, 'Perceptions of regional inequality and the geography of discontent: insights from the UK', *Regional Studies* liv (Jun 2019).
7. 'OECD Regions and Cities at a Glance', op cit.
8. McCann, op cit.
9. 'OECD Regional and Cities at a Glance 2018 – United Kingdom', OECD (Mar. 2019), https://www.oecd.org/cfe/UNITED-KINGDOM-Regions-and-Cities-2018.pdf
10. 'OECD Regions and Cities at a Glance', op cit.
11. 'OECD Regional Outlook 2016 – United Kingdom', OECD (2016), https://www.oecd-ilibrary.org/urban-rural-and-regional-development/oecd-regional-outlook-2016/regional-outlook-2016-united-kingdom_9789264260245-graph91-en
12. 'OECD Regional and Cities at a Glance 2018', op cit.
13. Ibid.
14. 'OECD Regions and Cities at a Glance', op cit.
15. 'Regional and subregional productivity comparisons, UK and selected EU countries: 2014', Office for National Statistics (Apr. 2018), https://www.ons.gov.uk/economy/nationalaccounts/uksectoraccounts/compendium/economicreview/april2018/regionalandsubregionalproductivitycomparisonsukandselectedeucountries2014
16. Ibid.
17. Philip Oltermann, 'Enemies everywhere: photos show absurdity of life under the Stasi', *Guardian* (Mar. 2020), https://www.theguardian.com/world/2020/mar/20/enemies-everywhere-photos-show-absurdity-life-under-stasi-east-germany
18. Charlotte Bailey, 'The Lingering Trauma of Stasi Surveillance', *Atlantic* (Nov. 2019), https://www.theatlantic.com/international/archive/2019/11/lingering-trauma-east-german-police-state/601669/

19. Ben Mauk, 'Did Eastern Germany Experience an Economic Miracle?', *New Yorker* (Nov. 2014), https://www.newyorker.com/business/currency/eastern-germany-experience-economic-miracle

20. John Gramlich, 'East Germany has narrowed economic gap with West Germany since fall of communism, but still lags', Pew Research Centre (Nov. 2019), https://www.pewresearch.org/fact-tank/2019/11/06/east-germany-has-narrowed-economic-gap-with-west-germany-since-fall-of-communism-but-still-lags/

21. Ibid.

22. 'Regional gross disposable household income, UK: 1997 to 2018', Office for National Statistics (June 2020), https://www.ons.gov.uk/economy/regionalaccounts/grossdisposablehouseholdincome/bulletins/regionalgrossdisposablehouseholdincomegdhi/1997to2018

23. Ibid.

24. Gramlich, op cit.

25. 'Regional gross disposable household income, UK', op cit.

26. John Kampfner, *Why the Germans Do it Better: Notes from a Grown-Up Country* (London: Atlantic Books, 2020), 87.

27. Clay Risen, 'Underestimating East Germany', *Atlantic* (Nov. 2009), https://www.theatlantic.com/magazine/archive/2009/11/underestimating-east-germany/307776/

28. Emma Yeomans, 'Levelling up Britain "will cost as much as reuniting Germany"', *The Times* (Aug. 2021), https://www.thetimes.co.uk/article/levelling-up-britain-will-cost-as-much-as-reuniting-germany-mpjbm23kf

29. Kampfner, op cit, 87

30. Risen, op cit.

31. 'OECD Regions and Cities at a Glance 2018 – Germany', OECD (Mar. 2019), https://www.oecd.org/cfe/GERMANY-Regions-and-Cities-2018.pdf

32. Luke Raikes, 'The Devolution Parliament: Devolving power to England's regions, towns and cities', IPPR North (Feb. 2020), https://www.ippr.org/research/publications/the-devolution-parliament

33. 'OECD Regions and Cities at a Glance 2018 – Germany', op cit.

34. Simon Jeffrey and Paul Swinney, 'Levelling up local government in England', Centre for Cities (Sep. 2020), https://www.centreforcities.org/publication/levelling-up-local-government-in-england/

35. 'OECD Regions and Cities at a Glance 2018 – Germany', op cit.

36. Raikes, op cit.

37. 'OECD Regions and Cities at a Glance 2018 – Germany', op cit; 'OECD Regional and Cities at a Glance 2018 – United Kingdom', OECD, https://www.oecd.org/cfe/UNITED-KINGDOM-Regions-and-Cities-2018.pdf

38. Raikes, op cit.
39. Ibid.
40. 'OECD Regions and Cities at a Glance 2018 – Germany', op cit.
41. Kampfner, op cit.
42. Ibid.
43. Gareth Dale, 'How divisions between East and West Germany persist 30 years after reunification', The Conversation (Nov. 2019), https://theconversation.com/how-divisions-between-east-and-west-germany-persist-30-years-after-reunification-126297
44. Ibid.
45. John T. Correll, 'The Cost of Schweinfurt', Air Force Magazine (Feb. 2010), https://www.airforcemag.com/article/0210 schweinfurt/
46. 'OECD Regions and Cities at a Glance 2018 – Germany', op cit.
47. D. Clark, 'Leading European cities by GDP in 2017/18', Statista (July, 2021), https://www.statista.com/statistics/923781/european-cities-by-gdp/
48. '10 Largest Ports in Europe', Shipa Freight (Sep. 2021), https://www.shipafreight.com/knowledge-series/largest-ports-in-europe/
49. 'Hamburg in Profile', Hamburg Chamber of Commerce, https://www.hk24.de/blueprint/servlet/resource/blob/1159512/ae7761e82883fdbefa171ab31c9f8f2b/hamburg-in-profile-a-dynamic-metropolis-data.pdf
50. 'Frankfurt. The financial centre of the continent', German Convention Bureau, https://english.hessen.de/economy/the-financial-center-frankfurt
51. 'History of the Frankfurt Stock Exchange', Deutsche Börse Group, https://www.deutsche-boerse.com/dbg-en/our-company/frankfurt-stock-exchange/history-of-the-frankfurt-stock-exchange
52. 'Records of the Liverpool Stock Exchange', The National Archives, https://discovery.nationalarchives.gov.uk/details/r/86d26393-f551-43dd-9e85-9b6aa82150c7
53. Harriet Ellwein and Hildegard Mai, 'Dortmund', in Leo van den Berg, Jan van der Meer and Luis Carvalho (eds), Cities as Engines of Sustainable Competitiveness: European Urban Policy in Practoce (London: Routledge, 2016), 141–55.
54. Volker Wagener, 'North Rhine-Westphalia: an overview', Deutsche Welle (Nov. 2009), https://www.dw.com/en/north-rhine-westphalia-an-overview/a-3901456
55. Kampfner, op cit., 31
56. 'OECD Regions and Cities at a Glance 2018 – Germany', op cit.
57. Jason Karaian, The Atlas (2016).
58. Mark Frary, 'How Berlin became the capital of cool', The Times (Apr. 2018), https://www.thetimes.co.uk/static/how-berlin-became-capital-of-cool/

59. Eliot Stein, 'How Berlin Became the World's Coolest Capital City', Conde Nast Traveller (Nov. 2017), https://www.cntraveler.com/story/how-berlin-became-the-worlds-coolest-capital-city

60. 'Internal Market, Industry, Entrepreneurship and SMEs: Berlin', European Commission, https://ec.europa.eu/growth/index_en

61. Jean-François Gravier, *Paris et le Désert Française* (Paris: 1947).

62. Alfonso Díez Minguela and M. Teresa Sanchis Llopis, 'Regional income inequality in France: What does history teach us?', Working Papers in Economic History (Jan. 2018), https://ideas.repec.org/p/cte/whrepe/26152.html

63. Ibid.

64. Jean-Louis Andréani, 'Paris et le desert français, le livre devenu une bible de la décentralisation', *Le Monde* (July 2008), https://www.lemonde.fr/idees/article/2008/07/15/paris-et-le-desert-francais-par-jean-louis-andreani_1073531_3232.html

65. Matthew Wendeln, 'Territorial Equality in France: A Historical Perspective', Metropolitics (June 2014), https://metropolitics.org/Territorial-Equality-in-France-A.html

66. Andréani, op cit.

67. Wendeln, op cit.

68. Ibid.

69. 'Dossiers: Les chiffres de la région Île-de-France', *Republique Française* (Jan. 2018), https://www.prefectures-regions.gouv.fr/ile-de-france/Region-et-institutions/Portrait-de-la-region/Chiffres-cles/Les-chiffres-de-la-region-Ile-de-France

70. Jack Brown, 'London is still the UK's golden goose – and that needs to change', *Guardian* (May 2019), https://www.theguardian.com/commentisfree/2019/may/20/london-uk-economy-decentralisation

71. 'Dossiers', op cit.

72. 'Migration Snap-shot of the city of Paris', OECD (2018), https://www.oecd-ilibrary.org/social-issues-migration-health/working-together-for-local-integration-of-migrants-and-refugees-in-paris/migration-snap-shot-of-the-city-of-paris_9789264305861-6-en

73. Ibid.

74. Victor Ginsburgh, Glenn Magerman and Ilaria Natali, 'COVID-19 and the role of inequality in French regional departments', *The European Journal of Health Economics* (Jan. 2021), 311–27

75. Andréani, op cit.

76. Angelique Chrisafis, 'Marine Le Pen rails against rampant globalisation after election success', *Guardian* (Apr. 2017), https://www.theguardian.com/world/2017/apr/24/marine-le-pen-rails-against-rampant-globalisation-after-election-success

77. Angelique Chrisafis, 'The real misery is in the countryside: support for Le Pen surges in rural France', *Guardian* (Apr. 2017),

theguardian.com/world/2017/apr/21/counryside-marine-le-pen-forgotten-france-presidential-election-2017

78. Clare Byrne, 'I support Marine. She is the only one we haven't tried: How "forgotten" rural France could influence the election', Business Insider (Apr. 2017), https://www.businessinsider.com/afp-forgotten-rural-france-seethes-over-big-city-bias-2017-4?r=US&IR=T

79. 'OECD Regions and Cities at a Glance 2018 – France', OECD (Mar. 2019), https://www.oecd.org/cfe/FRANCE-Regions-and-Cities-2018.pdf

80. 'Migration Snap-shot of the city of Paris', op cit.

81. Chrisafis, op cit.

82. Lauren Slagter, 'Detroit unemployment sits at 25% – lower than pandemic peak, twice pre-pandemic peak', University of Michigan News (Aug. 2021), https://news.umich.edu/detroit-unemployment-sits-at-25-lower-than-pandemic-peak-twice-pre-pandemic-rate/

83. Thomas H. Klier, 'From tail fins to hybrids: How Detroit lost its dominance of the U.S. auto market', Research Papers in Economics.

84. Simeon Alder, David Lagakos and Lee Ohanian, 'The Decline of the U.S. Rust Belt: A Macroeconomic Analysis', *Yale University* (Jan. 2013), https://economics.yale.edu/sites/default/files/lagakos-130212.pdf

85. Gwynn Guilford, 'The epic mistake about manufacturing that's cost Americans millions of jobs', Quartz (May 2018), https://qz.com/1269172/the-epic-mistake-about-manufacturing-thats-cost-americans-millions-of-jobs/

86. Timothy B. Lee, '27 charts that will change how you think about the American economy', Vox (Oct. 2016), https://www.vox.com/new-money/2016/10/10/12933426/27-charts-changing-economy

87. Michael McQuarrie, 'The revolt of the Rust Belt: place and politics in the age of anger', *British Journal of Sociology*, 68: 1 (Nov. 2017), 120-52.

88. Ibid.

89. Ibid.

90. 'OECD Regions and Cities at a Glance 2018 – France', op cit.

91. 'OECD Regional and Cities at a Glance 2018 – United Kingdom', op cit.

92. 'Regional Outlook 2019 – France', OECD (2019).

93. Ibid.

9. UNIFICATION

1. Kate Proctor, 'Rees-Mogg sorry for saying Grenfell victims lacked common sense', *Guardian* (Nov. 2019), https://www.theguardian.com/politics/2019/nov/05/jacob-rees-mogg-claims-grenfell-victims-lacked-common-sense

2. Jonathan Owen, 'Parliament refurbishment will cost at "least £12bn," chair of spending watchdog says', Building (Jan. 2021), https://www.building.co.uk/news/parliament-refurbishment-will-cost-at-least-12bn-chair-of-spending-watchdog-says/5109926.article; Kate Proctor, 'Jacob Rees-Mogg Predicts £20 Billion Cost of Parliament's Refurbishment', PoliticsHome (Mar. 2021), https://www.politicshome.com/news/article/jacob-reesmogg-predicts-20-billion-cost-of-parliaments-refurbishment

3. D. Clark, 'Value of claims made by companies from the job retention scheme in the UK 2020-2021', Statista (Sep. 2021) https://www.statista.com/statistics/1122100/uk-cost-of-furlough-scheme/; Noel Dempsey, 'UK defence expenditure', House of Commons Library (June 2021), https://commonslibrary.parliament.uk/research-briefings/cbp-8175/

4. Tim Wyatt, 'No, parliament should not move out of London while they rebuild the Palace of Westminster', CityMonitor (Feb. 2018).

5. Russell Brand, 'Russell Brand on parliament: "The whole joint is a deeply encoded temple of hegemonic power"', *Guardian* (May 2013), https://www.theguardian.com/politics/2013/may/24/russell-brand-parliament-illusion

6. Simon Jenkins, 'Parliament needs to leave London and reconnect with the people', *Guardian* (July 2017), https://www.theguardian.com/commentisfree/2017/jul/17/brexit-britain-needs-mps-out-of-westminster-provinces-neglected

7. Jonn Elledge, 'Here's why Britain should move its capital', CityMonitor (Aug. 2018), https://citymonitor.ai/government/why-britain-should-move-its-capital-london-manchester-4074

8. Danny Dorling, 'Should parliament move out of London?' *Guardian* (Mar. 2015), https://www.theguardian.com/commentisfree/2015/mar/07/should-parliament-move-out-of-london

9. Kate Lyons, 'Why is Indonesia moving its capital city? Everything you need to know', *Guardian* (Aug. 2019), https://www.theguardian.com/world/2019/aug/27/why-is-indonesia-moving-its-capital-city-everything-you-need-to-know

10. 'Jenrick confirms Housing Department Wolverhampton HQ in historic move', Gov.uk (Feb. 2021), https://www.gov.uk/government/news/jenrick-confirms-housing-department-

wolverhampton-hq-in-historic-move#:~:text=In%20a%20key%20
milestone%20for,Group%20roles%20set%20to%20be

11. 'UK Cabinet Office to shift civil servants to Scotland', *Financial Times* (Mar. 2021), https://www.ft.com/content/8063b3c2-387c-46e7-a9d0-3fca47dc6d07; Laura Nolan, 'First 300 Treasury workers to move to Darlington within a year', The Northern Echo (Mar. 2021), https://www.thenorthernecho.co.uk/news/19164523.first-300-treasury-workers-move-darlington-within-year-major-businesses-set-relocate/

12. 'House of Lords: Temporary move to York rejected by repairs body', BBC News (Aug. 2020), https://www.bbc.co.uk/news/uk-politics-53837718

13. '"Treasury North" leads march of civil servants out of London', *Financial Times* (Jan. 2021), https://www.ft.com/content/2f44cb25-ea8a-4a8e-8f83-86a8b2acb2e0; 'Civil Servant Statistics', Gov.uk (Mar. 2020), https://www.gov.uk/government/statistics/civil-service-statistics-2020

14. 'Drinks club "ritual" wrecks pub', BBC News (Dec. 2004), http://news.bbc.co.uk/1/hi/england/oxfordshire/4066329.stm

15. Tom Calver, 'How could a wealth tax work in the UK?', *The Times* (May 2021), https://www.thetimes.co.uk/article/how-wealth-tax-work-uk-xlq5v7qcm

16. Ibid.

17. George Monbiot, Robin Grey, Tom Kenny, Laurie Macfarlane, Anna Powell-Smith, Guy Shrubsole, and Beth Stratford, 'Land for the Many: Changing the way our fundamental asset is used, owned and governed', Labour (June 2019), https://labour.org.uk/wp-content/uploads/2019/06/12081_19-Land-for-the-Many.pdf

18. Ibid.

19. Dominic Caddick and Alfie Stirling, 'Half of UK families are £110 worse off a year since 2019 general election', New Economics Foundation (December 2021), https://neweconomics.org/2021/12/two-years-on-britain-has-been-torn-apart-not-levelled-up

20. Full methodological details and tables are available on the Omnisis website.

For more unmissable reads,
sign up to the HarperNorth newsletter at
www.harpernorth.co.uk

or find us on Twitter at
@HarperNorthUK

Harper
North